Web Page Design:
A Different
Multimedia

Mary E. S. Morris
Randy J. Hinrichs

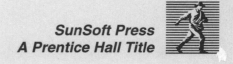

SunSoft Press
A Prentice Hall Title

The publisher offers discounts on this book when ordered in bulk quantities. For more information, contact: Corporate Sales Department, Prentice Hall PTR, One Lake Street, Upper Saddle River, NJ 07458 Phone: 800-382-3419; FAX: 201-236-7141; E-mail (Internet): corpsales@prenhall.com

Printed in the United States of America

Acquisitions editor: *Mary Franz*
Editorial assistant: *Noreen Regina*
Editorial production/supervision: *Joanne Anzalone,*
    Patti Guerrieri, Ann Sullivan, Camille Trentacoste
Cover design director: *Jerry Votta*
Cover designer: *Energy Energy Design*
Interior art direction and design: *Gail Cocker-Bogusz*
Web Site Story design: *Beverly Catli Design*
Manufacturing manager: *Alexis R. Heydt*
SunSoft Press publisher: *Rachel Borden*

10 9 8 7 6 5 4 3 2 1
ISBN 0-13-239880-X

SunSoft Press
A Prentice Hall Title

Web Page Design: A Different Multimedia

Contents

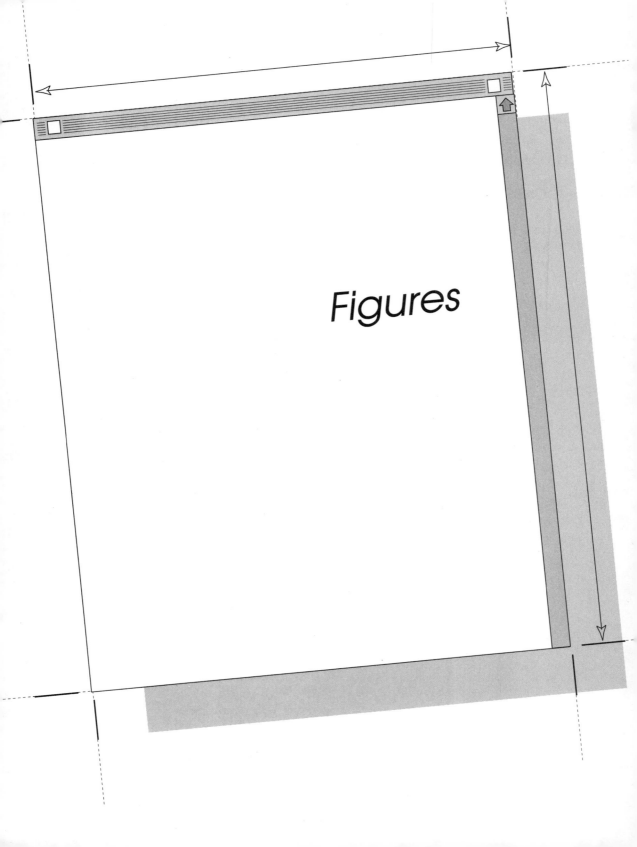

Figures

Acknowledgments

This book is the effort of many individuals. It demonstrates the work of dozens more. All of them deserve a hearty thank you.

This book was reviewed in whole or in part by many people from many disciplines. Their wide ranging perspectives kept us on track. Our review staff included Jay Lorenzo, Wayne Spivak, Paul van Oss, Francois Fluckiger, Thomas Powell, Scott Bascon, Marianne Cooley, Brian Behlendorf, and Michael Hutchins.

At the heart of this book are many good examples. They helped make this book what it is. We thank the following sites: Monster Board, Howard Rheingold, HotWired Ventures LLC, US PGA, Flex Net, Worlds, Inc's Alpha World, Discovery Communications, the Internet Society, C I Net : The Computer Network, Golfweb, Lycos, Inc's Point Communications, Sun Microsystems, Excite, World Access Yellow Pages's Infohiway, Saqqara Systems, the Tax Prophet, Time Warner's thePalace, MediaZones, Discovery, Sean Russell, Michael Bieber, Information Mapping, Sony (Japan), Wilson Internet Services's WilsonWeb, Ka-Ping Yee's Shodouka, the US Whitehouse, Cue Systems, Yahoo! Inc, Matterform Media's Qbullets and Market Central's Duke's Diner.

The other unsung heros include Rachel Borden, John Bortner, and Mary Franz.

I'd like to thank my incredible wife Janice. She is truly the wind beneath my wings. She is my soulmate and walks shoulder to shoulder with me through the pathways of the heart. I cannot ever thank my four children enough for being there for me, supporting me, and loving me through all the hard work in weaving the fabric of family and work. Thank you.

— *Randy J. Hinrichs*

No book ever gets published without the support of family and friends. In my case, Terry Haynes deserves all the credit for seeing me through the gestation and birth of this creation.

— *Mary E. S. Morris*

About This Book

WHO SHOULD USE THIS BOOK

Once you have learned HTML, you have only just begun. In the early days, it was enough to simply have a web page. This is no longer the case. When your competition numbers in the tens of millions of other web pages, you need to stand out. This is where good design comes in.

This book is for anyone who designs web pages, manages their design process, or reviews and approves web pages (such as the Marketing staff). This book goes a long way toward explaining what makes an *effective* web page and site—not just *cool* ones.

HOW THIS BOOK IS ORGANIZED

Chapter 1, "Web: A Different Multimedia," describes the similarities and differences between the Web and all other media.

Chapter 2, "Content Design," provides a high-level overview of creating content for the Web.

Chapter 3, "Cognitive Design," discusses the ways to get and keep users' attention without overwhelming them with Information Overload.

Chapter 4, "Audience Considerations," presents the varying needs of the audience and discusses how to analyze the audience and tailor the web design.

Chapter 5, "Navigational Design," provides background into hypertext structures and offers structure design philosophies to carry design to large scale and next generation sites.

Chapter 6, "Layout," presents guidelines for integrating standard desktop publishing with the Web, both at the basic level and with enhancements.

Chapter 7, "Designing Graphical Elements," offers insight into the biggest problems in cross-platform design—the graphics.

Chapter 8, "Meta-Information," provides an overview for the structure needed in next generation web creations to meet the needs of web agents as well as human surfers.

Chapter 9, "Interactivity Design," describes the design of forms and other interactive elements that start to create the coming *mass customization.*

Chapter 10, "Designing for Time," discusses the temporal aspects of page and site evolution.

Chapter 11, "Experiential Design," discusses design for web media other than HTML.

Chapter 12, "Testing Your Design," itemizes the areas that need to be tested before and after exposing your site to the public.

Case Study 1, "Sun and Java," tours the Sun® web site.

Case Study 2, "Point Communications," tours the Point Communication™ web site.

Case Study 3, "Golfweb," tours the Golfweb web site.

DESIGN PHILOSOPHIES

In writing this book, we tried to take on the perspective of all schools of thought that contribute to the Web. The Web is not just a technical programmer's playpen or the sandbox of the desktop publisher.

The Web brings together a wide range of disciplines, including cognitive design, desktop publishing layout (and eventually typography), graphics design, 3-D virtual world design, and interactivity challenges akin to computer game playing, hypertext theory, library sciences, and classical document management.

This book may seem a little scattered at times, but there is no way to reconcile all of these various disciplines into a coherent flowing whole—yet. Bear with us. This too is *evolving....*

■ MARY'S PHILOSOPHY

I have watched the various groups take to the Web as it moved from its research home to the commercial world. Those that designed it originally had a noble philosophy that has been handed down through generations of Internet design—make the stuff work everywhere. These people value the standards process and the creation of a tool that can and has reached critical mass.

However, the Web has gone far beyond the people that originally designed it. Thousands of people and hundreds of companies are contributing to this Stone Soup. Along the way they have made changes and enhancements. Those enhancements are not without value. They add a coherence that cannot be implemented with the existing standard. And they add this coherence in a far more timely fashion than a formal standards committee can respond to.

Therein lies the dilemma. Not only has the Web created a new multimedia out of various tinker toys, it has also devised a new way of measuring time—the web year.

Web years are similar to dog years in the fact that they are shorter than standard human processes. The initial 5 years of web evolution has followed the same path that it took television 75 years to traverse. The Web shows no sign of slowing this rampant evolutionary process.

Each year that you as a designer participate in the Web, you must revise your design strategy from the ground up.

- In 1994, it was enough to have a web page and start sharing information.

- In 1995, that web page met with stiff competition as the number of web sites climbed. At its peak, web sites doubled every 45 days. This rate of change has slowed but is still advancing at supersonic speeds. The design requirements here were to create some enticing aspect that would motivate users to return. Some sites added flashy graphics, others, cute hacks. Many relied on the tried and true: content.

- In 1996, interactivity is the rage. The Web is not a mass communications medium and the "any-color car—er, web page— as long as it is black" is no longer acceptable. People talk back now.

- In 1997, the evolution of interactivity will give way to full-fledged *mass customization*. If you thought your niches were small before, you are in for a surprise. The personalized newspaper, *The Daily Me*, will be the rule instead of the exception. Web sites will have to follow suit to stay in the game. Jakob Niesen has already forecast the end of surfing the Web. People are no longer reaching out to get information. It must come to them, prepackaged just as they like it.

- In 1998, there stands a good chance of having more web pages than there are people on the planet. This infoglut will be met head on with technology, namely agents.
  Agents will have been around for many years by this time. They will have crawled through the Web as spiders and robots in 1996, indexing web pages and searching for inexpensive CD-ROMS. Their first fledgling steps in 1997 will begin with simple *Daily Me* compilations and extended shopping trips for concert tickets. By 1998, the user will no longer depend on an information provider to compile and provide editorial content. Agents will have usurped even this role.

There is a shocking level of change in this forecast. That level of change is no greater than the previous evolution of the Web. It has sweeping ramifications for the future of design. The Age of the Knowledge Worker has really arrived.

■ RANDY'S DESIGN PHILOSOPHY

Communicating on the Internet via the World Wide Web has no other precedent. In the time it took the Gutenberg press to mass-produce and distribute books, years had elapsed. The World Wide Web is a mere infant in comparison, appearing on the scene less than two years ago. Yet it has grown to become one of the most superior technologies of communication and interaction we have ever seen. It is robust, personal, easy to use, international, and potentially larger in its offerings than radio, television, video, telephone, or cable. To design for it is to design the future.

I became interested in the World Wide Web because I am an educational technologist. Since my early days in college in the late 70s, I have been looking for a way to educate large numbers of people at the same time, on any subject. In doing so, I would be able to affect the way a market evolves, improve processes within an organization, open the potential and creativity of any student, and ultimately raise the consciousness of the individual. So, my academic history led me through one technology after another: laser disc technology, computer-assisted learning, artificial intelligence research, computer-based training, application software design, multimedia development, electronic performance support systems, CD-ROM, and now, the globally distributed, interactive World Wide Web.

Using these various educational technologies, I designed and developed different ways for students to learn and collaborate. But no matter what I tried, I kept hitting the same brick wall. I could only develop an environment as rich as the information that I found in libraries, books, and from other colleagues. I was intellectually bound by the content. If I used content experts, once the product was complete, the content expert returned to his own world of continuous learning, and I to my next project. What happened to the program? It became dated, then unused.

Like CD-ROM technology, I could produce different pieces of multimedia and show a little bit about a subject or delve into a subject in detail. But I had to continually authenticate the information, expanding my own weary knowledge on the subject and maintaining the quality and quantity of the information myself. And, without the classroom contact, I couldn't really get the students to collaborate well, even when e-mail came into existence. I needed something more robust, more distributed, more connected to expert systems. I needed content to be maintained by the originators, and the feedback mecha-

nisms to be integrated throughout the communication system. I needed an environment I could develop quickly without six months of
development and two months of testing.

When I joined Sun Microsystem's SunU, I was introduced to the Internet via Mosaic and the World Wide Web. SunU was intricately tied
into Icon Author and Gain's Momentum, both very good authoring
programs for computer-assisted learning. However, when I examined
these as development environments, I found the same old problems. I
had trouble quickly accessing content, collaborating with experts over
long periods of time, and shortening my development cycle. SunU
was on the cutting edge of electronic conferencing and electronic performance systems environments in which the internal users could
learn software through Rad Technology-driven tutorials. I liked the
technologies, but I found the same problems creeping up behind me; I
wanted to interact globally, over large populations, with diverse audiences, at various levels of learning. Marketing, sales, human resources, and engineers wanted to reach the same group.

I was assigned the task of training Sun Microsystems global sales
force and systems engineers on the Internet. The thought hit me immediately: why not use the tool to train and distribute the information? In doing so, I could reach critical mass very quickly and develop
in an environment that I could program myself and team with experts, rather than project manage a team of programmers, designers,
and developers. Within 11 weeks, using Sun's internal resources and a
telephone, I created Sun on the Net, which allowed Sun's sales force
and system engineers to be prepared for Sun's official launch of Internet Solutions at SunWorld '95.

Even more useful, the customers could be on the same page as
Sun's staff, collaborating in efforts to understand how to streamline
their business with Sun's client/server Internet solutions. Sun on the
Net provided users with training/information on what the Internet
was, what Sun's strategy on the Internet was, how to do business on
the Internet, who was doing business on the Internet, what Sun's solutions and configurations for different enterprises throughout the
world could be, etc. The training provided objectives, links to the key
features of Sun's Internet strategy (Netra™ and Java™), and criteria
that served as test answers if uses wanted to evaluate their understanding or key concepts. The site was distributed worldwide, with
an internal site mirroring the external site, enriched with proprietary
information, from prices to competitive information. The site was a
success.

I discovered all of the technical limitations, of course. I couldn't distribute Rad Technology's software across multiple platforms. I couldn't incorporate sound, video, or interactive test questions without halting most laptops and PC-based machines. I could get feedback from a user, but I had difficulty intelligently managing individual learning requirements. But despite these obstacles, I knew it would be a matter of a few months before the software tools were built to assist in developing the right kind of environment for interactive learning on-line. Right in the midst my enthusiasm, I saw Java develop and Netscape's wide distribution of quality software emerge as a way of adding on, or plugging in, to the rapid development of software applications to enhance interactivity.

And, now within a short nine months, I see Shockwave™, Real Audio, VRML, Java- enhanced sites, drag-and-drop manipulable objects, feedback mechanisms, testing environments, and real live connectivity to the experts in the field. The content I had at my fingertips was amazing. The quality of the content was coming from the best of the best. I saw the ability to navigate huge databases and develop elegant feedback environments and chatting sessions that would enable the learner and the master to communicate one on one, or one on many others. And, I saw that these environments could be designed quickly and efficiently, using the latest findings in educational psychology.

What really began to thrill me was seeing the introduction of entertainment elements, where students/learners/users could discovery new ways of seeing or doing things. I saw a playful game-like environment, in which the beginner, the intermediate, and the advanced student could dive into a world of interactive, focused information and come out knowing and being exposed to more than any environment I've ever developed in before. I saw learning and investigation igniting like a nova.

So, I dedicated myself to designing environments for learning, for communicating, for selling, for marketing, for playing, for discovering, for creating the future. I wanted to get my hands into HTML, CGI, JavaScript, Java, whatever was coming next. It was so easy to learn and so easy to reuse the best of the best. I don't simply surf the net anymore, I evaluate the effectiveness of the design. I examine every node on a page. I compare each site with a comparable site and haunt the sites that call themselves "Best of the Web," "Cool Sites," and, of course, "Weird Internet Site." I'm constantly comparing, analyzing, dialoguing with the creators.

My conclusion. We are only at the brink of where we're going. Design is completely relative to our creative potential and imagination. One month, and frames, VRML and Shockwave are born. Another month, and Java-enhanced sites allow us to manipulate objects on the screen. So far, we've spent a lot of time imitating the outside environment, the paper and pen, the mail, the television programming environment, and the classroom. However, we've just started to scratch the surface of how to accelerate experience in this new environment. Imagine having all information at your fingertips, with the ability to access it instantly and to reorganize it to fit your needs and to satisfy your audience's/student's/user's needs immediately. And, you get audio, video, virtual reality, bouncing, jamming interactive fun and discovery at the same time. Oh, and when you're not working, studying, or researching, you are surfing worlds you never imagined entering even a year ago.

We need to transition from our present experience on the Web to a more integrated experience. Up to this point, I designed for efficiency. I want to see users get information at a glance. I want to reduce cognitive overload. I want my designs to start like a movie, wide-angle view of an idea, topic, subject, and provide a quick overview that is clean, simple, elegant, and explains the topic in five to seven icons, sounds, movie clips, or whatever. Then, I like the user to be able to pick the area to focus on and be able to seamlessly move into the information, picking the kind of information he/she wants, manipulating it freely and digging in for more, until their thirst is quenched.

Users differ, their styles differ, their cognitive needs differ, and so the way they access, process, and reuse information varies. In the way I view design, there is a mode for every learner. There are visual modes, aural modes, tactile modes, experiential modes. The designs have to accommodate the variation with the global population, in language, approach, orientation, and delivery. The design has to be as varied as the global identities that make up its users. I see new sites articulating our collective unconsciousness daily.

As the Web develops, I am banking on simulated environments like SimCity™ and SimEarth™ from Maxis Software in Walnut Creek, California. I'm looking for Java to bring us SimSales, SimPsychology, SimHouseBuilding, SimMedicine, SimPoolRepair, SimGardening, SimBonsai. I want to see the user be able to enter an environment in which he can manipulate variables and immediately see the results. Instead of getting a list of the ten most important things that he has to do, he will instead be handed the ten most important tools and an environment in which discoveries must be made by himself. In short, he will receive the tests first, and the lessons afterward—kind of like life.

I want to see more fantasy on the Web, more playful environments, in which the user is pulled into the scene, much like we get pulled into a movie like Indiana Jones or Silence of the Lambs. In other words, when the environment engages our senses, our feelings, and perhaps even our instincts, then we'll be more alerted to the environment, so we'll have a reason and a need to discover how to manipulate the environment to survive. When real engagement happens and anything goes, you've got the user's attention!

I've been in school for more years than I care to count. I loved the interaction with the students and an occasional professor or two. But, I have to admit, most of the time I felt I was in an experiential ghetto. All the information was droning, presented with the technology of linearity, one solution for all the hundreds of people who have gone through this subject before. I never felt excited until I left the classroom and started hanging out in the student bars and interacting with information in apprenticeships. Then, I was introduced to the World Wide Web, and I feel as though my learning has begun all over again. I feel like a kid, pushing buttons, setting off reactions, communicating with anyone from the President to Timothy Leary, and getting responses. I feel I'm touching other cultures and interacting with information I'd never dreamed of before. I am excited. I am motivated. And, now I'm dedicated to finding how to improve it, how to learn more about it, and how to design and develop in it, with every new technology, every new twist in the road ahead.

There are some remarkable visionaries out there making predictions about the World Wide Web, the Super Information Highway. Bill Gates has a vision, Scott McNealy another, Jim Clark from Netscape another, Nicholas Negroponte another. And the fiction writer's visions, like Neal Stephenson's *Snow Crash* and Irwin Winkler's *The Net*, keep toying with our imaginations of how it's going to be. They're all right, and they're all pioneers barely scratching the surface of how this environment is going to change the way we do everything. Whatever happens, I'll be there, designing, developing and playing.

Visit me in my cybercube. Stop in and talk awhile; I always learned the most that way anyway.

TYPOGRAPHIC CONVENTIONS

Table PR-1 describes the typographic conventions used in this book.

Table PR-1

TYPEFACE OR STYLE	DESCRIPTION	EXAMPLE
AaBbCc123	The names of commands, files, tag attributes, and directories; on-screen computer output	Edit your `.login` file. Use `ls -a` to list all files. `system% You have mail.`
AaBbCc123	What you type, contrasted with on-screen computer output	`system% `**`su`**`  password:`
AaBbCc123	Command-line placeholder: replace with a real name or value	To delete a file, type `rm` *filename*.
AaBbCc123	Book titles, new words or terms, or words to be emphasized	Read Chapter 6 in *User's Guide*. These are called *class* options. You *must* be root to do this.

CHAPTER

1

Web - A Different Multimedia

The World Wide Web, WWW, or just plain Web, sprang from its birth place in the highly technical laboratory called the Internet about 1994. It has since become a tool of not only the technical literati that gave it birth, but of artists, marketeers, and even the kid down the street. Although its layout capabilities are primitive in comparison to a standard desktop, its potential is unfathomable.

Bigger than television, cable, multimedia, and even books, the Web may possess the ability to communicate and interact worldwide in an environment where no individual person or country can control the flow of information, without consensus from the users. The World Wide Web provides us the tools to communicate globally, the means to explore new ways of doing business, and the opportunity to access almost infinite education.

The World Wide Web has certainly gotten everyone's attention. There are few who have not dreamed about the meaning and potential of the Web to their organization or to themselves. The millennium is ending, the digital 21st century has its door open, welcoming you, the designer and developer, to help shape the future of the Web.

To the Heart of the Matter. In order to design and develop the Web, this book will explore the nature of the Web: its successes and failures, its effects on human psychology, commerce, and education. We'll identify the principles for good web design and provide you plenty of opportunity to use the Web itself to explore, visualize, and create. After all, you know it's great to have something to read while you wait for those intensive graphics to download.

Multimedia development provides us with CD-ROM environments that are unparalleled on the Web. The Microsoft® Encarta and Bookshelf '95 products are excellent examples. CD-ROM technology, however, lacks what makes the Web so seductive. CD-ROM cannot maintain up-to-date, live information. Once the CD is pressed, it requires time-consuming editing and repressing to update a single section on the CD-ROM. CD-ROM is not directly linked to e-mail or interactive forms, so no direct communication exists between the user and consumer.

Use multimedia as the user's eyes and ears.

Sega®, Nintendo®, and other "interactive" multimedia game environments are another exciting multimedia experience. But again, they lack an open communication between the user and the developer. Open communication fosters feedback, providing the developer with constant information on how to improve the site. In AlphaWorld™, for example, see Figure 1.1, users can build their own environment, and they can communicate with each other as physical avatars. This form of interactivity, where one web user is communicating directly with another web user, is moving us beyond the multimedia of CD-ROM.

Figure 1.1 AlphaWorld: Where Users Truly Interact

Video, audio, and animation excel in the multimedia environment. In fact, I haven't seen any web site as much fun as a Disney interactive CD. But, the Web is maturing quickly, integrating each multimedia technology into it almost daily. Multimedia presentations are now possible, Shockwave™ and Java™ provide animation, video, and audio. The Web is developing into the ultimate multimedia, bringing together all the technological capabilities of multimedia with the interactive capabilities of networks. A key design issue that you need to address, then, is how you design a web site that simulates reality. You use multimedia as the user's eyes and ears. Then provide multimedia tools for communicating and participating in the simulated world.

NEW RULES

Because the user communicates and interacts with others via the Web, new rules apply. Certain classic design features remain—form, color, content, sequencing of information. But, new design techniques for interaction and information handling must be employed. New ways of communicating need to be established. Unforeseen social implications must be considered. A new world has appeared, with new social, political, and artistic definitions. Finding out what these new rules are is what the Web pioneers of this decade are discovering.

DESIGN IMPLICATIONS

The rules of design include techniques for handling interaction. So we'll examine the psychological aspects of human interactions and human learning in order to help us design web sites.

Table 1-1 highlights some characteristics of the Web that will have implications for design. The **key difference** is the heightened level of **interactivity**, which combines various communication skills with media.

Table 1-1   Web Characteristics

WEB FEATURE:	DESIGN IMPLICATION
• alive, comprising millions of diverse people and cultures	• language, icons, and graphics must be global; audience tracking is vital
• proactive, growing daily, improving constantly and neverendingly	• robust maintenance must be designed; ISO standards need to be implemented
• the great communicator, seamless and vast	• content must be customized; depoliticalization must occur; world-wide network management is imperative
• a haven for experts on-line	• content management and authentication of information is crucial
• a learning place, a human school, a virtual performance	• solid instructional design is important, as well as production and broadcasting design
• unstable, one minute secure, the next highly exposed	• design security features into web sites
• a business consortium where millions can be made	• design a way to collect and distribute money
• an advertising, sales, and marketing showroom	• utilize the media to strengthen marketing and sales information
• a starting point where the future is taking place	• design for variety, for adding new features, for flexibility

If possible, create your site by using the Web as a collaborative tool. Post meetings on a page. Provide the mission statement, purpose, goals, action lists. List the people involved and ways to get hold of them. Provide a timeline with links to individual developer's pages. Create a bug page to monitor problems.

WEB DESIGN ISSUES

It is often assumed that the same artistic principles can be used in both multimedia and web development. Certainly because the Web is made up of multimedia pieces, a lot of the design and development will be the same. Great web design utilizes new design techniques for the average multimedia designer. Many fields of study have come together to provide the best design methodology for web development. Prepare to become multi-skilled. You'll need to learn a lot of new skills to produce web sites or to communicate with your development vendor.

■ NEW SKILLS

Among the disciplines that you'll need to understand are:

- Platform-independent multimedia development
- Self-directed learning techniques
- Communication, especially two-way feedback mechanisms
- Computer game development theory, virtual reality techniques, and simulation methodology
- Navigation science for both directional and psychological movement
- Expertise in content and content architecture
- Links and relationships management
- Pluralistic design, where you accommodate wide, diverse audiences
- Technology reuse
- Cognitive psychology, especially mind map development
- Video, audio, virtual reality, and emerging media production
- Human ergonomics
- Learning theory and human development

In short, design and development will require you to understand human experience such that you can provide a simulated environment in which the user feels comfortable, challenged, interested, productive, and entertained. But just think, you can start learning about these topics now. Start typing these topics into your favorite search site on the Web and away you go. (See `http://www.excite.com` in Figure 1.2 or `http://www.yahoo.com`)

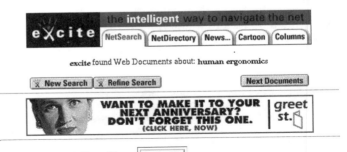

Figure 1.2 Excite: a Window to Training Yourself

■ THE DESIGN PROCESS

The design process for creating web sites will not differ much from the design and development of any multimedia product. The differences are in the components that are included into the web site. The process for creating the web site will follow traditional design principles.

Use the keywords in italics in the following section with the on-line search tools at http://www.yahoo.com or http://www.excite.com to learn more about the process.

Try This!

1.   **Analysis**: In this stage, you will identify the users. Users will vary considerably, so ensure that you perform an audience needs analysis, talk to users, get responses from e-mail, talk. Also, at this stage, you must identify the tasks that the web site will perform. For each audience, there are a basic set of task requirements

for each web site. For example, "How do I learn more?" "Who can I contact?" "How do I order products?" or "How do I download software?" Identify what users want to accomplish, what questions they'll ask, and what answers they'll expect. Set the objectives for the web site with the design team. *(Keywords: Needs Analysis, Task Analysis, Profiling).*

2. **Design:** Begin to identify the major high-level topics, break the topics into groups, then subgroups of information. Begin to see text, graphics, audio, video that will enhance the meaning or the message of each topic. Pick a theme and stick with it. If it doesn't work, change it, then stick with it. Brainstorm what the relationships are between the groups and how they support the theme. Get this information down in some form and get everyone on the team to review it and reach some level of consensus that the design is meeting the objectives set during the analysis phase. Plan for feedback. Design forms and databases to maintain the forms. Freeze your plan. Prepare for contingencies. Project manage and communicate to everyone at all times. Plan for internationalization. *(Keywords, Mind Mapping, Brainstorming, Design, Entity-Relationship Diagrams)*

3. **Development:** Build the pages based on the topics you designed in the previous stage. Build as much as you can as a stand-alone. Then, begin creating the links and relationships between each topic. Remember, you are the expert and you understand the relationships better than an occasional visitor. Trust yourself. You will check the validity and reliability of your information with your peers during usability testing. Build all the multimedia elements to meet the specifications in the design phase. Be prepared for change. Project manage and communicate to everyone at all times. *(Keywords, Development, Project Management, Partnering, Usability Testing).*

4. **Test:** Grab everyone you can and have them work through your site. Start with your team first, to avoid the embarrassing moments; we all have mental lapses—it's better to hear it from a colleague. Observe, discuss, use people from all different backgrounds, and look for different responses; don't simply try to validate your own expectations. Make sure it works for you, for novices, for experts, for casual users, and for hard-core critics. Then, try it on a kid. *(Keywords, Usability Testing, Quality Assurance)*

5. **Implement and Redo:** Launch the web site, but make sure you have included various feedback devices so you can constantly and neverendingly improve your site. Provide user statistics and

chatting capability when you can. Others should be able to watch the development of your site; take their advice very seriously. This is the environment in which the users and observers will be actively making required changes to your site. If it doesn't work, get rid of it. Constantly maintain the freshness of the site. (*Keywords, Launching/Marketing, Process Improvement, User Statistics*)

■ STAFFING CONSIDERATIONS

Conventional multimedia authoring teams already comprise a wide variety of professionals including:

Table 1-2　Print versus Web Comparison

Content Writer	Graphics Artist
Sound Artist	Content Architect
Video/Animation Specialist	Content Integrator
Interface Designer	Technical Support
Editor	Production Manager

Try This!

Use the Web to search on skills identified in the surrounding tables. Look at http://www.yahoo.com or http://www.excite.com or http://www.infoseek.com. You may find the results surprising.

To this extensive list, web development can add:

Table 1-3　Transfer Rates

•Programmer (CGI, Java, VRML)	•Database Analyst
•3-D Graphics Specialist	•EDI Integrator
•Networking Expert	•Web Marketing/Advertising
•Computer Specialist	•Web Master
•Web Lawyer/Copyright Specialist	•Media Specialist for Emerging Media
•Web Statistician	•Web Publisher

Everyone is the author

Each of the designers and developers makes up the "author" for a web site. The collaborative environment of the Web requires several individuals who work together to talk in one voice. You'll have to learn how to work in a collaborative environment, both technically and socially. The more you communicate with each other on-line, over the phone, in real meetings, the more you will mirror each other's attitudes and language into the site. Each member of the team must understand how the other members make their contributions to the overall design of a web page.

Consensus must prevail

Much like the "team meetings" or the "collaborative groups" in education, each individual contributes to the content, form, and design of the web site. Consensus must occur for decision making and is different than making a democratic decision. In consensus, each individual has the right to repeat a point of view to all the others. Once all sides have been heard and all the parties concerned agree that all the opinions have been heard, then a final decision is made by all. Consensus concedes that there is a right way of designing something and that everyone agrees. In this way, no individual point of view is excluded. This won't always be easy because of all the different backgrounds involved. Investigate conflict management skills.

■ USER CONSIDERATIONS

The user is the key to your designing success. Make sure you understand his needs, his thinking, his pleasures.

Invite participation

Make sure that the users of the web site have some way of communicating back to you to contribute their insights, programs, or content. The author and the user are much like Aristotle and Plato in that the student may surpass the expert status of the teacher, contributing unique and meaningful insights. If the readers have a way of communicating back to the site and becoming a member of the "authoring" team, they will certainly add more value than expected and will feel engaged with the information. This all-inclusive, global mentality adds vigor and realness to the site.

Contribute back

In the world of the Web, partnering is more important than ever. If a user contributes back to your site, you may be in a position to host that user at your site (especially if your site is well known and your user has developed a presence on the Web). Most users will encourage links back to their site. You may have to establish an agreement in order to ensure that the link is reliable, available, and serviceable.

Listen to others but make up your own mind

Just as an author or a painter will listen to peers, ultimately the best work comes from those who break the rules or try something that has never been done before. Read everything, listen to everyone, go to a conference, follow an e-mail group, but when you sit down to work up how your information would best be served in this environment, think about what pleases you. You know your audience best. Use your own reactions to the Web. Why does a site appeal to you? What features do you think are requirements? What are the innovators doing? Hold fast to this principle; it will keep your site fresh, focused, and vivid.

Principle

Design what delights you as a user. The design process is cyclical.

TOP DESIGN SPOTS

Before you go much further, you need to visit some of the sites designed to show you what a good web site is. PointCom's site, see Figure 1.3, breaks down the sites into most visited, top content, top presentation, and top experience. PointCom values users first by focusing on frequency and content. Presentation and top experience highlight users entertainment values, a key motivator for web visits .

Other sites worth a visit include Netscape's *What's Cool*, PC Computing's Top Sites at http://www.zdnet.com/~pccomp.

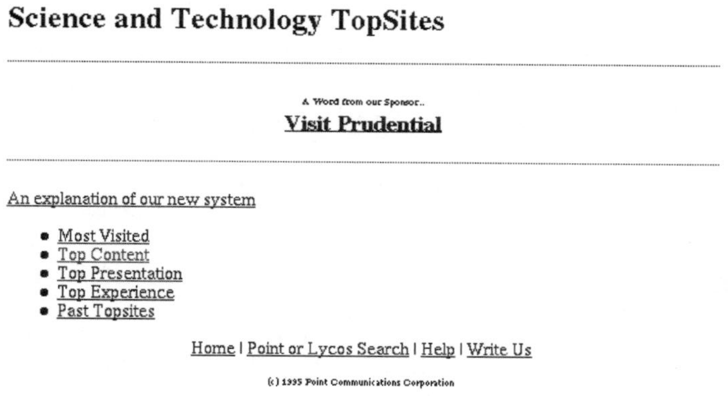

Science and Technology TopSites

A Word from our Sponsor...

Visit Prudential

An explanation of our new system

- Most Visited
- Top Content
- Top Presentation
- Top Experience
- Past Topsites

Home | Point or Lycos Search | Help | Write Us

(c) 1995 Point Communications Corporation

Figure 1.3 Doorway to Top Sites at PointCom
http://www.pointcom.com/text/topsites/

MIND MAPS

The Web works a lot like the brain. The user comes to an experience with a central core of stored-up experience and knowledge. The stimulus to the user's many senses are triggered by the interaction with the web site. The new experiences are spontaneous, chaotic, disparate. The journey through the links provides different approaches to thinking that may or may not logically follow a user's train of thought. Yet at each page, the user is drawing conclusions, filtering information, and asking more questions. Finally, a new mental map has been constructed, and the user acts on the information or conclusion that he has reached, and then, off to another URL. These mental maps, or mind maps, are what you need to link into when designing your site.

This book discusses mind maps frequently. If you can think of a mind map as a family tree, you can understand mind maps. An idea is like a root, a beginning. Branches emanate from the root, with various parent sites, with various children branching from that. All are interrelated. Both human mind maps and web mind maps are like these family trees. In order for a designer to link into the human mind map, there must has to be a set of common features they both share. What are the relationships, the connections between the user and the developer? What you are designing is the communication of these relationships.

> **Principle**
>
> Design sites that link human mind maps with web mind maps.

MEETING THE INTERACTIVE CHALLENGE

If you're going to design in this communication environment, it is imperative to learn how to design interactivity. People go on-line in order to communicate worldwide instantaneously. They are willing to sit through any interface in order to express an idea, anticipate and use responses, experience discussion with anyone with a good idea. A web experience is a social experience that can take place in the comfort of your favorite environment, at any time you choose.

■ MAKE IT INTERACTIVE

No one factor can be identified that continues to enhance the user's motivation to participate. However, since the web experience is participatory, the more you can make it interactive, the longer you will be tapping into the user's self-motivation. HotWired invites you to become a Netizen and get involved with them as a community member. As shown in Figure 1.4, you are encouraged to interact with the opinion polls and let your voice be heard.

HotPoll

See also:

Impolitic
by John
Hellemann
Floating
media
cocktail party
is grounded

O K, we get it. It isn't our carefully worded, scientifically calibrated political questions that turn you on. It's what kind of platform you prefer to use to launch your netsurfs! So we'll continue to ask our political–junkie questions, since politics is what The Netizen is about, but we'll throw in a few other surprises, too. Whatever turns you on.

Decency Undressed
CDA Special

....

Raising the Dead
N o i s e

....

**Surf
Report**
by Heather
Irwin
Clueless
candidates hit
the Web

The main thing to remember is to vote! HotPoll is definitely the hottest poll on the Net, and by participating, you become part of the global movement to inject

Last Week's
H o t P o l l

....

Figure 1.4 HotWired's Interactive Netizen World
http://vip.hotwired.com/netizenpoll/

■ IDENTIFY WITH THE USER

Motivation to participate is deterred when the user begins to feel that you are motivating him. You have to keep your site's motivational features subdued, so the user will never feel that he is attending a pep rally. Instead, you have to tap into the user's identification of himself, where you are enhancing his experience, providing stimulus that meets his needs and expectations. GolfWeb in Figure 1.5 is the personification of the typical golfer. The section Where to Play with a beautiful golf course pulls the reader into the world he wants to be in. The Pro Shop with its elegant architecture suggests to the user that there's a place where he can truly be himself and even do some socializing. And, for the more sportive, Golf Action. You can view the site in color in Color Plate 1-1. You may want to get your old irons out of the closet.

Figure 1.5 GolfWeb Engages the User

■ PROVIDE INTERACTIVE TOOLS

The more you can simulate the user's real environment, the more the user will be motivated to stay with you in your web site. The more you make the user think he is playing rather than working, the more your user will be glued to your web site. And, if you provide the user with tools to interact with your environment, you will begin to create a place where users define the space that they're in. When users become part of the site, they will remain loyal and avid users of your services. In Figure 1.6, the consummate job-finding site at Monster Board provides an interactive resume writer.

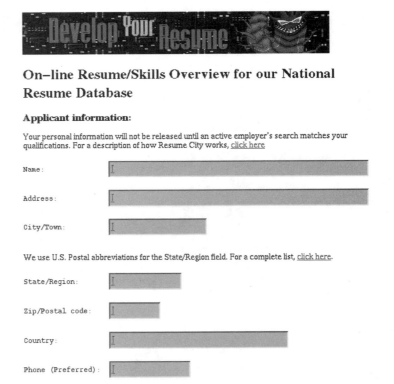

Figure 1.6 Monster Board Helps Write Your Resume - http://www.monster.com

CONTRASTING MEDIA

To design for the Web means to understand the two media from which the Web was born: print and CD-ROM. This section examines the differences and the design implications.

■ PRINT

Most web content comes from the print medium. This makes print an important medium to contrast with the Web. Print is in many ways the antithesis of the Web. They share a common method of communication, *words*. However, there the similarity ends. Do remember, there are individuals who still want to print "things" in order to recall them later. (I challenge them to find the printed copy, though, when they need it.)

Design Implication. Help transition these individuals to the Web with good screen design that will print good pages. Use book metaphors, page turning, contents, indexes, etc. Web sites with audio, video, virtual reality, and game scenarios will certainly attract their attention, too.

Table 1-4 summarizes the significant differences between print as a medium and the Web.

Table 1-4

PRINT...	WEB....
• Images are rendered with considerable detail, usually using a greater resolution than the eye can discern	• Images are often grainy and carry little detail. Reduce colors to improve quality
• Text and images can be assimilated by the user simultaneously	• User often views the text before the images have been displayed. Display text first that supports the graphic.
• Designer has complete control over presentation	• Software limitations and user preferences affect text justification, fonts, page layout, and even the display of images. Be creative.

Table 1-4 *(Continued)*

PRINT...	WEB....
•Content follows a linear path. It has a defined start, middle, and end.	•Users can enter a site at any point. The only content flow control is the management of hypertext links.
•Serif fonts are more readable	•Sans-serif fonts are more readable.
•Large visible area	•Limited visible material
•Instantaneous	•Often significant time delays between requesting and viewing a page
•High Impact	•High Content
•Single entity presentation (the page)	•Multiple links
•Static graphics	•Clickable graphics
•Telephone or mail communication	•User forms with e-mail
•Distribution through stores, libraries	•Distribution across global networks
•One or limited number of authors	•Multiple changing authors
•Information valid at date of publishing	•Information validated real time
•Passive access to further resources	•Active access to further resources

Design Implications. These differences mean that many paper-based designs will no longer have the powerful effect and impact that they used to. A web design that uses graphics, video, and audio elements gives users an environment in which to experience a topic in poignant detail. With the interaction that follows, discussions on material, e-mail to other participants, and to the author on a constant basis, the web environment will compel readers to interact with material in a collaborative environment. The effects will be stimulating.

■ CD-ROM-BASED MULTIMEDIA

CD-ROM technology produces excellent one-way, tutorial-like information meccas. The content is superb, the links are explicit, the graphics, audio, and video are excellent. In many ways, CD-ROM can be considered the parent of the Web environment. There are significant differences, however, that affect the design of a web site.

- Access hits
- Access speeds (bandwidth)
- Static links versus dynamic links
- Live Interaction with the content
- Database connectivity

Access hits

In the design process, unlike the case with CD-ROMs, the configuration/power of the server and its planned/possible evolution are critical parameters. With CD-ROM, the constraint on bandwidth is greatly reduced because of its stand-alone nature. Web pages, on the other hand, are accessed by various users at the same time. A key design goal is to anticipate the number of visits per day, per page. You must maintain web statistics to accommodate growth and ensure accessibility of your site.

The other critical parameter is the connection speed of the server (or servers) and the possible evolution of the speed. Your connection (T1, T3, ISDN) must be planned in advance. Many web server projects have failed because the system (or access bandwidth) could not scale enough technically or the funding for upgrade was not available. These constraints are often known at the inception of the projects but not always taken into account in the design.

Access Speed

The biggest difference between CD-ROM multimedia and the Web, is the speed with which data can be received and viewed. Table 1-5 shows the transfer rates of many current and future transfer methods. Realistic values can be as little as one-third of the ideal values listed there.

The first and foremost difference is speed. There is no comparison here. CD-ROMs are an order of magnitude faster than any currently available web access method, and they will continue to be for a long time.

Table 1-5

MEDIUM	IDEAL TRANSFER RATES	DATA TRANSFER METHOD
CD-ROM	300K/sec	Double-speed CD-ROM
	600K/sec	Quad-speed CD-ROM
	900K/sec	Six-speed CD-ROM
Web	1.8K/sec	14.4K modem
	7K/sec	Low-end cable modem – **Shared***
	7K/sec	56K ISDN
	14K/sec	128K ISDN
	62.5K/sec	Low-end cable modem – **Dedicated***
	80K/sec	T-1 – **Shared**
	125K/sec	High-end cable modem – **Shared***
	187K/sec	T-1 – **Dedicated**
	200K/sec	Ethernet – **Shared**
	1,200K/sec	Ethernet – **Dedicated**
	1,250K/sec	High-end cable modem – **Dedicated***

* - These methods will not be widely available until the late 1990s.

Bear in mind, the high-end web transfer speeds are usually shared among people in the same workgroup or neighborhood. At 2 a.m., one person may have all of the bandwidth to himself. However, during peak periods, the bandwidth must be shared.

These transfer limitations require an alternative to transferring all data from the server to the client. The method developed to meet this constraint is that only instructions about *how* to create a web page are transferred in HTML, in VRML, and, to a certain extent, in Java. The browser then builds or *renders* the web page and displays it on the screen.

WEB IS MORE THAN JUST HTML

HTML allowed the programming novice to enter the world of the Web quickly and nearly painlessly. The ease and simplicity of HTML built the Web's reputation and the vast libraries and knowledge warehouses. The Web has achieved a status beyond its maker. The Web has become a location where we socially interact, go to school, buy and sell, get our customized news, and communicate. The Web is the Global Network.

Below are some areas that you will need to explore and understand, and perhaps master, in developing a site.

E-Mail. E-mail can be imbedded in most HTML code. It is a rudimentary method for communicating with the web site. It will help target the right person if you include the e-mail address on the page. Not doing so can account for obsolescence. Not only can you improve your site through feedback, but you can have direct contact with clients, customers, and colleagues. E-mail is international, widely used, and an elegant way of sharing documents not on-line.

EDI (Electronic Data Interchange). You can form business partnerships and mutually create new ways of doing business. In the age of Internet commerce, EDI is the financial glue behind the scenes to verify and communicate credit card and debt purchases. Financial institutions have been using it for years to transfer funds. There are specific standards in place for how a transaction appears and what information it contains. EDI integration has become a major part of the Web.

Search Tools. Search tools are more than a nice-to-have. For pinpointing the right information in a flash, you need to search over vast databases quickly. Well, if you need them, so do your clients. Yahoo, Infoseek, and AltaVista maintain serious knowledge warehouses and simple front-end interfaces to search for any kind of information you're looking for. Hook up with them. As a designer, you'll need to consider adding search capability for your knowledge warehouses, too.

IRC (Internet Relay Chatting). Chatting on-line is coming into its own. The ability to get information in a real-time experience, something akin to a large, shared teleconference, is yet another reason so many are flocking to the Web. Not as elegant as it could be, IRC provides on-line experiences with experts in the field.

VRML. Virtual Reality Markup Language is moving users into the world of virtual reality. Instead of surfing the Web, users are flying through the Web. The implications are astounding. Now you are able to present information to the user in a 3-D environment in which discovery predominates. But, VRML has its limits. The user may manipulate the camera and follow links, but no other types of interaction are supported yet. There is only a very simple extension mechanism, and it does not allow one to specify the behavior of a new node type. See `http://rosebud.sdsc.edu/vrml/`.

Java. Java is bringing us closer to experiential designs. It allows users to fully explore a web site in full multimedia fashion, with the extra benefit of making the web site seamless. No longer is it necessary to watch the file transfer process between different stimuli. Audio, video, and on-the-fly development are invisible to the user. Instead, the user experiences sound, music, sight, art, and automatic behavior.

DESIGN PROBLEMS

The Web has created a new set of problems.

- Information overload
- Limits to the user's attention span
- Lost in cyberspace

The Web is all about movement. It is about the user moving from place to place like a rock climber scaling a cliff. Each step is a slow process of moving forward, testing the viability of the route, and moving forward again. Sometimes the climber cum websurfer may need to backtrack and start down another path to reach the goal. So, a websurfer will become lost in a wilderness of information relevant and not relevant to his information needs.

■ INFORMATION OVERLOAD

Information overload is becoming the industrial disease of the Information Age. Unfortunately, the title is something of a misnomer. A better description would be "data overload." The problem here is that the user is inundated by mountainous waves of data. The data rarely has enough structure and organization for information distillation without significant mind-numbing effort. How can communication take place effectively in a sea of confusion?

Information at Your Fingertips. Most people do not grasp the magnitude of the problem. They look upon the Web as a slick-cover magazine that discusses all the latest trends in the Internet. What they don't realize is that the information they need to do business, communicate ideas, make crucial policy decisions, understand financial implications is at their fingertips. They can find information on any subject, in depth, by experts who are willing to share interaction and who, in fact, encourage open discussion over the validity and reliability of their presented facts.

Information Mapping. Part of the reason for the obscurantism of the labyrinths of information is that most people have not been exposed to Information Mapping. Figure 1.7 shows a company devoted to training people in information structuring techniques. This company reports significant improvements of information recall when their techniques are applied.

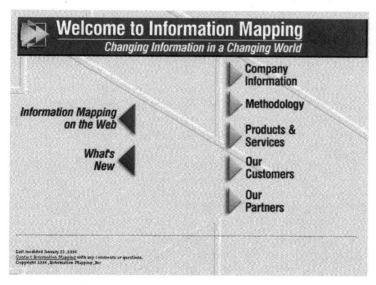

Figure 1.7 Information Mapping: A Solution to the Problem
http://www.infomap.com

Evaluations of the methodology have shown

- Reading time decreased 10%–50%
- Error rates decreased 54%
- Accuracy in retrieval increased 32%
- Questions to supervisors decreased 70%
- Initial learning improved 13%–83%
- Training time decreased 10%–50%
- Use of documentation increased 38%
- Rough draft time decreased by 90%
- High rates of users satisfaction
- Wide applicability of the method

The roots of Information Mapping can be traced to learning theory, human factors engineering, and cognitive science. Information Mapping can be applied to any medium: paper, on-line, and most recently the World Wide Web. More than 15,000 people attend Information Mapping seminars each year.

The best way to combat the disease of overload is to offer the user real, usable information in an intuitive framework. This means formatting and structuring the content for easy reference and assimilation. We'll talk about this in detail in the chapters on Content Design and Cognitive Design.

■ LIMITS TO THE USER'S ATTENTION

If there were only a few hundred or thousand web pages to visit, most web sites would have a captive audience. However, the Web has tens of thousands of sites and millions of web pages. The goal of all design is to attract and hold the user's attention. The differences noted in "Contrasting Media" on page 15 have a significant effect on the creation of web pages that capture users and hold them. Accommodate the users that need the information in your site. That way, you can design for their needs without including too much information for everyone.

Attention Space

A web page can be as long or short as the creator chooses to make it. A web page is displayed in a fixed window size, often rather small. Users will probably skim the visible screen; however, you cannot guarantee they'll read the whole thing. In fact, in many cases, people do not scroll. This makes the visible portion of a web page prime real estate. The middle of the screen is the most desirable real estate. The outside areas contain information that needs to be accessed only a few times. In many cases, if you don't interest the reader here in the prime real estate, you have lost the reader entirely.

The size of a visible web page varies from browser to browser and system to system. Add to this the fact that users can, but often do not, resize their browser window. This makes sizing images and managing whitespace a difficult proposition. In Figure 1.8, WilsonWeb creates a simple look, managing whitespace and conceptual load to identify itself clearly as a small business and effective web marketing newsletter.

Figure 1.8 WilsonWeb handles attention space well
http://www.wilsonweb.com/wmt/

Attention Span

Web pages are not instantly available. They take time to load and time to render, causing the user's attention to wander fairly quickly. Attention span depends upon the perceived value of the page but is nevertheless finite. Someone looking for data to make a large purchase is more motivated to wait than to explore.

Get them reading. Text takes up very few bytes., but images are significantly larger in byte size. This makes page design, especially image creation, a balancing act between fitting enough on a page to interest the user and keeping the user informed and entertained while the page transfers and renders. Always provide some light reading material while the user is waiting. Make sure scrolling can occur dur-

Principle

Design to the attention space.

ing downloading. Don't put so many links at the top that users want to jump off your page before it loads. The Bandwidth Conservation Society in Figure 1.9 handles this well.

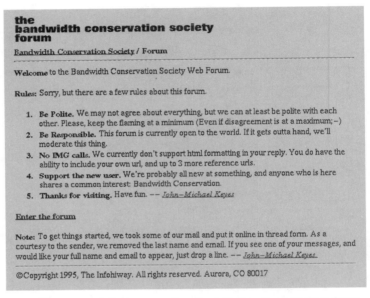

Figure 1.9 Bandwidth Conservation Society Handles Attention Span
http://www.infohiway.com/faster/threads/index.html

Zoom-in Principle. It doesn't matter if your audience is novice, occasional, or expert. Attention span works the same. Remember the zoom-in principle—start with a view of the site that is crisp, minimal, obvious, and aesthetically pleasing. Then provide links that focus or draw in the attention, zooming into the detail with each click of the mouse. HotWired in Figure 1.10 is very good at this. You've always got the BACK button to control recall.

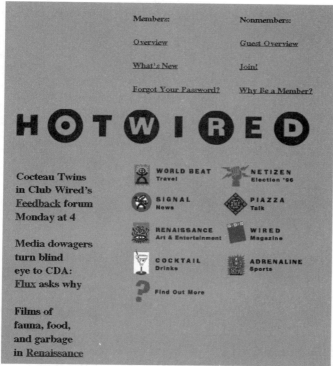

Figure 1.10 HotWired Uses the Zoom-in Principle
Copyright © 1994, 1995, 1996 HotWired Ventures LCC. All Rights Reserved.

■ LOST IN CYBERSPACE

The millions of web pages on thousands of different subjects is not very organized. People often have a problem figuring out where they want to go or how they got there in the first place. AOL, Prodigy, and CompuServe have attempted to created interfaces to allow some organization of the vast store of information. But they, too, launch you out to the World Wide Web with no guide. Since there is no formal structure to the Web, people get lost in cyberspace. A designer cannot save the world, but with appropriate logical linking strategies, a designer can at least guide the user through a single site relatively unscathed.

Sun Microsystems (see Figure 1.11) provides excellent linking strategies to keep you from floating off in cyberspace. They use a common look and feel, plus excellent navigation bars that tell you where you came from and where you're going at all times.

Figure 1.11 Sun Microsystems Doesn't Leave You Lost in Cyberspace

Strategies. Any site that provides some kind of tracking device for the user is a site that will reduce cognitive overload. Humans require seeing the whole picture. They do not need the detail to understand the basics, but they will investigate it if they feel they have an overall view of the subject. Your design can provide users with a way of seeing where they are with respect to your entire web structure. Then, as with a mind map, let the user see all the expert associations.

Link Fossilization. One of the oddest ways to get lost in cyberspace is to follow a link that goes nowhere. Either you get some arcane error or you are sent somewhere else that sends you somewhere else. It is like a wild goose chase. Fight back. Check your own links constantly, and report broken links back to any sites you visit.

KEY POINTS

- You must design web sites in tandem with the user's voice
- Web uses multimedia as the user's communication tool
- New web rules for design highlight internationalization, robust content maintenance, user customization, standards, authentication of information
- New skills are required—Java programming, database analysis, EDI Integration, web law, and web statistics
- Integrate human mind maps with web mind maps
- Interactive design is key to web success
- Concentrate on creating a site that will save the user from getting lost in cyberspace.
- Design problems, such as getting lost in cyberspace, information overload, limits to the user's attention span, have prescribed solutions but require your innovation

PART

one
design
principles

The design principles in this book have been culled from a wide range of disciplines. Each chapter presents a different perspective on meeting the design goals of:

- Designing pages that provide the user with a comfortable level of information, not boredom, not "Information Overload."

- Designing pages and sites that contain and present real information, not raw data.

- Developing the information structures and meta-information required for future generations of the Web including agents.

- Using media appropriate for the type of information conveyed.

- Creating a coherent navigation space.

CHAPTER

2
Content Design

On the Web, you are not just surfing in an electronic book. You are moving through a world of hypermedia, documents on-line, business on-line, education on-line, entertainment on-line, in short, experience on-line. Learning to manage the content will require some getting used to. Mastering what content to include will make your site a winner. Some sites look good but lack content. These sites see visitors once, maybe twice. Other sites are rich in content, trading T1 lines for T3 lines to keep up with the traffic.

■ REDESIGN CONTENT FOR THE MEDIUM

In order to bring you closer to a successful site, this chapter concerns itself with content design. You can use these design principles both for content you want to redesign and for new content. This chapter covers the following:

- What content to include in your web site
- Five different kinds of web sites
- Five content types
- Writing for the web culture
- Recommendations on redesigning text for the Web
- Recommendations on redesigning graphics for the Web
- Plan common look and feel

The Experienced. Watch a few experienced surfers. They know how to find a site, breeze through the links in under five minutes, examine every offering, send e-mail to the Webmaster, cut and paste important data to their web site, and then haul over to a Search Site to ten new references to other topics you suggested at your site but didn't link to.

These experienced people are not using the strategies learned from reading a book, or even from working on software programs. They are true web cruisers, who have learned a new set of skills for searching, consuming, and reusing content on the Web. To prepare the wide population to move onto the Web, you need to redesign the content for the medium.

Redesign Your Thinking. In order to build the best web site that meets and exceeds the customer's expectations, you must consider going back to square one. You must recognize that some of your design assumptions from text and graphics may not work in this environment. Many great companies have failed trying to transfer their success in marketing or advertising, losing sight of the way this medium truly works. You may have to rethink the way you have been representing yourself or your company. The way you write *text* has to change, and the way you use *graphics* must be modified.

Best of the Web. The best way to see how things are different is to look at sites that are successful at it. Several excellent or best of the web sites have cropped up, providing an Internet shorthand to the best design, best content, and best functionality at a site. Content seems to reign as the number one requirement of a good web site. Have it and succeed, lack it and fail.

Point Communications hosts a page of content winners (see Figure 2.1). Although very simple in their own layout, the springboard to excellent content is a must-see.

Look at the top ten sites; Go to
`http://www.pointcom.com/text/topsites/content.html`
Then, compare the content section to what PC Magazine and Netscape think of top design sites. See
`http://www.zdnet.com/~pcmag/special/web100/` and
`http://home.netscape.com/home/whats-cool.html`,

■ WHAT IS CONTENT?

Content is knowledge. The more different kinds of knowledge and information you provide at your site, the more well rounded and useful the site is.

Principle

Text and graphics work differently on the Web.

Try This!

Top Content

Our Sponsor...
Free Ride

These ten sites have the highest ratings for content in Point's **News and Information** catalog for the week of February 12, 1996. Rating Scale 0–50 points

1. Pathfinder
   Content: 48 – Presentation: 45 – Experience: 47
2. CNN Interactive
   Content: 47 – Presentation: 40 – Experience: 45
3. DejaNews Research Service
   Content: 47 – Presentation: 40 – Experience: 45
4. WWW Virtual Library: Electronic Journals
   Content: 47 – Presentation: 28 – Experience: 38
5. 1994 Statistical Abstract
   Content: 47 – Presentation: 31 – Experience: 37
6. Federal News Service
   Content: 47 – Presentation: 34 – Experience: 36
7. GPO Access on the Web
   Content: 47 – Presentation: 37 – Experience: 35
8. CNNfn (the financial network)
   Content: 46 – Presentation: 47 – Experience: 46
9. Bloomberg Online -- WBBR–AM 1130
   Content: 46 – Presentation: 30 – Experience: 42
10. The Newsroom
    Content: 46 – Presentation: 37 – Experience: 40

Next week's top ten listings will be for the category of **Science and Technology.**

Home | Point or Lycos Search | Help | Nominate Your Site

Figure 2.1 PointCom's Top Content Sites

Content is relationships or associations between information. Although you can't anticipate them all, you are the expert of the information, and you can provide the relationships and associations through links and link explanations.

An excellent example of great content can be found at the White House home page (see Figure 2.2). The page is resplendent with excellent information about the government, past and present presidents, government documents, and all the related government agencies.

Content causes thinking and exploration. Engage your users with issues, standards, controversy, new images, new language, and clearly stated goals to make them think critically about your content. Take a look at Joiner's *Team Handbook* materials to help you to state your goals effectively.

Figure 2.2 The White House Home Page Hosts Excellent Content

Content is clever navigation and orientation devices to help users explore your site effectively. (Review our chapter on navigation for some pointers.)

Content includes overviews, descriptions, maps, biographies, location information, glossaries and indexes, accomplishments, goals and missions, opinions, frequently asked questions (FAQs), critiques, and testimonials, and of course much more.

FIVE KINDS OF SITES

Before you try to include every bit of content everyone else is including: STOP! The content you provide depends upon the kind of site you are. Content is dictated by the definition of who you are and the reputation that you are the expert of the content. (See http://www.whitehouse.com) for an excellent example).

The content that you need to include at your site will depend upon the **purpose** of your site. We've identified five types of web sites that predominate on the World Wide Web. At each of these sites, different requirements must be met.

The following section is a recommendations section. Many of these suggestions can apply to more than one area. We are suggesting what to provide at each of these sites, in an attempt to get you thinking or brainstorming what could go into these areas.

- Internet Commerce (outside the firewall)
- Internal Intranet Sites (inside the firewall)
- Topical Sites
- Personal Sites
- Collaborative Work Sites

■ INTERNET COMMERCE (OUTSIDE THE FIRE WALL)

For the external site, you might be tempted to just use the information from the Corporate Communications. That level of content detail will leave many users wanting more. Users may already have seen the entire collection of print materials and be on the web site looking for *more info.* They will certainly be able to find information about you from other sources as well. So, provide them with the best of your world. Don't disappoint the users by offering them the same old stuff. The key here is to tell them who you really are. Users' cross-referencing skills are phenomenal. The number of corporate internet commerce sites is considerably small. Most of them are using the Web as an extension of their product catalogs. You want to go further than this and create a world of on-line commerce. In Figure 2.3, take a look at Sun Microsystems' creative and content-rich site.

Some winners who have helped inspire your choices have built effective, friendly, electronic townships in which you get to know the company as though you lived there. Try the following web sites for some of the best external-content-laden web sites.

`http://www.netscape.com` and `http://www.microsoft.com`, and `http://www.compaq.com`

Human resources

- **External job listings**
- Personnel or departmental listing

Try This!

Principle

Tell them who you really are.

Figure 2.3 Sun Microsystems, Inc.— A Successful Site Outside the Firewall

- Personnel home pages
- FAQs (Frequently Asked Questions)

Interactivity

- Forms to get acquainted with the customer
- Try-and-buy software
- What-if scenario building
- Relationship building
- Expert PreSales Configurator
    - with limitations/constraints
    - with benefits
    - with case studies and real-life examples

- links to tips
- links to the fulfillment system

Company Information

- Stock quotes
- Company prospectus
- Directions to company and subsidiaries
- Mission and goal
- Success stories
- **Columns from independent professionals (internet evangelists)**
- **Professional articles** — Has a magazine ever written an article about how to use your product in a new and interesting way? How about an article about how to tune up your product? It may not cost that much to reproduce some directly related articles, and it can't hurt to add some content that may be only distantly related or spontaneous suggestions.
- FAQs

Product Information

- Fact sheets
- New product announcements
- Benchmarks
- Trade show appearance — Calendar of Events
- FAQs

Sales Information

- Sales office locations
- Key salesman contacts in the area
- Fulfillment status
- Sales forms
- Tracking of shipments
- Sales cycle or philosophy

- **Case histories**

- **Real-life examples**

- FAQs

Support

- Technical Support information

- FAQs

- **Whitepapers**

- **Bug reports**

- **Hints, tips, and other trivia** — Most companies have a couple of people that know all the angles. If ever they left the company, a big hole would remain. There's nothing wrong with giving an expert five minutes of fame. Get your experts to chronicle their processes and principles. Showcase Expert of the Week. Allow others to capitalize on expert head starts.

Classical advertising is picking up some of the traits of the Web by augmenting standard brand and image creation with information distribution. The success of the infomercial is the most notable example. Information distribution can be as deep as a full product description and demonstrations or as simple as a tip like the instruction to cut flowers under water in the 1-800-FLOWERS TV ad.

■ INTRANET SITES (INSIDE THE FIREWALL)

If you are creating a web site for your company, you must consider that there is external information that you wish to share with your clients. And, there is internal company information that is reserved for your staff. The main purpose of an Intranet site is communication and information sharing among internal divisions and departments. The key to your site is how well you all are informed and the trust you build among each other. Communicating values is imperative.

Design Corporate Standards. Before you go too much further, it is important that you develop a statement regarding proprietary information. Certain levels of information cannot be cut and pasted and sent outside the firewall. This has to be made clear to all the employees creating and utilizing content. If you do not have these definitions well articulated and communicated throughout the company, you

Principle

Tell all internal users what you value.

could be headed for trouble. To clarify, consider identifying all departmental documents as *"For internal use only,"* to prevent accidental use on external (Internet) web sites.

Initiate Corporate Guidelines. To avoid everyone going helter-skelter, organize a committee to determine what the common elements on each page should be. Common elements include headers, footers, e-mail address, (i.e., the Webmaster should receive all known bugs or broken links on the page), posting dates, and common look and feel. You want to present one image inside the company, so any continued development that goes on the outside can be smooth and elegant.

Document Ownership. A key factor in maintaining a streamlined, well-oiled web site is to identify who owns what documents. A key method for doing so is to provide contact alias at the bottom of every page. When someone leaves the company, make sure these web pages are turned over to a working manager, so they can be updated regularly and so somebody can be responsible for the validity of the content.

Enhance your corporate culture. When creating a corporate information server, don't limit yourself to just product information and Human Resources manuals. The Web is a perfect place to create or enhance your corporate culture.

Personnel On-line. In addition, intelligent use of the security features of current commerce servers can allow management to share private information and employees to use on-line registration and changes of personnel information.

Keep proprietary information off the external site. Internal information includes sales quotes and payroll and accounting information. Keep the internal information off the outside web. Create your own policies of information sharing, if they don't already exist. Keep the maximum amount of information open.

Connections. The primary purpose of an internal site is to provide the organization a sense of "interconnectedness" (awareness of how things relate to one another in the corporation) and "connectedness" (how the individual relates to these connections, how they can contribute, and how they can learn from them).

Learning Organization. A great Intranet site helps users build shared vision and team learning across the organization. The purpose of the site is to develop creative tension and to avoid emotional tension among individuals. People can piece together new ideas, new ways of doing things, new insight to making their own work flow

Try This!

more easily in a collaborative web site. People begin speaking a common language, understanding the assumptions, actions, and consequences of other people or departments in the organization. This makes for better decision making and collaboration among the various groups within the organization. See Peter Senge's book *The Fifth Discipline*.

Take a look at Netscape at `http://www.netscape.com`. Look beyond the home page. Examine the structure of the entire site. The site is a learning organization for Netscape. They use the consumer as the usability tester, exponentially increasing their software development capability. But it is the web site that allows the communication to flow so freely. The internal staff uses the site to communicate, depositing new-found discoveries and learning what other departments are doing, and all the while history is maintained. Ancillary decision makers can enter into the process anywhere.

Contributions. The ability to publish on the Web has become quite simple. So, any member in an internal organization should be able to contribute to the Intranet site, defining it, refining it, challenging it, and improving it constantly.

Items to add:

Human resources

- Bulletin boards and chat groups

- Campus maps

- Policies and procedures

- Company calendar

- Company memos and communications

- Searchable company phone book

- Company program contacts — ride-sharing, company volleyball team, credit union contact info

- Corporate vision statement and goals

- Employee recognition

- Employee phone numbers and mail stops

- Employee web pages

- On-line training

- Org charts
- Procedure manuals and information manuals — how to use the phone system or request a replacement badge.
- Project descriptions
- Resource information (i.e., who deals with whom)
- FAQs

Product Information

- Fact sheets
- New product announcements
- Benchmarks
- FAQs

Sales Information

- Sales office locations
- Key salesman contacts in the area
- Fulfillment status
- Sales quotes sales forms
- Tracking of shipments
- Sales cycle or philosophy
- FAQs

Finance

- Nonsensitive payroll and accounting information
- FAQs
- Business and financial information

Interface to Company Databases

Many of these corporate/company functions can be tied together. Once you are entered into a corporate database, you can have access to various on-line job aids that continue to augment your identity in the corporation. Your history, skills, qualifications, education, projects, and a lot of your corporate activity become part of the entire organizational database.

Others can learn from this database. What are the successes within the company? What are the processes that can be streamlined, improved, or deleted?

- Benefits changes (401K changes, beneficiary changes, insurance changes)

- Company forms

- Conference room reservations

- Employee information changes (address, marital status)

- Employee surveys

- Travel expense reports and approvals

- FAQs

Topical Web Site

Topical sites vary along a spectrum. At one end, the site features a very specific organization of information: Jobs in America, Environmental Issues, Tourism in the Caribbean, or the Elvis site. These topical sites may be corporate businesses sites selling or promoting information on a particular subject. They are designed more for immediate information retrieval and/or amusement. On the other side, the sites can be composite sites that list category after category of information. The various groupings of topics are not necessarily related.

Topical Sites Spectrum

Specific Topic   Multiple Topics

E.g. Biking Information   Yahoo

At the other extreme, topical sites cover a wide range of topics. Yahoo (http://www.yahoo.com), Infoseek (http://www.infoseek.com), Excite (http://www.excite.com) or the World Wide Web Consortium (http://www.w3.org) are examples. These topical sites are information providers. They bring the user into them for the experience of many topics. They provide query-based searching and pull topics from multiple worldwide resources. Topical sites are also one of the most valuable places to put sponsorship-type advertising. Topical web sites are used by:

- Organizations devoted to unique areas of interest, such as Green Peace

- Consortium of related companies

- Web-indexing company serving as a point of focus for an industry such as GolfWeb for golf or Stellar Web for general business

Below are some recommendations for additions to topical sites:

- Company/site listings — Don't just make a list of sites. Add editorial value to make your list worth something. Add descriptions. Rank or evaluate the sites for quality content or specialty sites. Indicate such things as page size in bytes of the home page and an average page, whether special browsers or viewers are needed. In Figure 2.4, the new topical search company rates your search request by relevance, using concept-based searching.

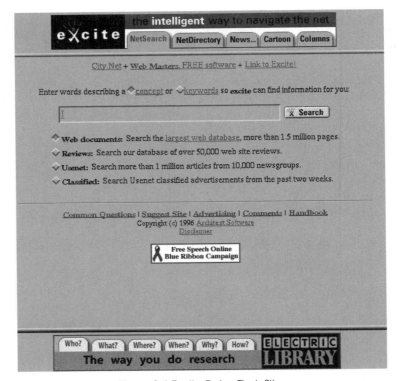

Figure 2.4 Excite Rates Their Sites

- New Happenings — Don't just follow the standard What's New listings of web sites and web happenings. Include information about conferences, guest appearances by professionals, unique findings.

- Add Bulletin Board services such as job-posting areas and want ads.

- Include information about local area groups. The Internet is by nature an international medium. As much as people organize on-line, they still appreciate being able to meet face-to-face. Create places to make the local connection, and broadcast events.

- Add regular columnists.

- Chat areas — Use hypermail, netnews, and webchat programs for user/site interaction and cross-communication between users.

- Add pointers to tutorials and Getting Started guides.

- Add resource listings — Support vendors. For a publishing site, this might be a list of printers, whereas a Mac-oriented place might have support addresses, phone, and site information.

- List sponsorships.

Personal Web Page

Just because companies and organizations are doing web pages doesn't mean that individuals are left out in the cold. A personal web site can be a place to hang your resume, publish papers to establish or enhance your professional reputation, or show off a portfolio of your work. It can be a place to introduce yourself to like-minded people that share your passion for Jimi Hendrix or Tai Kwan Do. In Figure 2.5, Howard Rheingold uses his concept of Brainstorms to pull the reader into his world.

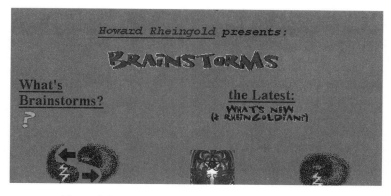

Figure 2.5 Howard Rheingold's Personal Web Page

There is an emerging method for becoming recognized in many professions and some hobbies as a resource or valuable person. In the old days, you were published (often a very hard task), spoke or networked at conferences, and … to establish a reputation. With the Web, publishing has become a piece of cake. It makes a good preliminary step to paper publication, and it can be a lucrative intermediate step as well.

Items to include:

- Biography
  - Who are you?
  - Classical resume timeline with two-liner job/company/buzz word descriptions. This can be linked to detailed job descriptions.
  - Education
  - Nonstandard experiences — hobbies, volunteer work, awards
- FAQs
- Writings
- Projects working on
- Experiences and personal information—travelogues, epiphanies, most influential book or music, role model, favorite food, sport, or hobby. This gives people insight into who you are, not just the dry facts. It also gives material for starting a discussion with a complete stranger, often a rocky business.

Collaborative Web Sites

Collaborative web sites allow a team to work on the same material at the same time. Since many products today are components of knowledge products, collaborative development can occur easily online. Sun-on-the-Net, in Figure 2.6, is a collaborative site issued to tell Sun's Internet story. On the outside of the firewall, however, much of the project management information and issues had to be deleted for security reasons.

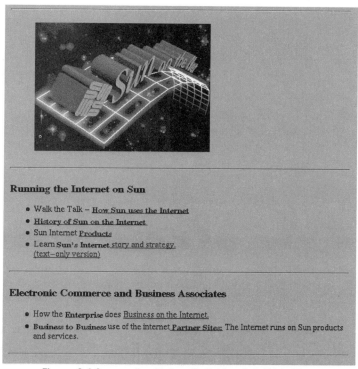

Running the Internet on Sun

- Walk the Talk – How Sun uses the Internet
- History of Sun on the Internet
- Sun Internet Products
- Learn Sun's Internet story and strategy.
  (text–only version)

Electronic Commerce and Business Associates

- How the Enterprise does Business on the Internet.
- Business to Business use of the internet Partner Sites: The Internet runs on Sun products and services.

Figure 2.6 Sun-on-the-Net, a Collaborative Web Site

Some recommended inclusions:

- Goal statement, strategy, and ground rules for the site

- Project management information (track status, resources, costs, constraints, overview, breakdown of the tasks); you may not want to include these if they are out of the firewall

- Full biographical information about each member

- To Do list, so action items can be monitored by the group, and the project scope can be measured

- Meeting section, with minutes to provide collaborators with key history and action items

- Links to appropriate associative information

- Graphics, diagrams, and figures directory and an index in the directory

- Directory for templates
- Technical or any related documents with searchable tools to sort through the documents
- Bugs list, or Problems list with solutions and names of the persons who both submitted and/or solved the problem
- Glossary to explain terms and acronyms
- Consider password protection so only a given group of individuals can see the collaborative site; the information may be proprietary and you would not want others to see it.
- FAQs

WHAT CONTENT GOES ON-LINE?

Content, Content, Content. Web readers like content. But, not everything you have stored in the file rooms of your business, home, or office needs to go on-line. As a matter of fact, only the right content that helps people make decisions or have fun should be included. Certainly, content needs to be plentiful, but it also needs to be meaningful.

In order to determine what meaningful is, you have to spend some serious time in meeting rooms, brainstorming and including everyone's needs and wants. You'll need to talk to the consumers of your site and sites like yours. See Chapter 4, *Audience Considerations* for details.

Consolidate content from all sources

Your site is much more than just an advertisement for your services or products. If you design the top page simply as an ad, you will probably attract few readers. However, if you provide content from all the sources, you widen the range of users interacting with your site.

- Let people know who you are.
- Tell them what you do.
- Explain why you do it.
- Show them how you do it.
- Offer what others think of what you are doing.

Take a look at the Sun Microsystems pages in Color Plate 1-1. It is clear what this company does, why they're doing it, and how you can find out more about the company, the products, and what others think of the company, just from their home page. Once you get moving through Sun's web pages, you gain a clear understanding of the company and know why it is a successful player in the Internet and networking market.

Partners. You can either create all your own content, or you can partner with content providers who are expert in certain areas of your field. This is a more practical and reliable way of ensuring expertise at your site. Content providers offer an objective view of your product or service and provide up-to-date marketing information from the consumer's point of view. More importantly, you can sign up your partners to maintain the quality and accuracy of the information. This distributed model allows you to share the management of the web site, the only way you'll be able to manage expert content.

Full Content, Full Media. In addition to making sure that all different kinds of content are available about you or your product at your site, make sure you've included sound, motion, animation, or video. The user will want to experience you with as many senses as possible. The Web is a haven for multimedia and user experience. Make the experience as rich as possible. Remember, go light on bandwidth while you're creating full media, at least for now.

Take a look at Rad Technology's Tester page at `http://www-dsed.llnl.gov/documents/WWWtest.html` to view the potential full media of the Internet.

Principle

Include content in sound, motion, animation, or video to enrich the user's experience.

Try This!

FIVE CONTENT TYPES

Grouping content among the five types of web sites is a great start. Having supercategories to fit all your content provides the kind of structure you need to get the various contributors working on the presentation. This section explains five content types to assist you in designing and developing your content. Users come to the Web in search of knowledge. What users benefit from in the quest of that knowledge is:

- education (learning about something)
- performance (learning **how to do** something).

Designing with content types allows you to create pages that educate and help users perform. The five content types are:

- Facts
- Concepts
- Procedures

- Processes

- Principles

Facts are specific information in the form of a statement or data. Facts are unique, requiring no explanation. For example, that the IP address for Gunter's machine is 192.102.249.3 is a fact. It requires no explanation; the relationship is one to one. That statistics about the Web can be located at `ftp//nis.nsf.net/statistics/nsfnet/` is a fact. Users crave facts because they represent fundamental knowledge and provide the building blocks for more critical thinking. You must provide lots of relevant facts in your content.

Concepts or definitions are necessary for understanding what something is and what it is not. Concepts and definitions can be concrete, like "What is client/server hardware?" Users can grasp the concept with multimedia animations that provide a visual picture of a client/server system. Concepts can be abstract, like "What is Java?" Users can understand what Java is by an explanation of the components of Java's functionality, by a demonstration of Java applets, by downloading Java to their site, or by a connection to chatting sessions or newsgroups to discuss the concept of Java. Users rely on concepts and definitions to penetrate expert content.

Procedures identify a sequential number of steps that tell you how to do something specific. For example, adding a bookmark in the Netscape browser is a three-step procedure. First, you open the URL you want to record. Second, you select Bookmark from the menu. Third, you select Add Bookmark. That's it. Procedural information is highly valued on the Web. It educates users to do something they want or need. It is not enough to simply tell a user where a tool is located at your site. You must provide procedural content, so they know how to download it and use it. The success of the Web is, in fact, dependent upon content providers writing good procedural instructions.

Rad Technology at `http//www.rad.com` utilizes procedural information frequently to explain software installation and setup. Rad Technology uses sequential steps to explain software configuration.

Try This!

Processes explain how something works. This is a little different from procedures, which tell you the steps to making something work. Processes involve a flow of multiple events that describe how a system works. Processes are usually technical, like "How do you configure a Web Server for security on the Internet?" or they can be business oriented, like "How do you increase sales revenue by developing a presence on the We?" This process requires more than a sequential se-

Try This!

ries of steps and may have not been successfully executed by anyone yet. Explaining processes requires a more detailed design to identify all the individual parts and how they are interconnected.

In order to help users understand how to write HTML code, the HTML Literary Guild at `http://www.mindspring.com` developed an apprenticeship program to assist users in walking through the process with mentors.

At Sun Microsystems, a section called Sun on the Net `http://www.Sun.COM:80/sun-on-net/index.html` walks users through the process of setting up a server and configuring it for doing business on the Internet. In Figure 2.7, Sun Microsystems uses processes on their pages to explain how to use the Internet at Sun.

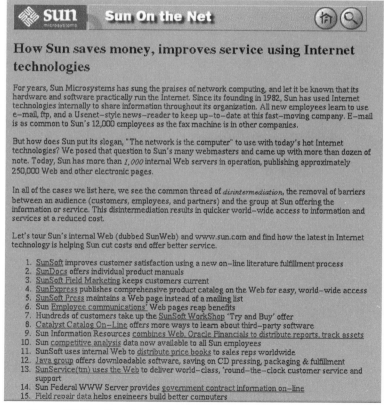

Figure 2.7 Sun Explains the Process of Using the Internet at Sun

Users visit your sites to find out how the processes work in your organizations. How your products work is a process. The more time you take to identify these processes and put them on the Web, the more users you'll have.

Principles and guidelines are general advice given by experts who have developed a knack for doing something well. The experts use "gut instinct," "intuition," "feelings." Experts follow certain guiding ideas and insights, tweaking here and there when something differs. They use procedures and processes, but in different ways each time.

A typical principle is how to sell a client/server system to an oil and gas customer. The content needs to include all competitive information on the client/server systems, an in-depth knowledge of the oil and gas customers' needs, prices, potential uses of the product, and a host of other things that only an expert would guess. You can create on-line experiences with the experts, package expert procedures and processes, relate success stories, tell anecdotes, create a database of like experiences. Principles are proven experience that web users will want to take advantage of to accelerate their performance. To date, we haven't seen a good site that identifies principles on-line. We believe the next killer consumer product will, indeed, utilize principles on-line. They separate experts from novices.

■ REPRESENTING CONTENT TYPES ON THE WEB

This section suggests some ways to create the five content types online. Some of these suggestions are relatively basic. Ample literature has been written concerning the appropriate way to represent the content types in multimedia (see Ruth Clark, 1992). Following are recommendations for displaying them on the Web.

Facts
Which is which?

- Use color graphical images to display facts.
- Use tables or other job aids to show codes, numbers, data, places, times, etc.
- Search on Job Aids in Yahoo.

Concept/Definitions
What is it?

- Use graphics, JPEG images, photographs to explain new terms, ideas.
- Use text for short, brief glossary links.
- Take time to explain what the concept is not.
- Test your users with games, trivia questions, contests, etc.

Procedure/Steps
How do you do it?

- Provide numbered lists that explain how to do the procedure.
- Write one step per line.
- Use short, terse sentences with action verbs.
- Insert small graphical screen shots to emphasize "which one."
- Use links to show possible decisions or actions you might take.
- Include reasons to perform a step.

Process/Stages
How does it work?

- Use animation and video to dramatize how the process works.
- Rely on audio for quick reviews.
- Provide text that explains how the process works or what happens during the process.
- Separate process into phases or stages.
- Focus on functions, movements, conditions and their results.

Principle/Guidelines
What would an expert do?

- Explain the cause and effect of the principle.
- Identify the experts and introduced them asap.
- Identify guidelines and encourage flexibility.
- Provide varying opposing opinions, not a single rule or order.
- Get users on-line chatting, e-mailing, responding to newsgroups.
- Provide a success database.

These five content types assist the user in learning about something or learning how to do something at your web site. Users appreciate seeing this kind of content at a site because it is concrete, easy to follow, and encourages the user to take some kind of action. In short, it encourages interactivity and develops a relationship between you and the user.

■ MEET THE AUDIENCE'S GOALS

Content types help meet audience goals. Use them to add rich content to your site. Using all of your currently available materials may not be sufficient. Some materials may not be appropriate for the web audience. Read Chapter 4, *Audience Considerations* to guide you in getting to know your audience well, so the content you provide hits the mark.

WRITING FOR THE WEB CULTURE

The Internet culture has developed different communication methods to combat the problems found in the information-intensive environment. They value substance over fluff.

Avoid descriptors, go for meat. Users are more autonomous and trust in their own values. They make their own decisions. Instead of saying things are "better," "improved," "great," or other expansive adjectives, give them the facts and let them decide for themselves.

Speed up! Internet culture values signal over noise. You must focus on the topic. Long, meandering sidetracks or deliberate nontopic interruptions are very time consuming to this culture. Time is the currency of the 90s.

Use nonverbal communication. Use graphical bullets that say something and are not gratuitous. Graphics need to tell a story, not pretty up the page. Chatting groups use human icons to portray personality (look at Sega's chatting area, `http://www.segaoa.com/live/`. Internet culture values the nonverbal communications methods (i.e., smileys, SHOUTING, *emphasizing*, _pausing or effect_ and `<smirk>` emoticons   :   >) a happy smiling face or   ;   >) a happy winking face.

Write lots of FAQs. FAQs (Frequently Asked Questions), in essence, are just that: facts. Break them into chunks, allowing for quick reference. Makes your FAQ appear intimate, as though you were talking to a friend or companion. Write persuasively with little discussion. The document persuades you with facts but doesn't force a decision upon a reader.

Consider interactive content. Your content requires interaction. You need to get information from your users or provide ways for them to order products and services, talk to you, and play. Interactive capabilities include forms, surveys, registration, ordering forms, customized analytical responses to user input. See Chapter 9, *Interactivity Design* for more. You can benefit greatly from these interactive web pages. Users are attracted to them first because interactive pages give them something to do instead of read.

Try This!

Go to `http://www.niyp.com/`and try the interactivity on the Internet yellow pages, or the U. S Post Offices service for zip codes at `http://www.usps.gov/ncsc/lookups/lookup_zip+4.html`

REDESIGNING TEXT FOR THE WEB

Readers don't read web pages in the same way as they do a book. Most users scan a web page, looking across the page for cues. Since they're not reading, you have to accommodate for the new scanning skills being applied to moving around on the Web. Your content messages need to be delivered via text for now.

Many of these subjects have been covered in length in other places in the book. The focus here is the impact redesigning text has on content. Here are several tips for redesigning the way you write text for the Web.

1. Emphasize the important up front.
2. Focus on the links.
3. Shorten the text.
4. Format text effectively.
5. Remove transitional rhetoric.
6. Avoid overstimulus.
7. Break content into chunks.
8. Remove transitional rhetoric
9. Change the tone.
10. Beware of web cliches.
11. Add meta-information.

■ EMPHASIZE THE IMPORTANT

Your audience has little time to waste. They are not reading anything from beginning to end. If they can't find what they want immediately, they are out of there. Try to resist the temptation to refer your readers elsewhere. If you bring something up, tell it to them NOW. Now is when they're paying attention. Now is when it is important. Keep them at the same place with information, instead of redirecting them to "above," "below," or "will be explained later."

■ Focus on the Links

Design the links on your pages as though the reader were only reading the links. Identify patterns in your links and make sure you're telling a story with the links. Use both internal and external links.

Parts of Speech. Don't get hung up using nouns and verbs to link. Make other parts of speech link as well. Make some of your links nouns and verbs, but use some pronouns, adjective, and phrases for variety.

Examples:

We'd like to hear from you, so please write us.
(verb phrase)

Try downloading this hot VRML help application.
(adjective phrase)

Learning about you is fun, take a personality test.
(pronoun)

■ Shorten Text

Don't be verbose. Users will simply not take time to read a lot of text. Use the command verbs to suggest to readers what to do next. Command verbs are like orders. Make very word count.

Examples:

Click on the BACK button in your browser.

Provide more info on next screen.

Choose a CD title.

■ Text Formatting

Make text brief, use active voice. Limit length to 60 (64 x 20 pixels) per line. Use bullets to format a list. Use whitespace. Not less than 10-point. Use sans-serif fonts for the main text to ensure that the audience can read the text. Avoid uppercase. Left-justify. Use bold and italics sparingly.

■ REMOVE TRANSITIONAL RHETORIC

You just don't know where users came onto your web site. They may have gone directly to the URLs home page. They might have linked to one of your product pages. You can't even be sure if readers are reading the paragraph from start to finish; they could be scanning the links. So, write clearly, in short sentences, and remove the common transitional devices between paragraphs. Avoid words like "consequently," "subsequently," "on the other hand," and "it follows that." They are based on information that either precedes or follows them. You can't be sure the audience read the preceding sentence or thought. Users may not be following you in a linear fashion, so keep each idea or small grouping of words unique in itself. In the Bandwidth Conservation Society, in Figure 2.8, look a the text flow. The site is easy to read because of the absence of transitional rhetoric.

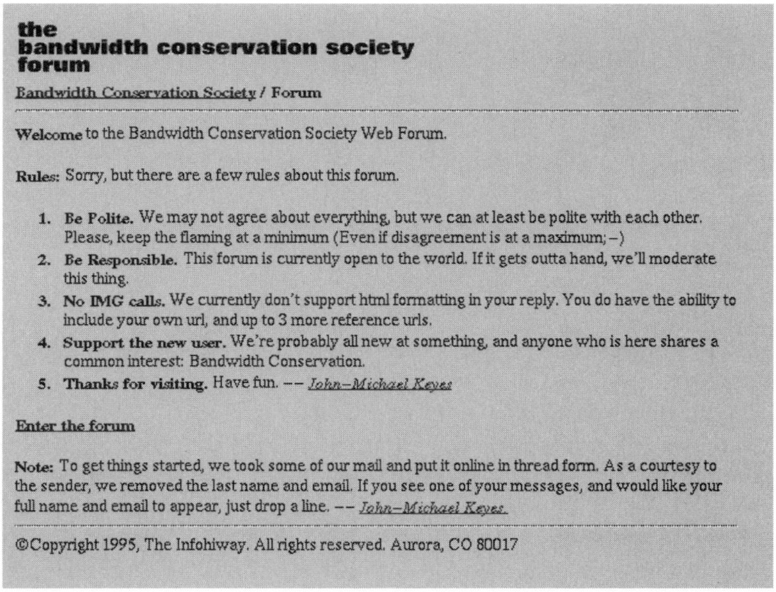

the bandwidth conservation society forum

Bandwidth Conservation Society / Forum

Welcome to the Bandwidth Conservation Society Web Forum.

Rules: Sorry, but there are a few rules about this forum.

1. **Be Polite.** We may not agree about everything, but we can at least be polite with each other. Please, keep the flaming at a minimum (Even if disagreement is at a maximum; –)
2. **Be Responsible.** This forum is currently open to the world. If it gets outta hand, we'll moderate this thing.
3. **No IMG calls.** We currently don't support html formatting in your reply. You do have the ability to include your own url, and up to 3 more reference urls.
4. **Support the new user.** We're probably all new at something, and anyone who is here shares a common interest: Bandwidth Conservation.
5. **Thanks for visiting.** Have fun. –– *John–Michael Keyes*

Enter the forum

Note: To get things started, we took some of our mail and put it online in thread form. As a courtesy to the sender, we removed the last name and email. If you see one of your messages, and would like your full name and email to appear, just drop a line. –– *John–Michael Keyes.*

©Copyright 1995, The Infohiway. All rights reserved. Aurora, CO 80017

Figure 2.8 Bandwidth Conservation Society Tight Text

■ REWRITE REFERENCES

Rewrite references so the user knows where the reference is located. Implicit references don't work well on the Web. You can't assume where information is going to fall on any given browser, so when you are referring to another block of text on the Web, you need to be explicit about its location, description, or the number of steps you're referring to. The user may have to go searching or scrolling for the complete reference.

Example:
Using a phrase like "as can be seen in the figure below" to introduce a figure doesn't work well on the Web. You can't tell whether the figure is on the screen or not. Instead place a Clickable graphic on the page and beside it tell exactly what the image is, with a link to click on for more detail. Figure 2.9 provides an easy design to accommodate referencing that works on any browser.

Fishing is great in the `Great Lakes` area.

Figure 2.9 Using Text with Graphics for Immediate Referencing

An example:
Book Reference: The procedure below explains how to order the product.
Web Reference: `Order` your product.

Book Reference: After you've filled out your form, it should look like the one in Table 5.
Web Reference: `Fill out` this form. Or, see a <u>completed form</u>.

■ AVOID OVERSTIMULUS

Many designers want you to link to other wonderful sites that you can't live without. References and links are good, but if you start a list of too many unrelated links, with short, unqualified comments beneath them, you will be overdoing it. You are overstimulating your users. They can't see the associations, and the links aren't telling them a story. So, their brains refuse to take in information, they feel uncomfortable, leave, and won't return.

Avoid this:

Favorite Spots

Barabbas Site. Good, it's full of stuff.
Kennedy Page. Everything you wanted to know about the family.
My Favorite Search Tool. Gotta use this to find anything.
Exercise Site. Order products, meet people, take a test.

Instead group your sites under a category, and write simple explanatory text. List a few of the best, rather than everyone you can find. For example:

Jobs and Career Placement

Monster Board provides on-line job searching by state and a resume generator.
Careers on-line focuses on a career orientation, and searching by industry.
9000 hi-tech jobs are listed at this site.

■ CHANGE THE TONE FOR THE INTERNET AUDIENCE

Readability on the Web is different than in other media. You must be conversational, speaking to readers as though you've known them for a long time., like family members. Familiarity on the Web makes up for the isolation in a global maelstrom of images, text, suggestions, and recommendations about what to do with your time on the Web.

Modernize the language. Use language appropriate to the audience. Lean, however, toward modern language, rather than formal businesslike English. Using terms like "check it out," or "Cool Sites" is appealing to a generation transitioning to this new medium. Be careful to keep the language fresh and not full of overused, overexposed terms. Be original and mature. Let the language grow with the site. Let new words modernize or *webecize* your site.

> This "whopping 600-plus page Webmagazine devoted to arts and entertainment" definitely delivers the gigagoods: excellent coverage of film, music, food, theater, and photography, among other fields. (See http://www.pointcom.com/text/reviews/zzsh_018.htm

Try This!

Visit http://www.wired.com and look at the way they use language. Also, try http://www.suck.com and see a sister site that uses a strong, modern tone. Also look at Netly News at Pathfinder (http://www.pathfinder..com) or WebReview at GNN (http://gnn.com/wr/), which are modern sites writing wise but not as "trendy."

Assume educated users. You can speak directly to users as though they were educated. Most likely, they can read fairly well if they are browsing the text-laden web. So, assume you can speak in an educated tone. Try to make users understand that you are providing them with the best information you've got, so they can make their own decision about what to do with it.

■ COPYEDIT TEXT

In this new medium, users are intolerant of anything less than superior. They do not allow a single error anymore in any medium without a barrage of mail admonishing the producers for misspellings, grammatical errors, or inaccurate facts. Errors equal incompetence to users. Worse yet, the quality of your services and/or skills are being evaluated by such damning criteria as a single misspelling. Read everything you write and check it twice for correctness and appropriateness.

■ WEB CLICHES

Sharing ideas, graphics, formats, etc., is good on the Web. Just because you see other sites doing something though, doesn't mean that it is good and you should copy it.

Under Construction. Many sites often say that their site is under construction. Every site is under construction, really. Web sites are in a constant state of growing, refining, and improving. If you don't have any content at your site, don't put a site out there. If you have limited content, put what you've got out there and start working on it daily. Users are in the habit of coming back to check out a site to see how it has improved.

Page Access. Page access counters are another cliche that can be avoided. Many sites add them to the home page to let people know how many hits the site is getting daily. In same cases, it is good to know how many people are hitting the site, but it may dissuade others from staying at the site because the access number is too small. Consider first why you are using a page access counter. Use one if it does your site some good.

Netscape Now. Linking to sponsor sites is good. But, what is the point of letting users know which browser a site is designed for? If you're using Netscape, you'll see the Netscape enhancements. If you've Javatized your page, Java users will see it. Otherwise, you're telling everyone else, We've got something that you don't. What's the point?

Top 5 Percent or Cool Site. Unless you can provide criteria for why a site is in the top 5 percent or is a cool site, then saying so is meaningless. It is purely subjective on your part. You must explain what features the site has that make it good, and you should show several examples identifying the features you've highlighted.

■ To Understand the Web, Use the Web

If you're going to design a site on the Web, make sure you spend some serious time cruising the Web finding out what kind of content you prefer yourself. You are probably the best critic for the quality of your site.

Study Hot List patterns. You will undoubtedly start creating a Hot List or Favorite Places list. After you've created a dozen or so, go back over them and find out what you like about them. What features do they have in common? What do you think they did that pulled you in? What functionality did these different sites provide that you thought were have-tos. You'll discover a lot about what you think is good on the Web.

■ An International Note

Write your work for translation. Many international sites prefer translating the best web sites. Every site is not intended for international audiences. But if you are planning on communicating with people from other cultures, make sure you spend some time getting to know that culture.

Pay special attention to customs about religion, gender, politics, and language differences.

- Stay away from jargon, acronyms (without explanations), slang, colloquialisms. They'll be misunderstood.

- Use fewer clauses in your sentences. Second language users often have limited vocabulary and translate when they read.

- Try to keep Subject-Verb-Object format. This is not an international format, but English is quite common around the world, thus a common format.

- Avoid prepositional phrases. Prepositions translate poorly into other languages.

- Write in a conversational but business-like tone. Try to be modern, but a lot of "trendy" phrases just don't translate.

- Include glossaries and indexes.

- Provide more content and detail; it is highly appreciated.

- Format numbers and dates. Some sites allow you to choose a language, then all the numbers, dates, etc., format at the site. Know your audience, and use their formats. Rarely will you consider using both formats.

    - $2.50 vs. 2,50

    - Month Day, Year vs. Day, Month, Year

- Use metric measurements if possible

REVISE GRAPHICS FOR MEDIUM

Reduce the size of the graphics. Large splashy graphics at the top of the page don't work on the Web. They work great in magazines, but most users won't have enough patience to wait for them to load. There are so many other places to go and since time is the currency of the 90s, you will most likely lose many of the people you're trying to attract. Keep your graphics small or at least not bandwidth intensive. You can stay innovative; just design keeping the limitation of the medium in mind.

Table 2-1 provides some basic rules about graphics for the web page. For a more detailed explanation of graphics, see Chapter 7, *Designing Graphical Elements*

Table 2-1   Web Element Sizing

POSITION ON WEB PAGE	SIZE CONSTRAINTS
Background Images	4K
Site Logo	12K
Image Map	60K for Full Image Map 30K for Image Map with Text
Main Image	30K (or generate it on-the-fly with Java)
Bullets	2K
Custom Icons	10K
Custom Horizontal Rules	5-10K
Banners and Navigation Bars	
Photos	30K

Provide explanations with the graphics

Graphics require clear, simple meaningful explanations why they are on your page. The Web is a graphical environment, and users are bombarded with images constantly. Some of the images are self-explanatory, others are befuddling. Provide explanations with your site; the user shouldn't have to guess why the graphic is there. Limit the number of words to describe the graphic and increase the user's comprehension of the graphic.

▪ ILLUSTRATIONS

Keep illustrations simple. Compromise reality for clarity. Provide various views into an illustration, zoom, angle turning, etc. Again, make sure all illustrations are clearly identified with accompanying text.

▪ CHARTS

Consider how much of the chart the audience will see on the screen. Cycle and bar and line must be seen completely. Rechunk the chart if it is too big. Test the charts on different screens with different browsers to ensure that they come out as you expect them to. Make sure all data is labelled correctly. Much of a chart can be clickable for further information.

▪ TABLES

Provide a sentence between table and text. Try to make sure there is no clicking or scrolling to see best information. Use two or a maximum of three columns and no more than 10 rows. Make the rows and columns substantially wide. Keep rows to a minimum. Always use table headings and keep them down to 1–4 words max. Use plenty of whitespace around the table to show off the content inside.

▪ WHITESPACE

In order to avoid a graphically cumbersome page, include substantial whitespace around your graphics. The more whitespace, the stronger the message. Compare the two graphics in Figure 2.10 to examine how text and graphics can be combined with the proper amount of whitespace to enhance a page.

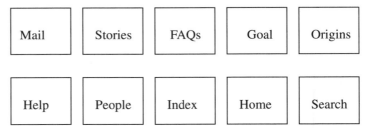

BAD EXAMPLE

Mail	Stories	FAQs	Goal	Origins

Help	People	Index	Home	Search

GOOD EXAMPLE

Get to know our people. Find out about our origins
and our goals. Read about our FAQs and stories.
Always feel free to e-mail us.

Home		Index		Search

Figure 2.10 Whitespace Used Properly

Originality

It would be better to strive for originality in your graphical images
than to rely on cut-and-paste graphics that you can retrieve or download out of any graphical library. If you want to be distinguished as a
good web designer, spend some time with a graphics artist and find a
way to represent your product or service that best supports your
needs.

PLAN COMMON LOOK AND FEEL

You built the web site and you have hundreds of links to excellent content. Your users are surfing forward and backward, searching for appropriate terms that they find immediately. Forms are coming in with database information, products are being ordered, and you're receiving e-mails that praise your site.

You want your users to know which pages are yours. You want to remind them that all the design and development that is making their lives easier came from your web site. In order to provide the users with a sense of knowing where they are within your site at all times, you need to develop a common look and feel for all pages.

Logo or Brand Identification. Many sites repeat their name across all of their pages, so you know when you are in the domain of their information. Repeating a logo or a graphic that identifies you is a form of branding.

Look around the corporate sites, Sun (`http://www.sun.com`), Apple (`http://www.apple.com`), Netscape (`http://www.netscape.com`), Microsoft (`http://www.microsoft.com`). Notice the omnipresence of their logo and how it is repeated to indicate presence.

Navigation Bars. Some sites (`http://www.sun.com`) use a series of navigation bars. These bars across the top of the page tell you what subgroups of information you are located in, as well as where you came from. This provides you the ability to track or manage the content you're investigating. Navigation bars are an important look-and-feel feature. In Figure 2.11, Sun sports a navigation bar to say where in SunSoft you just came from: "WorkShop Developer's Products," which originated on "Products and Solutions" page. And, within this navigation bar, how to return to Sun's Home Page, SunSoft's home page, and a search tool.

Principle

Provide a repeating element throughout your web site.

Try This!

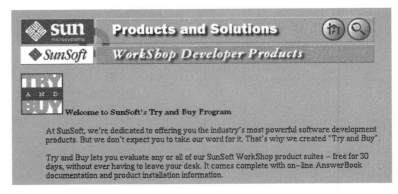

Figure 2.11 Navigational Bars in a Common Look and Feel

Banners. Like navigation bars, banners go across the top of the page, repeating certain functions. Banners can be image maps or textual menus. They perform the same function as menus in most of the software you use. The tools for operating at the site are located here. Often, the banners include a way to get back home, use a search tool, a table of contents, a glossary, an index. Frequently, banners repeat the overall structure of the site.

Repeating Icons. At some sites, you can use a repeating icon or graphic to identify that the site belongs to your URL. The color or shape of the icon can be easily recognized by the user. This can be the company logo or can be a unique set of graphics you develop for the web site. In Figure 2.12 the Discovery web page relies on repeating icons.

Figure 2.12 Repeating Icons

Incoming Links. Another useful look-and-feel feature is to explain to users that they are looking at a link that originated from a mother page. You can use text that indicates the origin of an incoming link or you can use a graphic. You can also use menus that branch off from a main menu, and repeat for each subsequent page. See http://space.njit.edu:5080/papers/overview.html.

Whatever you choose, make sure the user can easily identify the common features on each page, so they can easily move through the content.

■ PLAN COLOR SCHEME

Choose a color scheme that makes reading text easy. Colored text does not have the same legibility as black and white text. If you have a lot of text to read, consider black and white first, with two colors for links: blue for unread links and red for visited links. If you are considering color, provide a significant lightness difference between the information (text) and the background. With palettes of 8 bits (256 colors) or more, you have a wide range of colors to use be used while preserving good legibility. Take at look at GolfWeb in the Color Plates section to experience a powerful use of color. Is green not appropriate for a site called GolfWeb?

Link Colors. Link color choices can be turned on and off with Options -> General Preferences -> Colors -> Always Use My Colors -> Overriding Documents (in Netscape). Other browsers have other ways to change the colors. So be aware that color is not necessarily a driver for your site. Users have control over the colors that they want to see on the screen.

Backgrounds. The background color affects the reading of data significantly. Choose a neutral background color, like white, black, or gray if you are going to use a lot of different-colored text. You may very likely need to use the color scheme of the company look and feel. Make sure this combination translates well to the computer screen.

A Word About Commercial On-line Services

On-line services have taken a great step in making information on-line available to everyone. The format, the presentation, and the quality of the information is fairly decent.

Most of the on-line services prepackage the kind of information that you might want to see. Because their libraries are so extensive, they offer a considerable amount of content. And, the content is updated frequently. They tend to be graphic intensive, but provide some well-laid-out sites. They chunk information well and manage the cognitive overload issues substantially well.

◼ WORD OF WARNING

Like magazines, or television programs, an on-line site carries its own political credo that dictates both the content availability and the political correctness of the information. On-line services streamline information in such a way as to promote their own credo and philosophy. This is admirable in terms of freedom of speech. Do remember that the information you are receiving from these sites carry with it the limitations of information accessibility. What you see is what you get, and the censure or political focus of the site dictates the content you are permitted to see.

Many of these sites have added Internet access to their sites, so there is a door from the political hotbed of information conservatism to the wild, wild west environment of the World Wide Web. The point here is to confirm and substantiate any facts or information that is provided to you from any site.

◼ PUBLISH CURRENT MATERIAL REGULARLY

Many web sites have taken on the appearance of an electronic magazine. The front home page differs every time. In this way, the user can look forward to the changing graphic, information, and content. The basic underlying structure remains the same, but the feature articles change. Not only should you publish current material regularly, but you should change the structure of site as well. Users habituate themselves to scanning over sites that haven't changed their look and feel.

For example, `http://home.netscape.com` uses frames and JavaScript extensively with the release of Netscape 2.0 to express content more effectively. Netscape can update the different frames independently, keeping users abreast of new angles or aspects of the main window.

◼ UPDATE STALE CONTENT

Timeliness is very important on the Web. In the print world, a piece of literature might be used even if it is six months old because of the expense of updating and reprinting. The Web doesn't have that kind of cost overhead; thus, audiences expect timely content.

If you have content sitting out there that is not being read or has no new information in it or has out-of-date information, change it. Update the information with the latest or collapse the information under a link. Don't let it sit out there.

■ THE *MORE INFO* SYNDROME

Often when a person receives information electronically, they ask for "More Info." Sometimes they are asking "How do I know this product is right for me?" and sometimes they're asking "How does it compare to other products of the same kind?" A sales person can often answer these questions tactfully, making the client feel that they've satisfied their need to know more. Spell out in detail what you do offer and what you don't. This saves everyone's time in the long run.

Simple Solutions. Tactfully educating the customer without losing the sale is very difficult. On-line, you can provide several solutions to the More Info syndrome. A simple solution is to provide the interested party with a Lessons Learned document or Success Stories area. This proves that you have been through the same process and can help guide the user along through personal anecdotes and customer testimonials. You can use case studies that the user can identify with.

Try and Buy. You can provide try-and-buy sessions, so users can get a feel for what your product does (this is mostly true for knowledge products or software products). Users will feel more comfortable with your site knowing they can get a feel for the product and what the hidden gotchas are. Trying can answer the question "What do I really need to upgrade to get and use this product?"

Virtual Reality. You can put together a virtual version of your product or service and create an interactive environment to play "what if" with the product. This is the purpose of much of the research in VRML and will be seen a lot in the near future. Break out those eye goggles and data gloves.

Observe Users. In order to answer the question "What other information is needed?" follow several prospective customers through the sales cycle. See what questions they ask. Find out what areas they are looking at.

No matter how you did it, make sure that more information is always available to your net surfers. Content consists of more information. Users are sifting through hundreds and hundreds of topics, styles, textual cues, and graphics to figure out what you're all about. This chapter has provided you with some strong suggestions for organization, designing, and developing content.

SUMMARY

The World Wide Web is more than a place to hang out. You can perform quite a lot of normal human functions via the Web. You can download software, test it, and play on it for hours. You can chat with experts, you can e-mail anyone with an e-mail address. You can handle business the Internet, buying, selling, advertising, marketing. You can educate over the Web. But, most alluring, you can play with information—increasing your knowledge about anything, enriching your knowledge, and promising growth for you, your family, and your business.

Content reigns supreme at a web site. Users will overlook bad format if you have a wealth of content. Content comes in many forms and services. Think variety. Think defining your company culture or providing the best quality you can to your site, so users will come back for more, buy, offer new information, and observe your corporate culture through the browsers and other web-related tools.

KEY POINTS

- Excellent, well-maintained content is a core success factor in a web site
- The kind of content depends upon the kind of site you are
- Content must include facts, concepts, procedures, processes, and principles
- Writing for the Web culture improves communication at your site
- Focus on writing the links in such a way as to make them tell the story, keep text at a minimum, and use the rules of clear writing
- Design your graphics for manageable bandwidth and let the graphics and text reflect the same story
- Plan for a common look and feel

CHAPTER

3
Cognitive Design

Human brain studies have revealed how individuals process information. Cognitive psychologists, educators, and marketing gurus have been studying the effects of information processing for several decades. Much of this research impacts the way we design on the World Wide Web. The web experience combines the worlds of learning, self-actualizing, research, shopping, filtering, and consuming. Information on the Web is both a commodity and psychological tool. We want to influence, persuade, convince, excite, direct, assist, promote, and politicize. So, we need to examine how an individual deals with the vast load of information in a web experience. Specifically, we need to concern ourselves with how a user:

- Receives information
- Stores and recalls information
- Analyzes information
- Acts upon information
- Manages information

THE HUMAN BRAIN: A WORKING DEFINITION

At a web site, users are engaged in all of the activities listed above. Gaining attention is fundamental at a web site (receive information). Because brain capacity is limited, you'll need to help the user get the whole picture quickly (store and recall information). Users will ques-

Principle

Find out how people think, and design to their needs and desires.

tion you, challenge you (analyze information), and want reasons or motivations to use your information (act upon information). Helping the user properly manage the information is a designer's challenge (manage information).

Designing for any user requires a good understanding of how a user thinks. Understand what users need to see. Delve into the intricacies of the human mind, and you'll create a web site that people can use and that can spur them on to creativity, action, and a thirst for more.

Trade-offs. As any designer knows, trade-offs always have to be made in designing. In order to tap into the main activities of the brain, designers must consider what absolutely has to be included for effective information processing and what would be nice to have. Users have limitations on what they can focus on and how much they can assimilate, so choose a few features to design well.

Principle

At the very least, concentrate on what the user's brain expects to experience at each web

Needs and Wants. Good web page design takes these limitations into account. You cannot design every element into your web pages. Therefore, evaluate and choose between what the brain needs and brain wants in satisfying the cognitive requirements of your audience.

Table 3-1   Needs and Wants

BRAIN NEEDS	BRAIN WANTS
Language	Order
Imagery	Questioning/Challenge
Numbers	Reinforcement
Logic	Preparation
Rhythm	Clarity
Color	Personalization
Spatial Awareness	Change

Satisfying or even delighting web viewers may be calculated and formulaic or may just be accidental. Good designers plan for it.

■ USER NEEDS

Language is a requirement for communication. Keep the user's experience reflecting the real world of language as much as possible. Follow all the grammar rules, spelling rules, and common uses of language. Reduce your user's brain load by providing expected language. Explain everything, always.

Imagery provides so much information to a user. Graphics, charts, tables, symbols, icons, video all are a major part of the viewer's world. Provide clean, meaningful images that create powerful messages or emotions inside the reader. The entertainment and advertising industry excel at the use of imagery. Web sites will profit as well. Look at the effect of imagery in Sun Microsystems, Inc. site in Figure 3.1. It looks like a magazine cover. It draws in the reader.

Figure 3.1 Sun Microsystems Use of Imagery

Numbers offer organization to users. They also are used for priority and sequencing. Users need to know what comes first, second, and so on. Telephone numbers are a requirement in sales and marketing. Numbers help to group information and help the user sort out the overall structure.

Logic must prevail at a web site. Even if your web site is trying to be chaotic and breaking the system, it must do so in a way the user can understand. The user must see information sequenced properly. Certain information comes first, then second, and so on. A good brainstorming session with your content experts will identify the logical patterns.

Rhythm allows your site to flow. Like the zoom effect in film production, you must start with a single message or image, then your site must draw the user into the headings, subheadings, or graphical images that move them to the next level of understanding. Then the rhythm explodes into a melody of detail. Think of "web as Theater" to imagine how web sites will look when Hollywood gets on the 'net.'

Color motivates, excites, draws attention, provides emphasis. Users are affected by colors differently. Cultures have different reactions to color. Find out what the different reactions are if you are targeting a particular culture. You may inadvertently be sending a different message than you think. Red may mean warning, passion, or do this first. Use colors that work together, but that don't tax the user's sense of what works.

Spatial Awareness is whitespace. Users have to have plenty of it. Like Japanese flower arrangements, the whitespace defines the objects around it. When a user goes to your web site, the whitespace makes him feel secure. Then, he focuses on the colors, images, and text. Whitespace allows users to be able to tell one thing from another quickly. Don't clutter the page. Observe how the magazine HotWired in Figure 3.2 uses whitespace to provide a sense of organization.

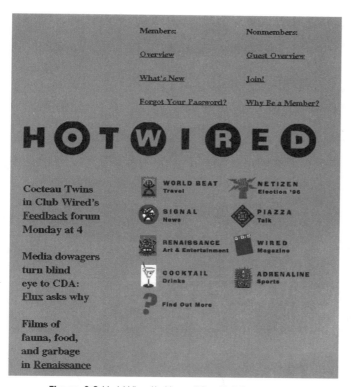

Figure 3.2 Hot Wired's Use of Spatial Awareness
Copyright © 1994, 1995, 1996 HotWired Ventures LCC. All Rights Reserved.

■ DELIGHT THE USER

Once you have provided for the basic cognitive needs of the user, you will want to consider the treats. Users can live without these features in your design if content is rich and complete. Use these design features, and you'll delight your users.

Order. Try to provide the users with the most elegant breakdown of your site. There is a central message, motive, or reason for your site. Tell them what it is. Break down the major categories and design around them. Provide an overall system view, with no more than five to seven basic ordered subsections. Keep users aware of this order at all times.

Principle

Allow users to e-mail with
questions and challenges.
Then, answer them.

Question/Challenge. Users want to be in control of their information. They'll want to communicate with the site to ask questions or challenge the information. Provide e-mail connections to somebody at your site. And, answer all inquiries. Encourage users to tell you if you are satisfying their needs or not. And, listen to them.

Reinforcement. User want to know they've submitted the form correctly. They want to know what you're doing with information you collect. Provide cues to them that reinforce that they've take the right action. Tell users forms have been submitted. Tell them what you're doing with the information you collect from them. If you change your site's structure, allow users a glimpse of what your superstructure is now, reinforcing why you've decided to change on them all of a sudden.

Preparation means that the user is aware that you know what his needs and desires are. You are prepared with the right information, at the right time. You provide the right content, because you know the user and you're the expert. The user wants to see that you are well prepared. It adds reliability to the content.

Clarity means your words, messages, text, graphics, and navigational paths are clear. Anything unusual is explained. You get to the point and avoid fluff. For example, don't just throw things on the Web because they're there. Make sure they support your overall structure, and fit into the five to seven categories you have designed for your site. Also, avoid jargon. Explain acronyms. Add hypertext links to your terms and quick return to the point where the user asked for the definition.

Personalization enables the user to customize the site. Users can choose which topics they want to see, rather than wading through the entire superstructure. Even the graphical user interface you provide can be altered to match the user's needs more directly. Users feel in control when they can modify the presentation. It also keeps them from getting bored. Look at HotWired's way of handling customization in Figure 3.3.

Customize Your "What's New" Page

Create your own view of HotWired. See what you want to see on your custom home page every time you visit. Make your selections in the form below. You start with all content being selected. Click the boxes you want to ignore, then click save. (You can change your selections at any time.)

NETIZEN
Election '96

☐ Columns
☐ HotPoll
☐ Noise
☐ Visual Clue

RENAISSANCE
Art & Entertainment

☐ Surf du Jour
☐ Upgrade
☐ Open Site
☐ Workshop
☐ Who's Who and When
☐ Event
☐ TeeVee
☐ Gallery
☐ Zines
☐ Reading
☐ Movies

Figure 3.3 Hot Wired's Customized Web Site
Copyright © 1994, 1995, 1996 HotWired Ventures LCC. All Rights Reserved.

Change is essential to users. They must feel that your site is growing and alive. Change your site, and your users will visit you frequently. Make sure the good stuff is always available at all times, but always add something novel. Change the layout, the colors, the headings, the topics, the content, the graphics. Users love variety and spontaneity.

RECEIVING INFORMATION

The brain can't focus on everything in the environment equally. When viewing a page, attention is selectively centered on one item, then another. In classical design, the terms **figure** and **ground** are used to attract the user's attention.

The term figure refers to the words or images that are brought to the attention of the reader. Ground refers to the area that contrasts with the words to make them visible to the reader. Without a sufficiently contrasting ground, the figure isn't visible.

For this book, the terms foreground (*figure*), background (*ground*) and a new term, middleground, are used to describe how users receive information in the web site.

■ WORKING DEFINITIONS

The **foreground** holds the best spot as the attention grabber. Use it only for the blatant, in-your-face messages. The **middleground** is where all the action takes place. Content and organization dominate this area. The **background** is reserved for just that: the background. Table 3-2 provides examples.

Table 3-2 Element Priority

	FOREGROUND	MIDDLEGROUND	BACKGROUND
PURPOSE	**ATTENTION GRABBING**	**ORGANIZATION & STRUCTURE**	**FOUNDATION**
Definition	Items on a page that stand out; catch the eye immediately	Individual items that the user must focus on.	Items not noticed on the page; subliminal information.
Example	Blinking, motion, <H1> headings, tables, frames	<h2> through <h6> Headings, Links, bullets, icons	Background; graphics part of the background

DESIGNING IN THE FOREGROUND

Minimal Use of Foreground Items. Try to keep your foreground items to a minimum. Having too many items in the foreground can cause *Information Overload* and is not a good thing.

Foreground Techniques. Table 3-3 shows how to gain attention from the reader. Use foreground items sparingly. Put your main message, hot selling item, or key activity in the foreground.

Table 3-3 Foreground, Middleground and Background Elements

FOREGROUND	MIDDLEGROUND	BACKGROUND
Blinking	Color	Background Color
Motion	Colorful Graphics	Background Graphics
Animation	Blocking Out Info	
Marque	Whitespace	
Splash Graphics	Text and Formats	

Principle

Limit the number of items in the foreground.

Blinking

A designer should only use blinking text in rare occasions where the message is very important **and** there is little other content on the page. Many usability studies suggest users are distracted by the blinking after they've read it once.

Some examples for blinking are to update something, to overwrite data when you've updated something very important on your site, or when the user is about to overwrite data.

There are other situations that aren't as clearly black and white. An example of this would be an announcement of a sale. If the blinking text is a link to a page of sale items, blinking might be appropriate. However, if the blinking text is a headline for a section of sale items, the headline will detract from the display of the sale items.

> **Principle**
>
> Use blinking text in the foreground only when there isn't conflict with other content.

Motion

Motion consists of blinking, simple one-dimensional animation, (e.g., an arrow moving), or text moving from one location to another. A moving image or flashing word is often the first thing that people focus on. It is very difficult to tune out motion and focus attention on another item. Motion will become key in future Java-enhanced sites. Use it sparingly at first.

> **Principle**
>
> Use only *one* motion item per page where text is the primary communication method.

Shockwave. Shockwave for Director enables playback of high-impact multimedia on the World Wide Web, setting a new level of interactive performance on the Internet. Shockwave is likely in the short run to be the primary way to animate, given the expertise and system requirements for Java. Look for it at http://www.macromedia.com/Tools/Shockwave/index.html

Unwanted Motion. Graphics loading before text is also considered motion and can be distracting to the user. Place some text before memory-intensive graphics to lessen the impact of meaningless information on the screen. Once the graphic loads, it becomes foreground and focuses the user's attention on its meaning.

> **Principle**
>
> Place descriptive text before memory-intensive graphics.

Animation

Animations are wonderful things. When you want to draw attention to part of the screen, you can use an animation that starts from somewhere else, moves toward the important part of the screen, and stops. Java applications excel in animation. Expect to compete with sites that use a lot of animation.

Principle

Pause animation to allow the reader to read the text.

Pause animation. Animation is a foreground feature, and users will concentrate on it until it stops. Pause the animation to allow the reader to grasp the whole meaning of the page. Pausing has a dramatic effect. Also, pause to allow reading of text if you're combining animation with text.

Add sound over text. If animation is continuous, let it tell the whole story of the web site without the written word. Introduce audio elements if you want language to clarify meaning.

Marque

Microsoft has created a marque for their Internet Explorer 2.0 browser. Marques are animated text, like the scrolling text at the end of a movie. Many people read marques in detail. They provide spontaneous information and can provide users with an unexpected solution to their problem.

Principle

Marques must scroll in the direction of the language they're written in. English scrolls left to right, top to bottom.

Continuous Marques. Remember, marques are animation and capture the attention and continually draw the eye back to it. Thus, continuous use of a marque will be an attention grabber on many pages, perhaps distracting from other, more important, content. A marque would be good in cases where the web site is designed to be experiential and the marque is the only text on the page. Some marques are placed in frames, acting as tables of contents or menu items. Shareware.com in Figure 3.4, is an example.

Figure 3.4 Marquees Used as a Table of Content
http://www.shareware.com

A Java Marque. Java can implement something similar to a marque but with the added ability to define clickable regions. Such an application can be used to consolidate pages of information into a single viewable screen. Consider this an opportunity to reduce user scrolling.

Graphics in the Foreground

Graphics in the foreground are the attention grabbers. Netscape (`http://www.netscape.com`) and SGI (`http://www.sgi.com`) rely on graphics to attract your attention. They are bold, dominating, and pull the user in immediately.

Foreground graphics suggest the style and quality of the site. Like marketing and advertising, however, be careful that you are attracting to the graphic and not the content. Users look at foreground graphics as a whole.

Graphics are discussed in depth in Chapter 7, *Designing Graphical Elements.*

Which graphics are not in the foreground? All the graphics you use on your web site are not necessarily in the foreground attracting the user's attention. Some of the graphics are in the middleground because user's don't concentrate on them until they are pulled into them by the other foreground elements. Graphics used for menu items, for bullets, and to adorn forms are in this category.

■ MIDDLEGROUND

The middleground is where the more loyal users will proceed. Once you've gotten their attention by using foreground techniques, you'll want to continue to support those foreground items with middleground ones. This is akin to newspapers that use headlines to draw you into the content.

The middleground shows the structure and functionality of your site. It uses small graphics and text to accomplish this task. The middleground houses all the content, so it must be complemented with a well-designed structure that assists users in quickly figuring out how the site is organized. Look at GolfWeb in Figure 3.5 for example; notice how the middleground graphics break the site into its individual parts. They support the main graphic, which in this case is the title GolfWeb

Principle

Use the middleground (MG) to support the foreground (FG).

Figure 3.5 GolfWeb's Use of the Middleground

Middleground items will come to the front of the user's attention when he begins to focus on them. The user is seeking additional information to supplement the broader, overall message of the foreground. Now the user is looking to find out how your site is organized, coded, structured. The user will most likely first focus on graphics, then on text links, and finally on the written text.

Techniques for Middleground Design. Whether you use graphics or text to show the user the structure of your site, you can use various techniques to design your site so it is effective, by allowing the user to quickly see what your site has to offer.

Some of the techniques you can use to design the middleground effectively are:

- complementary color graphics
- blocking out information
- Whitespace

•Textual cues
•Fonts

Use Color to Show Structure

Use color in the middleground to draw attention to the various levels of structure at your web site. A quick glance down the page should show the five or six items that you're trying to focus on. Some examples:

•All <H1> headings the same color
•Colored bullets
•Color groups of menu items in long lists
•Color to show sequence or priority functions. Notice how GolfWeb, Color Plate 1-1, cleverly uses green, a color every golfer is familiar with. It repeats into the bullets and onto every page.

Color Warning. Many browsers allow users to override your designed color choices. In Netscape, for example, Options, General Preferences, Color, Always Use My Colors, Overriding Document, allow users to customize all your web pages colors to their own liking.

Color Conventions. Ensure that you use color conventions. For example, in finance, red means loss and black means gain. Any unconventional use of colors may confuse the reader. Some basics to remember:

•Red is a dominant, aggressive color that screams for attention.
•Yellow is activity; use it against black for best effect.
•Green conveys information readily. It's user friendly.
•Blue is best as a background color to soothe and pacify.
•Black text on a white background is easiest to read.
•Place colored text on a neutral background (white, black, gray).
•Limit the number of highlight colors to two or three.
•Be clear why you are coloring the text.

International Meaning of Color. Find out what color conventions are used in other countries. Some colors carry significant different meanings. If your audience is international, spend some time finding out about the meaning of color. You could avoid offending someone. For example, red means danger in the U.S., death in Egypt, and life in India. White means purity in the U.S., but death in China and Japan. Choose your colors well. (See "How Fluent is Your Interface? Designing for International Uses" by Stephen Boor and Patricia Russo.)

Avoid Color Overload. The brain can only handle so many thoughts or concepts at a time. Using color to augment communication is good, to a point. However, after a certain number of colors,

> **Principle**
>
> Use small, colored graphics to show the organization of your site.

> **Principle**
>
> Be prepared for different cultural interpretations.

Principle

Limit the number of colors
used in text and figures
to ~4.

many users are not able to distinguish color variations, nor are they able to keep the color meaning associations straight in their head. The number of colors that a user can track varies, but a good ballpark figure is three to four colors.

ISO Standards. Use the formulas found in the colorspace FAQ at `ftp://ftp.wmin.ac.uk/pub/itrg/coloureq.txt` to define the contrast. ISO standard 9241 part 3 recommends that the luminance difference between text and background shall be a minimum of 3:1, and 10:1 is preferred, (e.g., yellow is 10 and black is 100 giving a 1:10 contrast ratio). (cf. Jackson, Richard, et. al. *Computer Generated Color*).

Monochrome Screens. All of this talk about color is meaningless on a monochrome screen. Monochrome users are not the majority of the Internet users. If your private web has a large number of monochrome users, go easy on the color augmentations and make sure that they are readable on a monochrome screen.

Blocking Out Information

Tables. One of the major forms of organizing information in blocks is to use tables. Tables are middleground items, because users will not focus on them unless they understand the overall meaning of the site. Tables usually indicate the breakdown of a larger structure into its components. Tables condense information to make it easier to consume, reducing cognitive overhead. In the site in Figure 3.6, Randy used tables to separate his own web page into three distinct groups; see how the information is broken down into three clear sections, with appropriate links in a table.

Welcome. *This site is designed as a personal, knowledge repository. I use it for collaborating with my colleagues. This page is shorthand to my mindmap.*

WebUcation	Web Design	Parallel Universes
Tutorials, virtual classes	Theory, top design sites, book.	A home away from home
Color Tags	Internet Experience	Trump Taj Mahal
Virtual Tours	Style Guide	Trump Castle
Excite Yahoo and Alta Vista	Book	CNN fn Homepage
Yahoo	Human Computer Interaction	Houston
Class	Web Development Cyberbase	Ohm's law in Java

Feel free to E–mail Me! or read my Resume **This page has been read 33 times since Mon Feb 5**

This page powered by FLEXnet!

Figure 3.6 Using Tables to Separate Groups

Keep the table columns and rows to a minimum, again, about five to seven rows, and three to four columns. Always provide table headings and, if appropriate, column headings.

Graphic Grouping. Another method of blocking out information is to group a set of graphics or icons together to show off the organization of your web site. Keep them all the same size and color within color groups. Make their functionality clear. Take a look at SunSoft's use of graphic grouping in Figure 3.7. This common look-and-feel set of graphics makes this page easy to use and easy to understand.

Figure 3.7 SunSoft's Graphic Groupings

Frames. Breaking information into different frames is very useful. The user can use one frame to maintain a view of the overall site, while in another frame, the user can scroll through more specific information. Don't expect to see frames in every browser. Look at the graphic below to see how PC Computing magazine used frames to break up information.

Go to http://www.shareware.com or http://cool.infi.net/oldcool.html and play with the frames. It is the only way to experience them. Of course, you'll need Netscape 2.0.

Other Blocking Methods. Below is a list of other techniques to help you block out large amounts of information, making it easier for the user to focus on the structure of your web site. You are familiar

with all of them. The list is a reminder for you to provide visual images for the user, which are certainly easier to remember than long passages of text.

- Bulleted lists with keywords
- Charts
- Diagrams
- Labels
- Maps
- Repeated icons or symbols
- Menus

Manage Whitespace

Whitespace is the unused portion of the web page. As learned during the desktop publishing era, whitespace has a powerful effect on the printed message. Learning to use whitespace effectively is an art. Use it around graphics, between text items, between bullets and text, between headings.

Some whitespace organizes information; other whitespace separates information. See Table 3-4.

Table 3-4   Whitespace Control

ORGANIZING W/ WHITESPACE	SEPARATING W/ WHITESPACE
Double-spacing*	Outside margins
Space between columns	Space around single graphic
Space around multiple graphics	Space between continuous paragraphs
*Unfortunately double-spacing and space between continuous paragraphs cannot be commonly implemented now with HTML. It may in the future be doable with stylesheets. You'll need to wait for stylesheets.	

Textual Cues

Text is all the written accumulated knowledge you have collected. You may think of putting all this wisdom right up front in the foreground, because you'd like your readers to know everything immediately. Lead them in with big word splashes, then five to seven major groupings of words. Then use precise, explanatory text to explain what to do or why they're doing it. Users need to be led into the logic and up to the conclusions you have made over the years. You are simulating your personal or professional world for them.

Keep text to a minimum. In the foreground, keep text to a bare minimum. In the middleground, write enough text to explain your overall site and structure. Introduce your links with text. Then, point the way to the library of information you have waiting for your avid readers.

Provide a lot of content. When your audience is ready for your wisdom, i.e., the well-written, grammatically correct text you've prepared for detail, they'll want lots of it. Many sites have been called "Best of the Web" because they provide hundreds or thousands of hyperlinks to detailed documentation. The text lies behind the scenes. It is the well-written, minimalist text and links in the middleground that draw the reader into the detail.

For a look at top content sites on the Web, see
`http://www.pointcom.com/text/topsites/content.html/`.

Arranging Text. Arrange text on a web page by using principles similar to those for arranging text on the printed page. The placement has a psychological effect on the user, making your site more friendly and communicative. In Table 3-5, we've summarized some of the cognitive effects of text placement.

Principle

Middleground text provides the wisdom of your site.

Try This!

Table 3-5   Orgranizing Elements

TEXT FEATURE	COGNITIVE EFFECT
Sequence items in a straight line	Focuses on priority
Left-justify text	Blocks text visually
Use ragged right edges, not right-justified text	Reduces eye strain in readers
Position comparisons and contrasts side by side	Provides a right brain/left brain analysis of text
Put key items in the center, the Park Place of the screen	Focuses attention
Place less-important information on the outside	Makes it available, but subordinate, to the eye
Call users' attention to the bottom of the screen	Provides choice to scroll
Indent explanatory information	Sequences the importance of information
Repeat text menus on top/bottom	Assists in orientation
Rotate text	Adds variety

Principle

Transition users from linear book model to the multidimensional web

Principle

Use fonts as graphical images for now. Wait for the browsers to catch up.

These features appeal to the need for logical development. Users expect these design elements, and without them they grow disconcerted and disoriented in this cyberenvironment. These techniques will work when we investigate virtual reality and other nontextual simulation environments.

Fonts. When they are more readily available, font modifications can also be used to focus attention and send subliminal messages. Century Schoolbook and Palatino, for example, are used often in technical school books, adding an air of the scholarly to your site. Font choices are only available via Microsoft and stylesheets now, neither of which is readily available. So, on the Web, you're not going to be able to rely on fonts as much as you can in the printed world. You can use fonts in your graphical images to accomplish what you may need for now.

Case. Figure 3.8 has both uppercase and lowercase letters, what you're probably used to reading. Readers anticipate this case and can scan through it fairly quickly. Figure 3.9 has only uppercase letters. All uppercase is considered "shouting" on the Web. Use it only if you want to really get someone's attention. It is a foreground feature, so use it sparingly.

Studies have shown that mixed-case letters are easier to read because the human eye uses the top of the letters first to distinguish. Thus, the "*t*" and the "*e*" in Figure 3.8 are decidedly different from each other. In Figure 3.9, the "*T*" and the "*E*" are the same size horizontally and vertically.

Letters have a variety of shapes

Figure 3.8 Normal case or Proper Case

LETTERS HAVE A VARIETY OF

Figure 3.9 Uppercase or "Shouting" on the Web

The faster a person can distinguish the letters, the faster they can read the words. This makes mixed-case writing the method of choice for most things.

Mixing Case

One of the more recent experiments has been in the area of abnormally mixing cases. Figure 3.10 demonstrates the *ransom note* method of mixing case. We are not accustomed to reading uppercase letters directly after lowercase letters. This style of writing can be very disturbing. Some people even need to regress to sounding out the letters to identify the word. This has ceased to be an item of text and takes on the impact and assimilation time of a graphical image. Use it sparingly, if you want to communicate.

LeTtERs

Figure 3.10 Mixed-Case Letters

Treat mixed-case words as graphics not text.

Shouting. Uppercase-only words have a nonverbal meaning on the Internet, namely shouting. Raising your voice to someone for an extended period of time is considered rude and obnoxious. Use it for that.

It is appropriate to use an all-uppercase word to emphasize a particular point. For example, the word NOT or STOP can be used. Acronyms are also an exception to this rule.

Other Recommendations for Minimizing Text. The recommendations in Table 3-6 are extremely useful when you want to minimize the amount of text on a web page. These recommendations apply to the middleground area of the web site. Users are still looking for shortened forms of communication at this level. Maintain a link to the detail.

Principle

Don't use more than a word or two of uppercase letters in a row. Don't shout.

Principle

Use nouns and verbs to focus on concrete action. The user wants to perform.

Table 3-6 Minimizing Text Recommendations

RECOMMENDATION	EFFECT
One keyword per line	Allows reader to scan text
Minimum number of words	Lessens overload
Explain acronyms	Internationalizes the text
Use nouns and action verbs	Adds concrete action

Table 3-6   Minimizing Text Recommendations (Continued)

RECOMMENDATION	EFFECT
Pare down adjectives, adverbs, and prepositions	Reduces verbosity
Active voice, not passive voice	Enlivens the text
Concentrate on the positive	Motivates user to act

■ BACKGROUND

The background consists of two simple elements, summarized in Table 3-7:

Table 3-7   Background Elements

BACKGROUND	DESIGN ISSUE
Background Color	Affects the user's emotions
Background Graphics	Sends subliminal information

Background Color. Simple backgrounds provide stability, strength, confidence. Complex backgrounds counter with impulse, risk, and excitement. Look at http://www.netscape.com. The colors are simple and strong, blue and white. They suggest confidence. Look at http://www.yahoo.com. The colors titillate like a ferris wheel.

Avoid bizarre color combinations. Blue on magenta is painful. You may want to have an impact, but quite often, uncommon color combinations can obscure your message. Place strong colors with extreme care. Remember, your users have been surfing for a while, and color images have been bombarding them intensely.

Try This!

http://mirsky.turnpike.net/wow/Worst.html Mirsky's Worst of the Web. Here you'll find a category for the sites that just ain't got it right.

The right background color can be alluring. So take some time to ask a few users what they think of your creation. As always, the right background could be the masterstroke of your site.

Background Graphics. You can use your logo in a background to help brand you as a major name, product, or site. Keep it subdued. Background images can be subliminal, but remember that they are in the background and the message should be subtle. Use the features of the foreground to attract your reader's attention.

MEMORY AND RECALL

In order for users to be able to memorize or recall the information at your site, especially the URL, you need to design certain cues or features into your web site. Many of these cues will provide ways to enhance memory to navigate your site to meet these needs.

Read the chapter on Audience Considerations to understand how to meet user needs.

URL Name. Design your URL to say something about you that is unique, easy to remember, and carries your highest values. `http://www.yahoo.com` or `http://www.excite.com` says it all. If you've created value or brand recognition, use the brand name. If not, start creating a reputation with clarity, content, and support. These two names probably mean a lot to most people on the Internet: `http://www.netscape.com`. and `http://www.microsoft.com`.

Site Name. To hook users who get to your URL, create a single image to etch into their memories. Use a logo if it's well known, but keep it small and simple. Look at `http://www.compaq.com` for an example of a site name and graphic that is simple and easy to understand and use. Use a word or two, or a small phrase, no more than seven words long, to create a memory impression. Go beyond seven and you'll drop out of memory for the user.

Balance. Once you've captured your user's attention and impressed his memory, maintain the balance between powerful messages and skillful design. Messages are powerful when they're structured. Design is skillful when it uses basic principles. The magic happens when something creative is born from the balance.

Table 3-8 combines the elements of memory and recall design features. Look at the examples; they excel in helping users recall information from a site.

Table 3-8 Cognitive Design Features

DESIGN FEATURE	COGNITIVE BENEFIT	EXAMPLE
Create a whole system overview. Make it available at all times, via a link.	Provides holistic impact and ability to zoom in.	http://www.golfweb.com
Use only 5–7 subtopics, or groups at any time.	Limits amount of memory storage	http://www.sun.com
Use one keyword per line	Reduces time in analyzing content	http://www.infoseek.com
Chunk the data with buttons, icons, TOCs, indexes, and search tools	Avoids confusion with too much information.	http://www.yahoo.com
Use emphasis, whitespace, unusual style	Focuses attention directly on key points of information	http://www.hotwired.com

Users will mature quickly. A final note on memory (for those of you reading linearly). Cognitive overload disorients web users. Many will avoid the technology. Some will never enter cyberspace. They will be *home-page-less*. As web skills improve, and they will, users will maneuver information without taxing their memory. Their recall capabilities will improve as their usage increases. They'll learn more. They'll perform more.

The design issues you are grappling with now are transitional devices for memory storage and recall. Users will benefit greatly from them and will soon demand more sophisticated ones.

ANALYZING INFORMATION

In order for the user to analyze the information at your web site, design in elements to help speed up analysis. In short, users analyze information so they can determine if they can use it or not. A few easy-to-implement tips:

- Date the material so the user knows the timeliness of the data
- Use file names and URLs that summarize

For example,
```
/education/SeaWorld/baleen_whales/scien.class
```

• Discriminate clearly between relevant and supportive information

At `http://www.thejournal.com/contents/current.html` you see a clear distinction between the article, the author, and the supportive information about the article. Plus, the links at the bottom provide appropriate links for even more additional topical information.

• Be accurate so the user doesn't have to cross-reference

A simple example is at `http://www.excite.com` where the search results are sorted by Confidence level. Excite uses *relevance indicators* to provide a percentage of confidence that describe how well the search results match your request.

▪ COGNITIVE OVERLOAD

When a user is confronted with so much knowledge, so many different forms, colors, structures, breakdowns, and graphics, the result can be cognitive overload. The brain feels like it is fried, and the information becomes meaningless.

In order to reduce the cognitive overload, allow time to analyze. There are certain design issues to consider. Implementing them is an art, but the result is well worth it.

Table 3-9 examines design features that help reduce cognitive overload. These features help the user analyze the material at the web site, reducing the amount of information processing required.

> **Principle**
>
> Perform as much analysis as possible for the user to save his time.

Table 3-9 Information Control Features

ANALYZER FEATURE	COGNITIVE BENEFIT	EXAMPLE
State goal of site	Focuses on key language units	`http://www.micro soft.com`
Break info into chunks	Allows instant categorization	`http://www-elc.gnn.com/gnn/wic/botn/awards.1995.html`
Group like items together	Provides analysis of the relationships	`http://www.neoso ft.com/sbanks/xf iles/xmap1.html`

Table 3-9 Information Control Features (Continued)

ANALYZER FEATURE	COGNITIVE BENEFIT	EXAMPLE
Keep chunks in clusters of 4–6 (i.e., 5 1)	Frees memory for analysis	`http://www.ibm.com`
Use tables and bullets to visually organize data	Initiates comparison and contrast; suggests priority	`http://cwsapps.texas.net/`
Rely on visual images	Encapsulates large amounts of data	`http://www.netscape.com`
Use logo or branding	Creates instant association to quality, service, and reliability	`http://www.sun.com`
Naming	Brings meaning of deep-rooted structure (the link) to the surface	`http://www.discovery.com`

State the Goal

Don't waste the users' time. Tell them the purpose of the site as soon as possible. This can easily be done with a word like "Weather." For more complex sites, you'll need to provide an explanation, like "Classes on the World Wide Web." Keep the descriptions of your site down to few words or graphics. Make them universal, so the user can immediately determine whether you can satisfy his own personal goals. *When in doubt, leave it out.*

Look at `http://www.microsoft.com` to see how they stated the purpose of each of their links on the home page.

Break Up Info into Chunks

Chunking is the process of breaking up information into separate topics. It is akin to outlining. But on the Web, you can chunk with headings, with text, with color, or with graphics. Make sure all the information in the chunk refers to the overall message in the goal statement or title of the site. Use a label for each chunk, and keep the formats, verbs, colors consistent, so the user concentrates on the structure.

Breaking items into chunks can be difficult. Try some brainstorming techniques to help you breakdown the information.

At GNNs 1995 award site, `http://www.elc.gnn.com/gnn/wic/botn/awards.1995.html`, the categories are broken into topical chunks. Further on down the page, they are broken up again, with more detail and explanation.

To practice breaking a topic into chunks, try this brainstorming technique. Select a key topic, like Health. Draw a circle around it. Now, draw 5 to 10 lines from the circle out, like the spokes of a wheel. At the end of each line, write down one word that breaks down the topic more. You are chunking. You may not choose to use all the categories, but you'll get an idea of the major areas you want to cover.

Try This!

You can then take the next subject, i.e., Hospitals, put it in the center of the diagram, and start to break it down into the 5–10 topics.

Note

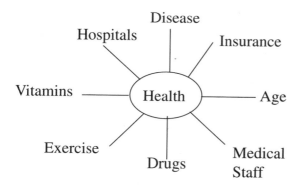

Figure 3.11 Chunking Topics into Main Subtopics

Group Like Items

Group items by using the same heading or the same font size. If you're grouping items by graphical image, make the graphics share the same color or shape. Use lines or geometric figures to group items together. In the XFiles site, `http://www.neosoft.com/sbanks/xfiles/xmap1.html`, a Macintosh® screenshot was used to break information into like items.

Keep Chunks in Clusters of Five to Seven

Chunking in clusters of five to seven is much easier for processing. At a glance, the user can determine how the information relates to his needs. This rule goes for lists, bullets, headings, chapters, graphics, diagrams, tables, and sections. The human brain is capable of only putting five to seven items into short-term memory. IBM excels at simplification; see `http://www.ibm.com`. The six key graphics represent the entire body of IBM on the Web. No more than four additional links are listed. And in keeping with the international flair of IBM, an index to International HomePages.

Use Tables and Bullets to Visually Organize Data

> **Principle**
>
> Tables speed up the process of analysis.

Tables accelerate analysis of a site. They convey information quickly, allow for categorization, and provide the ability to compare and contrast information. They speed up visual processing and enable the brain to perform a quicker mind map to help the user determine if the information is usable or not. At `http://cwsapps.texas.net/` the table helps to break up the wealth of Winsock applications available on-line. It's all here on the same page, separated by three columns.

Overflow. If the lists or tables begin to exceed seven items per column, consider breaking the information into subcategories. If you can show all your topics in a 3 x 7 table, you are making it a lot easier for the user to analyze what is on your site.

Visual Images

> **Principle**
>
> Textual graphics load faster and provide input more quickly to the reader.

Visual images encapsulate enormous amounts of information. In a single visual image, textual or graphical, the user can determine many attributes or characteristics of a web site. Once a user determines the usefulness of information, he will decide more readily how to act upon it.

Visual images are both graphical and textual. Lean toward textual imagery to help lessen the need to analyze data. We get the majority of our "intellectual" input from text. We make decisions with intellectual input. Allow more time for users to decide because they don't have to break down the components of your site themselves.

The main goal of most web sites is to get users to act upon the information: Buy, sell, improve the quality of their lives, or learn how to do something better. Table 3-10 lists the visual images that help web users analyze the information at your site more quickly. Sites that use these features abound on the Web.

Table 3-10   Text and Graphic Elements

GRAPHICAL IMAGE	TEXTUAL IMAGE
Bullets	Color headings
Arrows	Centered titles
Symbols	Uppercase text
Boxes	Blinking text
Horizontal lines	Numbers
Small graphics/icons	Links

Logos and Branding

Logos tell a story. They carry a reputation. Branding your product makes it very well known by the use of the logo, an audio piece, or a unique quality that no other product has (Sun Microsystems uses Network, the dog). Logos help users to identify information—the stop sign being the most conspicuous worldwide. Logos reduce analysis.

Look at some of the major corporation sites, `http://www.sun.com`, `http://www.microsoft.com`, `http://www.digital.com` and `http://www.apple.com`. Once you hit these pages, the logo downloads into memory everything you've heard about that company.

Logos help establish brand name and recognition. However, most logos have limited international recognition. They convey ownership, but rarely provide more information to the unfamiliar user. They convey ownership of the page and the information. They don't convey the information itself.

Logos need to share the prime foreground real estate area. This is especially true for laptops where the visible screen can be as little as half a regular-sized page. Any logo that takes up one-third or more of the top of your page will take up two-thirds or more of a laptop screen. Most of your screen should be devoted to conveying the message, not the ownership of the message.

See `http://www.inconcert.com` to see how a site uses logs to endorse the site.

Try This!

Try This!

Try This!

■ NAMING

Naming Graphics. Graphical images need explanation. Some graphics are self-explanatory, but since your site is international, don't count on the graphical images, symbols, or icons to send out universal meaning. Name the graphics, and provide short explanations of what the graphics are for.

See `http://www.aidsquilt.org/index.html` for a great example of naming graphics, which occurs below the graphic as an additional navigational device.

Gratuitous Graphics

Web design isn't any different than the game world. Gratuitous graphics are something to see once, or maybe twice, but they aren't something to keep a person returning to a site. The term "eye candy" has been used a few times to describe web sites, and that description is on the rise. See `http://park.org` for the appropriateness of graphics.

> HTML and other text-based web pages are not the place for meaningless gratuitous graphics. If you feel the need to create an experiential site, use media better designed for the task, such as VRML.

What is gratuitous? Gratuitous graphics include graphics that are not conceptually recognized by an independent observer as augmenting or relating to the text. Gratuitous graphics include graphics that are so large that the user has finished reading the page and is ready to go on to the next page before the graphic is loaded.

Summary

Analysis of your site leads to action. If you can ease the burden of analyzing what your site is about, you can save the user considerable time, frustration, and loss of good information.

ACTING UPON INFORMATION

Web surfers are explorers. They may not know exactly what they are looking for, but when they find it, they know. First, they seek knowledge. Then, they acquire it. Then, they act upon it.

Mind Mapping. The process of sifting through information, chunking it, finding associations, and acting upon it to meet personal needs or goals is called mind mapping. Surfers are unconsciously mind mapping the entire time they are cruising the Web. You can assist in the process.

Create central themes. Users want to act upon the information they have discovered. To act upon it, they must take the information and add it to a *central theme* or concept. If you create a site with a theme, e.g., GolfWeb (see Case Study No. 3, *GolfWeb*) or AutoWeb, you can hook in to the users needs, desires, and fantasies. You can provide the all-inclusive content on the subject or theme and become the only spot users go to get something specific done.

Figure 3.12 A Site with a Theme

Use the Web to complete the mind map. If a user wants to buy something, for example, he'll place the item in the center of his mind map. Then, he'll search the World Wide Web to bring information back to the center to help define why the product is good, useful, or economical. Each bit of information is a part of the overall mind map. The user will flip through web sites, picking and pruning until the picture is complete.

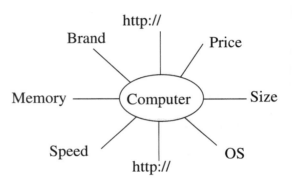

Deviations. Users may deviate from the central purpose several times. But the reason for this deviation is no different from doodling or nervously twisting their hair. They are thinking, pondering, looking for remote connections and associations—spontaneous or coincidental—that will suddenly help them finish their mind map.

Completed mind maps equal performance. When users finish the mind map, they will certainly go into action. In this case, they will buy the product they were considering, for the best price, with the most functionality, quality, and service. They will have multiple connections to the product and feel good about their decision. They will recommend it to someone else.

Techniques for Completing Mind Maps

In order to help the user complete his mind map, it is essential that you provide the best, most expert, reliable, authentic, up-to-date information you can at your site.

Techniques

- Provide an entire world view at your site.
- Provide a map for moving through your world.
- Link to related known expert sites for support and for benchmarking views.
- Brainstorm with experts in your field before designing your site.
- Provide on-line chatting with experts, and post the history.
- Be clear what you're about. Your theme must be durable.
- Be complete.

Let the user handle all the complexity of the multiple associations and "nice-to-haves." You cannot add everything at the site. What you can add is all the best information on the topic.

Expert Sites. You are the expert of your site. The user is either coming to your site to borrow the expertise to finish his mind map or linking to your site because you are the authority on the subject of a lesser part of his mind map. Either way, continuously explore your site, treating it like a mind map and adding to it whenever you fish something awesome off the Web.

See `http://www.w3.com` to see an expert site on UNIX® web development tools to build, upgrade, and maintain your web site.

Reasons Users Come to Your Site

Current HTTP protocol, as defined by CERN, offers only limited information on Web visitors: domain name, type of browser, and time of day. While this information is sufficient to track global site traffic patterns, it dos not say who is visiting your site.

You need to collect personal information, or user profiles, on your visitors as they travel through your site. You need to find out when they entered and when they leave. From this information, you can design position information at well-travelled locations.

■ ENCOURAGE USERS TO GIVE BACK

If users come with a goal, a purpose, or an objective in mind, especially if trying to complete a mind map, you can tap into their needs and provide them with just want they want. They will often reward you by spreading the word, e-mailing your URL to others, buying your product, or offering something in return.

Principle

Constantly improve your site with better information.

Try This!

MANAGE INFORMATION

Users need to control the information that is splattering in their faces. Some of the web sites provide direct contacts, products, or services that help solve a problem or achieve a goal. But, what do the surfers do with all of that other information that is bombarding them?

Web Site Customization. HTML pages can be computer generated to find the needs of the individual user. The relevant text, sound, video, or graphic images can be sent to a user, based upon biographies or profiles. http://www.hotwired.com allows you to customize your pages to suit your needs.

You can customize your site by using registration-based information (such as gender, age, location, or domain extension name). The diversity of customization is up to you.

Web Site Administration. You will want to analyze and monitor your user base in order to define their needs and manage the information appropriately. Use a Search, View, Edit, Add and Delete member tool. Send group e-mail to define segments of your audience base.

URL Web Statistics. Gather statistics for mastery over the page, for platform, for access to domain names, and for access by date. Run reports on membership activity at the site, separate active users from idle users. Record where visitors leave your site.

A LAST WORD—OTHER COGNITIVE NEEDS

Table 3-11 is some final food for thought. You certainly have enough to do in creating a meaningful, easy-to-use, content-rich site, using the vast and limiting resources of 21st century technology. However, the items listed here will provide you insight into designing to help the user better manage the Web.

Table 3-11   Cognitive Needs

Cognitive Needs	Key Attributes	Design Issue
Real-world experience	Time efficiency Insecurity Conflict	Don't waste time. Acknowledge limitations. Communicate openly.
Emotional empathy	Need for recognition Need to dream Need to identify	Reward users. Use fantasy. Target your audience.
Enjoyment of art and science	Aesthetics Culture Discovery	Strive for elegance. Be international. Never tell all.
Love of language	Eloquence Clarity New perspectives	Polish your language. Concentrate on meaning. Dare to reveal.
Learning	Doing something new Recognizing systems Ease of use User control	Provide many procedures. Provide many processes. Make it all obvious. Let the user do it.
Playing	Challenge Rules Winning	Play games. Explain the rules. Reward users.

■ REAL WORLD EXPERIENCES

Users want to experience the real world in cyberspace. They want to sell, buy, learn, play, socialize, and self-actualize. VRML will move us closer to that world. Simulate the real world as much as you can in your site, so the user can interact with it in as real a way as possible. Prepare for Sega/Nintendo/Sony Playstation Internet sites.

■ EMPATHY

Show the reader that you understand him and have had his experiences. Make the user feel he is the author, the voice speaking to himself. You can do this with person-to-person communication. Your site understands the user's needs, and desires. Your site understands why the user has come, solves the user's problem. Create experience. See Chapter 11, *Experiential Design* for a more in-depth discussion.

■ ART AND SCIENCE

Let technology and the human soul mingle in an expression of art and science. Use graphic artists who know color and form. Use only the best video and audio quality methods. Emulate the factual world when dealing with the mechanical causes of things.

Create art. Although some dull-looking sites can get by without art because of the superiority of their content, the first impression of a site tells a story that will never be forgotten. If the average user doesn't find the site aesthetically pleasing, you may never see him again. Look for what Nicholas Negroponte (*Being Digital*, 1995) calls the "New E-xpressionists," the electronic artists of the next generation, to create new artistic expressions at your site.

User expectations for visual quality have been handed down through television, video, and MTV. Maintain their level of quality and you'll win a large audience. Overdo the graphics and minimize the content, again, you'll lose your fans. TV has lost a lot of fans because of the lack of content.

■ LANGUAGE

Be personal. Be specific. Discriminate in your use of good language. Use the rhapsody of language, anecdotes, metaphors, poetry, eloquence, argument, and logic. Use modern language, borrowing from current language development. Stay away from jargon, but stay on the cutting edge of communication.

■ LEARNING

Users love to learn. Learning is doing something new. The user must feel he is learning. He must feel an impulse to go into action as a result of learning. While learning he must feel competent, in control. His tools must be easy to use. The user must feel that feedback is always available and that he can challenge any idea.

Ease of Use demands attention. The user must intuitively understand how your site works. She must immediately recognize the function of the buttons, the value of the menu, the genuine use of the graphics. The maps must be obviously clickable, and the user must be able to navigate in several different ways.

■ SUMMARY

Awareness of human cognitive needs enables you to design sites that will help the user recall, analyze, act upon, and manage information. Information is best managed by a user when he perceives that it has been designed to satisfy some need or desire. Appeal to the user as a whole person, in a whole world, and create a world where the user can experience you in every form he can in the real world.

KEY POINTS

- Cognitive design is understanding the needs and wants of human information processing. (Definition)
- Gain attention by using the foreground, middleground, and background elements appropriately. (Receiving)
- Enhance memory and recall by chunking information. (Storing)
- Create a visual impact by organizing information into chunks and making the information easily accessible. (Analyzing)
- Mind maps help users act upon information to achieve some goal or solve some problem. Be an expert site. (Acting Upon)
- Dealing with cyberspace requires management of information. Find a place for all the information. (Managing)
- Motivate your readers to return by allowing them control, freedom, and flexibility.

CHAPTER

4

Audience Considerations

The Web is a form of communication. It is empowered by and limited by its users. The Web depends upon human interaction and must be concerned with what the users expect. Like software development or any kind of multimedia development, knowing what the user thinks, expects, and desires is the number one requirement for browser and web site designers.

Audience Considerations examines:

- Categorizing your web audience
- Defining goals and expectations
- Identifying web skills
- Considering the international audience

CATEGORIZE THE AUDIENCE

Everyone is not your audience. When asking *who is your audience?*, the answer *everyone* is a little bit too broad for the nature of the Internet. On the Internet, the audience isn't a single homogeneous mass. It comprises groups of individuals. And, since it is difficult to tailor any communication to a million or more individuals, start by grouping their expectations into categories.

- Skill level
- Technology level
- Surfing experience
- Search strategies
- Age and computer experience

SKILL LEVEL

Users come in all sorts of combinations, with all sorts of skills. Their expectations vary, depending upon their skill level. Novices will want everything explained; experts will want to accelerate movement through your site.

*Table 4-1　**User Skills***

SKILL	NOVICE	EXPERT
Basic computer skills	Use definition; explain when to tab; use glossaries, guides, or tutorials	Avoid telling an expert to click, to fill out a form, to select text, etc.
Typing skills	Reduce the amount of typing; add buttons	Expect excellent typists or, at least, people who backspace quickly
Navigating	Keep navigation pages to one screen. Explain scrolling, moving your mouse, selecting text, clicking in forms boxes. Use imagemaps sparingly.	Provide jumps through text. Use imagemaps. Consider moving to Java or VRML. Push the limits. These people are stimulus hungry.
Forms	Use directions to fill out forms. Limit the number of fields to one screen, Fill out parts of the form for them if possible. Make the Submit button always visible.	Length is not an issue, so ask for open responses whenever you can. Use radio buttons and check boxes heavily.
Time	Take time to explain, show, demonstrate, teach. Explain everything, even the simplest functions.	Waste no time. Use simplicity but increase functionality. Include time cues, e.g., this will only take a few minutes or seconds.

Table 4-1 User Skills (Continued)

SKILL	NOVICE	EXPERT
Reading	Rely on very easy to understand text. Use 5–7 word bullets or graphics to call attention to one thought. Novices tire easily. Limit links. Rely on headers or key graphics to tell the story. Describe how you feel, identify with the audience.	Make your links tell a story. The experts read links first. Integrate the high content between the links. Use short sentences. Rely on noun, action verb, object. Avoid adjectives, adverbs, and prepositional phrases. Describe what things do or how they work.
E-mail	May not know how to use e-mail. Create easy forms to help use of e-mail. Encourage the use. Provide feedback to support the move to e-mail.	Expect sophisticated e-mail functionality. E-mail is a tool, not a toy.

Ranges of Skill Level. Certainly, users vary in their skill levels. Since the Web is a new medium for many, you can expect a wide range of skill level. Learning who your audience is for your site will help you develop just the right combination of design elements.

See `http://www.golfweb.com`. This is a site designed specifically for golfers. Imagine this audience's requirements, goals, and expectations: novice users, educated, decision makers with little time for surfing.

Other Skills. Also, consider other skills that define your audience. Some people have uncanny discovery skills, others don't. Some have good organizational skills and are judging your presentation by organization. Priority skills characterize some, pushing them to want the important information only, at the top, in limited space. Again, find out who your audience is and design to them.

■ TECHNOLOGY LEVEL

Your audience (which you know from hours of audience analysis) have different computers that they're surfing on. Some have different desktops with different icons. Users learn these interfaces and automate their use. They don't even see the icon or metaphor; they use it as though it were invisible, e.g., dropping an icon into a trash can. Appeal to your audience's technological skill level. Know their systems, its limitations and special features.

Type of System

The type of system that the user has will determine many graphical decisions. The Web was originally designed to be system-independent. Unfortunately, system idiosyncracies do cause design problems. Know your audience's systems.

Apple Macintoshes. Macintosh computers usually have monitors designed for Macintoshes. These monitors usually have a much higher *gamma value* than other platforms. This difference in gamma values causes significant lighting problems in images.

Macintoshes also come with 16 million color capability by default. Although all images must be reduced to 8 bits of color to be rendered as standard GIF images, the enhanced dithering capabilities of a Macintosh can hide many color problems that appear on systems with a limited color map. Web pages designed in this environment may appear different on other platforms.

VGA and SVGA. The Microsoft® Windows™ suite of operating systems is the most popular platform to date. Unfortunately, Windows is often limited by the PC hardware underneath. One of the biggest limitations for the user is the video. With SVGA, the standard video on a PC, the user must often choose between a high-resolution screen or a large color palette. Although the cost of memory-intensive video cards and high scan rate monitors is dropping, a large population is still running on last year's video. Colormaps and page layout need to be adjusted to work within a limited video capability range.

Principle

Design for a reasonable common denominator, 500-550 pixels wide, 64 colors preferred, ~220 colors max.

Laptops. Laptops are becoming more common, but they face many video restrictions similar to the older VGA configurations on PCs. Prepare for widespread laptop web access. Consider the limitations. Test your web site on the laptop screens. Any users moving around in real space doesn't want to lug a monitor around to see your cool graphics.

Sun SPARCstations and SGI Machines. Keep on developing those awesome, multimedia-rich web sites. Your audience is counting on your information innovation. Go boldly into the future. Just accommodate for your PC and Macintosh crew members; they're upgrading and downloading.

Screen Size. You can never be sure how large a window the audience is using to view your application. If you want to keep their attention, make sure you present the most important content in the top part of your window. This is true for novices and experts. Time and information are the gold.

■ SURFING EXPERIENCE

Your audience may simply be surfing around and wanting to see *neat* sites. They might want to get a quick fact. They might want to research for supporting evidence. They may be scanning and skimming to enhance their knowledge.

When considering your audience, determine how people will use your site. If it's for a quick fact, put the quick fact out there. Surfers with little experience need the information as close to them as you'll provide it.

Your users vary widely in knowing how to surf the Web. Those who have seen hundreds of sites develop an intuition for how to get information fast. Novices will, however, read every line of text, follow only a few links, and may become confused and disoriented. Guide them by designing sites that are easily surfed. The experts have their places to go.

When designing, include "cool stuff," or "what's new," or "did you know that?" or "test yourself" or "random pick of the day." Design in search tools or link to them.

Go to http://www.pointcom.com/text/topsites/. Look at the top sites and look for similarities between the sites. What makes one site better for you? That is the kind of feature for your site.

> **Principle**
>
> Lay out the most important content in the first vertical 300 pixels.

Try This!

■ SEARCH SKILLS

As you've analyzed your audience, you understand what search skills they have. Few of us ever learned how to search in the library effectively. Most of us used the reference librarian—it was faster. Your user may be searching for a specific item at your site. Make sure you have search capability if you have large amounts of data. If you are supporting catalogs, long lists of data, product information, cross-references, etc., you'll need search tools at your site.

Find out how your audience wants to search data. The W3 Search Engine page may be just the thing you are looking for. See `http://stargate.jpl.nasa.gov/meta-index.html`.

Use both textual and graphical devices for searching. Users are used to common searching metaphors: maps, subway maps, street maps, atlases, address books, alphabetical lists, tabbed file folders. The closer you stick to common search tools and metaphors, the faster your users will be satisfied.

Some search ideas to try for different audiences.

Table 4-2   Search Aides

TEXT SEARCH STRATEGIES	GRAPHIC SEARCH STRATEGIES
Table of Contents	Maps with key points
Index	Subway maps
Alphabetical lists	Alphabetical tabs
Keyword search (by product, by class, by part)	Tree structures
Forms with Boolean logic	Icons (magnifying glass)

Try This!

Use Sun's magnifying glass icon to search around and learn how Sun is building the Internet. See `http://www.sun.com`

Topic Searching

Users must understand how to search by topic. Depending upon the audience, provide guidance for searching. Help identify keywords. Consult on how to narrow down a search. Realize there are different kinds of search tools, so the results may depend upon who is maintaining the databases. Study the topical searching tools to determine how to use them for your site.

•Some of the topical search tools generate their sites by using researchers, who study, catalog, and package the databases so the searches are rich in human interpretation.

• Other search tools are generated by a machine that simply searches throughout a document, finds the corresponding string, and reports those multitudes back to you.

Visit these three topical sites and look up your favorite subject. Yahoo at `http://www.yahoo.com`; AltaVista at `http://altavista.digital.com`, and Infoseek at `http://www.infoseek.com`

Try This!

■ AGE AND GENERAL COMPUTER EXPERIENCE

The age of your target group will have a definite impact on your site. Usually, the younger the set, the more computer savvy. The younger the set, the more discovery and play goes on. Play is learning, though, in cyberspace. It is not like Sega—fighting and selecting weaponless multiple channels. But the information highway will probably have street gangs, so there is probably value in that too.

The younger people are when starting to work with computers, the more easily they adapt to new concepts and paradigms. And, they'll be able to take anything you throw at them. To see a site designed for a specific age group visit `http://www.hotwired`.

If your grandparents can't use the Web, sooner or later it will fall into "toy" status. The idea here is to make sure the interfaces and the designs are so self-explanatory that they dazzle with simplicity and delight with functionality.

It is the ability and interest to learn a new system, use its advanced features, and actively do exploratory learning, and not just age, that distinguishes the advanced or experienced computer user from the novice.

Categorizing your audience will assist you greatly in determining what design features you need to include. Important considerations for categorizing your audience include skill level, technology level, surfing experience, search strategies, age and computer experience.

DEFINE GOALS AND EXPECTATIONS

The cause of almost all disappointments on the Web is rooted in conflicting or ambiguous expectations that web users have. Some of these expectations are clear, precise, and expressed in many of the newsgroups. Some of the expectations are rooted in the human sciences, e.g., users need certain psychological cues but can't explain why. They just recognize good stuff when they see it (like good structure and meaningful language).

Principle

When an age characteristic of the audience is known, design pages that address the capabilities of the majority of that age group.

Consider these expectations that all users have.

- Cognitive
- Technical
- Content
- Functional
- Linguistic

■ COGNITIVE EXPECTATIONS

Your audience will expect some very basic elements of human information processing to be present in your web sites. They may or may not be conscious of these needs, but make sure they are addressed. Addressing these needs between novice users and expert users differs somewhat. Study your audience well.

Table 4-3 Novice and Expert Cognitive Needs

GOTTA HAVES	NOVICES	EXPERTS
Facts and definitions	Provide immediate access on same page. Use glossary. Limit supplementary links.	Create link to definitions or glossary. Link to related articles or diagrams.
Concepts explained; e.g., What is VRML?	Tell them what things are and what they're not; give examples on same page.	Create link to an expert site. Or, provide a glossary. Suggest a newsgroup or ftp site.
Procedural steps How do you do this task?	1) Put one link away from origin. 2) Use standard numbering. 3) Speak in the command form 4) Provide direct link back to site.	Use link to expert sites on the topic. Experts will return to your site later, using their own way.
Processes How does this whole thing work?	Use graphics to show overall process. Include maps so users know what's next. Put one link away from origin. Provide direct link back to site	Use graphics and links to expert sites on the process. Experts will explore it, then return to your site. Provide additional or opposing view links.
Principles How would you best handle something? How would an expert decide what to do?	List three or four bullet items. Identify clearly as a principle.	Use e-mail to collaborators or experts. Include chatting sessions.

■ TECHNICAL EXPECTATIONS

The web audience in general will expect quality fonts, well laid out screens, colors that are aesthetic, and icons and graphics that communicate clearly. Similarly, if you're going to use sound or video, they'll expect the quality they get from CDs and television. Finally, if you're going for pizazz, you need to make sure you're at least meeting the MTV standards. Etch these in your mind when designing.

- Desktop publishing quality
- Artistic graphic quality
- Superior screen layout
- CD quality sound
- Broadcast quality video (bandwidth restrictive)
- MTV pizazz (bandwidth restrictive)
- Speed

Alternative Graphics Usage

GIF is a very popular standard graphics format. However, it does have some drawbacks. Photo-quality images are large (byte size), it is currently limited to 256 colors, and the compression method is proprietary.

JPEG (aka JPG) and PNG are evolving as alternative graphics formats for inline images. JPG is available on Netscape Navigator. When creating a Netscape-specific page, evaluate whether a JPG image is more effective. Do not offer JPG as the default for a single, ***all-audiences*** web page.

It is a good idea to customize graphics usage where browser capabilities can be identified and custom alternatives can be created, such as with Netscape Navigator and frames or client-pull.

■ CONTENT EXPECTATIONS.

Whether designed for novices, occasional visitors, or experts, your site must contain content and lots of it. Skimp, and disappear off the Web. Provide tomes of content, well structured, of course, and become a "Best Web Site" contender. Your audience will expect it, if not demand it. There are so many different places to go on the Web, so much competition for expert content, that the only way you can excel is to ensure you have good, reliable, verifiable, up-to-date content. Remember, you are the expert of your site. Users will excuse slow loading, mediocre graphics, absence of high-tech features, if you provide deep, meaningful, plentiful content.

Content and the content design are so important to web success that we have dedicated an entire chapter to it. See Chapter 2, *Content Design.*

When considering the audience, interview users to determine what content they'd like to see. Talk to content experts and determine what they think needs to be on the site on the top level, then at the subordinate levels. Research the literature, and make the information on your subject available at the user's fingertips.

■ FUNCTIONAL EXPECTATIONS

All your users will expect everything to work right the first time. All links must work, all navigational devices must do what is expected. The tolerance level of the average web user is very low: There are so many places to visit. If you don't have almost 100 percent functionality, you'll lose your audience very quickly. See *Validate HTML* on page 260, for URLs for web tools that check your functionality.

■ DEFINING EXPECTATIONS

The Web is an environment where users actively participate. This means that the web page needs to motivate users to take specific actions. This action can be as simple as scrolling to see more information or as difficult as getting users to register themselves or to buy a product. To enrich the participation, make sure you define the users' goals and expectations. Analyze your users. Then, create a site so that top goals can be completed within a few clicks.

Talk to your users. In order to get to know the users, talk to them, interview them, survey them, and get to know their processes, if possible. This may not always be easy, but information gathering is where we excel today, so start finding out.

Two-way Communication. Does your audience require feedback from you when they do communicate with you? Ask them. How fast do they need it, and how often? What form do they need the feedback in? Be specific here. Users have strong preferences.

Check it, then check it again. Once you have this information, feed it back to the user again to see if you understood correctly. Always keep open communication lines with the user to modify or clarify goals and expectations.

Professionalism and Entertainment. Find out if your users are professionals and want to see information in a classical format. Or, are they progressive, looking for sites that push the very edges of the technology and standard communication devices? And, do they want no-nonsense data or entertainment?

Compare `http://www.suck.com` with `http://www.golfweb.com`. Can you identify the audience's expectations at these two sites?

Try This!

■ LINGUISTIC EXPECTATIONS

Language is a major part of communicating on the Web. Whatever the language, you need to satisfy the user's expectations for its effective use. And, as graphics replace text for faster communication, the language of visual images needs to be tended to as well.

Writing for the Novice Audience

The less experienced a person is, the more likely that he will miss the subtleties of your design. If your audience is novice, you must spell things out more often. You must make things blatantly obvious. You must lean toward textual explanations.

Subtleties versus the Blatant. Clickable images without borders are a subtlety. Imagemaps without clearly defined areas to click on are a subtlety because they lack written procedural instructions. Keep the colors simple, the graphics easy to decipher. Add lots of whitespace for the novice user. Avoid using high-end graphics; adding too much visual choice usually confuses the novice.

What is a neophyte? The computer neophyte can be a user who just purchased a computer, who is looking at on-line services for the first time. New users may have seen some multimedia either in advertising or in a computer store. They may have seen friends or colleagues use technology and have expressed the need for getting on-line. They will comprise about 50 percent of the Internet audience for the next few years Prepare to update and upgrade your site, however. Things will change rapidly.

Maintain their respect. Since many of the users are adult, educated, and knowledgable in many different areas, it is important to remember how to communicate with them, maintain their respect, their interest, and raise their level of capability. Speak to them professionally, but experiment with the language of the Web. New ideas require new language.

Principle

Be blatant when developing for the computer neophyte audience.

Principle

Develop a more linear site
for the novice user.

Linear Sites. You are going to have to transition the neophyte to the Web way of thinking. Be linear at first. Reduce your screens to one topic with a clear title or heading. Then, show the next top three to five subtopics in crisp, clean text. Link and branch rather than over-complicate the screen. Look at the Tax Prophet site in Figure 4.1 to show how graphics and text combine to provide a very easy linear site.

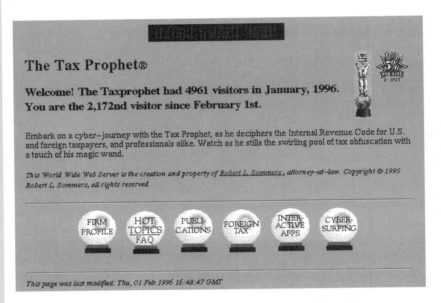

Figure 4.1 Tax Prophet Site Integrates Text and Graphics

Use hierarchies. Only the top items need to be included in lists for the novice. Sure, there are other considerations, more choices, and longer lists, but either refer to them as a choice, such as **More** . . . or provide a link with a specific keyword that will draw them to the detail. Rely on headings, bullets, and lists.

Keep with traditional symbols. Stick to text; novices are used to it. Add small icons to start transitioning the novice user to graphic choices. Use navigational features users recognize, e.g., VCR icons and directional arrows.

Writing for the Advanced Audience

If the audience is experienced, you risk offending them with *obvious* instructions, such as *"Click on the items in the image above."* The advanced group knows how to surf, navigate, read scrolling text, skim links, and cross-reference anything on your site in seconds.

Write less text for the experts, using the language of the Web, but provide more detail behind the scenes. Advanced users like detail, but only when they want to navigate down to it. Rely on graphics to speak for you, and complex, interactive graphics are even better.

Write clear, plain English sentences without any hype. They like easy access to facts. State the facts, then move on.

Nonlinearity for the Advanced. Not only do advanced users require a different user interface, they can accommodate a more nonlinear site. They have more exposure to the channel surfing of a TV, flying around in virtual worlds, or soaring through the heavy graphic sites of video arcade games that rely on speed and sound.

Remember, the Sega/Nintendo generation are playing on the Web, too. Their discovery skills in text are disproportionately limited. Their reading level is minimal. Identify this audience, and design for it.

Tools. This group is also used to tools to perform activities. Provide libraries, forms to reuse, downloading tools, faxing tools, etc.

■ JARGON

Jargon is one of the biggest problems with many web pages. Most web developers are too close to the material to realize the communication gap that they create with undefined or poorly defined terms. Especially notorious is the use of acronyms. The Web has added to those acronyms, and at the same time developed a kind of jargon web speak—web surfing, lurker, HTML, VRML, URL, web site, Webmaster, oh, the list grows and grows. Even the term "browser" is truly foreign to many.

When analyzing your audience, do some testing to find out if they know what is meant by some of your sentences and paragraphs that contain company information. Many developers don't even realize they're speaking in jargon.

Jargon. Avoid it! Unless of course, your site is designed for the people from planet Jargon.

> **Principle**
>
> Add detail for the more experienced audience.

> **Principle**
>
> Create more variety in the links and graphics for an experienced audience.

Branding

One of the most common forms of jargon is unexplained branding. It is wonderful to create a brand name for your product or service. Some brands can be self-descriptive such as Toys R Us®. Other brands are internationally known: Xerox®, IBM®, Apple®. Many marketers would like to believe that their brand is common knowledge, at least within their audience. Unfortunately, many people may recognize that a brand name is a product of a specific company, but the they will be unable to explain or describe what the branded product or service really is.

Unless your brand name is self-describing, or the average user is already familiar with the brand, you create a communication gap by using but not explaining a brand name. Web pages don't have the limitations of the print media. You *can* take the time and space to explain what a brand really is.

Explain Terms

It is vital that unknown words be defined if the audience is to get the message. This means explaining every proprietary word. Proprietary words are acronyms, trademarks, servicemarks, product names, and basically any proper noun not found in a standard dictionary. Your customized dictionary does not count.

You can't always verify that readers have covered preliminary material in other web pages. Each page must stand alone. This may mean reexplaining terms on every page. This is a good motivating factor for keeping undefined terms off most pages. It also tends to increase verbosity. In some cases, it is better to use the word and create a link to a glossary to define the word.

■ HUMOR

Humor works, and since good humor is timing of the truth, use it as much as you can. Humor has turned many a dry site exciting. Comics are beginning to appear more than as supplemental to a site—necessary, in fact, to explain things that just can't be presented any other way. Remember, localized humor won't go very far past a local set of users. However, if your audience is specific, then more power to you.

Most importantly, humor is not international. Word humor rarely translates. However, humorous graphics tend to more international.

■ FEEDBACK

Feedback is information about past behavior, delivered in the present, and influencing future behavior. If you're going to use e-mail, and it would be much better if you did so at your web site, you need to understand feedback. Feedback encourages user participation, engages the user to provide information back to your site, and improves the quality of your site.

Without feedback, you've created a flat noninteractive, one-way communication, like television and radio—these are the media we are moving away from. Consider some of the following when designing feedback for your audience.

Table 4-4   Feedback Implications

FEEDBACK REQUIREMENTS	DESIGN IMPLICATIONS
Make feedback known to others to enhance the quality of your content	Post FAQs (Frequently Asked Questions). Maintain e-mail list. Consider chatting sessions. Link to client web sites.
Users have to want feedback	Provide yes-or-no cues when necessary. Provide options to withdraw from participation.
Feedback is universal, but you must be aware of cultural differences. How do you respond to individuals?	Provide translation if audience is predominantly of that language. Respond according to the cultural and social norms of the individual.
Caution! Some feedback has risks.	Create disclaimers that the information from other sources may not be the opinion of the Web site
Users will refuse feedback that threatens their world view. If you disagree strongly with a user, tempering your feedback will help.	Encourage fair and open communication, stating that this is just an opinion. State your respect for opposing points of view.
Make sure you know from whom the feedback is coming.	Encourage use of real names
Clarity and facts reinforce feedback.	Make your feedback brief, and stick with facts, not opinions. Encourage users to add content.

Feedback is essential to improving your site's content and the quality of the information. Users feel engaged and effective when knowing it is they who are truly designing the site. Notice, in Figure 4.2, a simple Feedback and Update capability. It allows users to include

URLs to update the content of the site. This capability allows the site to grow beyond the original contributors and opens the knowledge domain to a wider audience.

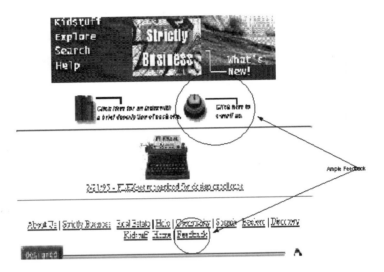

Figure 4.2 Feedback Takes Many Forms

Identify your users' goals and expectations. In doing so, you will be able to develop the right design elements, links, and features that will address their needs more readily.

WEB SKILLS

There are some audience considerations to take into account regarding web skills. The assimilation of these skills makes for expert web surfers. Your audience will mature, and quickly, too. They will possess these skills within a short period of time. Be prepared, yet remember to transition the novice. Web skills include:

- Navigational skills
- Browser skills
- Relationship awareness
- Software skills

■ NAVIGATIONAL SKILLS

Navigational skills have been honed by the many graphical user interfaces of the past couple of decades. Navigating with scroll bars is a skill some users are good at and others are still struggling with. Determine your audience's average skills set, and increase or decrease the amount of scrolling at your site.

Navigating through a web page. What skills are required to navigate a page? Web pages offer tables of content, indexes, and glossaries. But they appear in many different formats than in a book. If you put them at the top, a little scrolling makes them invisible. If you design them in Netscape frames, you have access to them at all times. For transitioning the novice, limit the page length to one screenful so these navigational devices can be seen.

Navigating through Web Sites. Users need some way of following their train of thought on the Web. Experienced users have learned to open more than one browser window at a time. In one browser, they'll keep a top-level page as an "Information Overview," and they'll surf in the other window. Netscape frames offers the capability to do this in one window. Use frames to improve navigational quality.

Tutorials, read me first, or how to navigate this site is a welcome addition on any page.

■ BROWSER SKILLS

Do you users know how to change options in their browser? You may want to tell them. Often as much as 80 percent of the web surfing population uses Netscape. There is no better time to provide Netscape hints throughout your site to enhance the user's surfing experience.

Browser Tools. Does your reader know which menu items are important? That is, can they `Save to Disk`, `Print`, or send e-mail from the browser? You may want to provide some procedural directions that explain how to download software, fax, or set color preferences in their browsers. A Netscape tip on top of a few selected pages could improve your site's readability.

Different Browsers. Sometimes things may be done differently between browsers. Use the power of the hyperlinks. Link to a Mosaic section, a Netscape section, or a Microsoft Internet Explorer section (that is if you have Windows 95). Use moderation, though. You don't need to go into extensive detail, mapping each function in every browser. The idea is to encourage people to expand their browser skill experience.

Try This!

Keep your eye on browser differences at
`http://www.ski.mskcc.org/browserwatch/index.html`.

■ RELATIONSHIP AWARENESS

How are you going to get users to understand the relationships
you have built on your site? In many cases, a nice graphical image or
a map of your entire site can show the overall site's relationships.
Take a look at the Figure 4.3. You get an overall impression of what to
expect at each turn.

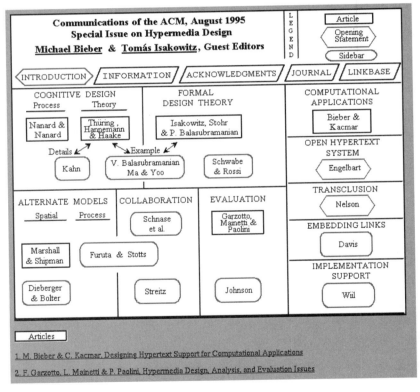

Figure 4.3 Show the Relationships Among Links

Overall Picture. Another way to establish meaning between relationships is to keep the home page very simple. Repeat the same obvious five or six main ideas over and over again. Put them on every page, so the user knows this is a relationship.

Use the same graphics, the same color, the exact same layout, page after page after page. The links and the way you think will become obvious, and the users will drive you without seeing what's under the hood. GolfWeb site handles this very well in Figure 4.4.

Figure 4.4 GolfWeb Makes It Simple and Easy

Clickable Graphics. Make clickable graphics obvious. So many pages have graphics. Some click in one spot, some are clickable all over the graphic. Others do nothing when clicked, and, worse, some self-load when you click on them, making the user wonder what just happened. In a few browsers, a blue line surrounds a clickable graphic. Do your users know this? Find out when you do an audience or market analysis.

URL Addresses on Screen. In some browsers, you can place your cursor over an item, and you'll see the URL referenced somewhere on the screen. Some users know this and can predetermine when they want to go to that spot. Novices need to be told where to look for information additional screen cues. They need to be told to wait when files are downloaded. Find out again if your audiences know the basics, then teach them accordingly.

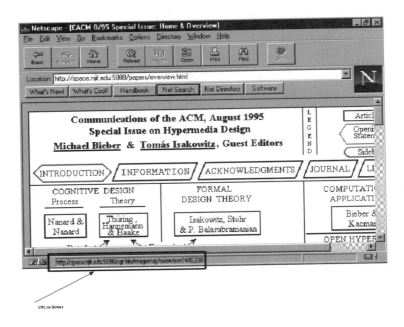

Figure 4.5 Destination URLs Are Displayed as Cues

■ ARE PAGES SIMPLE/COMPLEX ENOUGH?

Simple screens are excellent. Sophistication still reigns supreme in any medium. Remember one thing: Your biggest opponent is complexity. You don't know how far the user has come, what his experiences are, what his level of sophistication is. Study your users during audience analysis and testing for simplicity and complexity in your pages. Adhere to the principles of good screen design (Galitz, 1989), good CBT design (Clark, 1994), good multimedia design (Burger, 1993), good electronic performance support systems design (Gloria Gery, 1991), and good instructional design (Gagne, Briggs, Wager, 1992). These are discussed in the upcoming chapters.

■ TYPE OF BROWSER

The type of browser that the user has determines layout and formatting decisions. HTML standards are evolving at a phenomenal rate, but the HTML is rarely fixed in stone before one or more browser vendors implement it. In some cases, browser vendors implement enhancements that aren't even agreed upon by the standards working groups. Vendors add enhancements with each version of software, turning a wide variety of browsers into an even wider range of implementations.

There are too many browser variations to design for and test each variant. As of August, 1995, there were over 800 different versions of browser products found in the agent files of large sites that watch for browsers. This number increases every month, since there are always one or two people that will not upgrade.

If you have a captive audience, such as an intranet, designing a standard web page doesn't fall into the feats-of-Hercules category. However, it is humanly impossible to develop special pages to meet each and every browser variation in use on the Internet. The best alternative is to study the audience and develop pages that meet the common needs of large groups.

■ MAILTO: CAPABILITY

`mailto:` capability is quickly becoming a standard on web pages. At least make sure you can get hold of the Webmaster.

If you don't have a Webmaster, try the content expert for that page or topic. Most content experts are happy to help people in their favorite subject area. See `http://www.synet.net/hwg/ma.html` for an excellent example of using mailto: with *HTML Writer's Guild Mentor/Apprenticeship* program.

Not all browsers allow mailing capability. If you feel a need to use this form of feedback, convince your users to upgrade or change their browser. They'll take it from you if you add instructions, links, or how-tos.

Check your browser for `mailto:` capability. For many systems, `mailto:` requires users to configure a browser to forward e-mail. This process, however, is not always straightforward, so provide instructions.

■ TABLE USAGE

Tables organize data in remarkable ways. Use them whenever and wherever you can. However, don't forget that the `<pre>` tag in HTML can be used to create the most rudimentary table for any browser.

Table 4-5   Enhancing Cognitive Effects with Tables

TABLE FEATURE	IMPACT
Table caption	Quick explanation of table
Columns and rows	Divide information into manageable groups
Column heads	Label top-level categories
Cells	Focus on single item
Borders	Separate the information visibly

■ NETSCAPISMS

Netscape offers significant additional layout capabilities for you to consider with your audience. These Netscape enhancements can add to the value of the pages. However, Netscape is not universal. There are dozens of other browser makers that don't offer equivalent features.

Because of the dominance of Netscape in the marketplace (60–80 percent of browsers on monitored sites are Netscape), many designers automatically design with Netscape enhancements. This disenfranchises some 20–40 percent of the audience that may not have the option of using Netscape.

The ideal workaround to offer all users access at their browser level is to offer an HTML 2.0-compliant page as the base page. See `ftp://ds.internic.net/rfc/rfc1866.txt`. Use frame or a client-pull `<META>` tag in the base page to automatically load a Netscape-enhanced page as needed. This is documented fully in Chapter 8, *Adding Meta-Information*.

■ BANDWIDTH

Bandwidth is a critical consideration for the audience because of the attention span of the average user. Use Table 1-5 on page 18 to compute estimated speeds in determining how much to put in a web page. In the case of the corporate user, do remember that other traffic obstacles such as firewalls and proxy servers can slow transfer times beyond these ideal values.

Consider the "weakest link," namely, the limit for speed of transmission across the Internet is determined by the slowest link on the path from client to server plus some overhead for latency, particularly when satellite links are concerned. Proxy servers and firewalls don't limit things nearly as much as the restrictions of the Internet. In fact, proxy servers tend to cache documents locally, thus making things much faster than they would normally be on successive uses in an organization.

CONSIDER THE INTERNATIONAL AUDIENCE

The Web is a tool of the international community. Language, especially jargon, acronyms, proprietary terms, and colloquialisms, carry heavy cultural content. The use of this language most likely will be lost to a reader of a different culture. Design with global comprehension in mind. Be aware of religious differences, sexual differences, age differences, and skill differences. You can rarely assume the global audience will understand culturally bound terminology.

Some Considerations

- Understand the international audience needs before creating your site; remember, not everybody is your audience.
- Placement of international symbols on your site has an impact.
- Assume business practices, content, and image appropriateness are different around the world.
- Assume cultural borders between information cultures, especially information freedom.
- Learn by interacting with experts from different cultures.
- Start surfing the internationalized sites now.
- Consider government regulations.
- Interact with the technology and language of the country.
- Time is perceived differently in many countries.
- Organization is essentially linear across the globe. Surprising, isn't it?
- Allow yourself to innovate, but consider evolution, not revolution.

Lowest Common Denominator Audience

Your audience is international. You may not always need to accommodate every member of every culture. As you identify your audience, you will be able to determine the common characteristics of your audience. You need to speak to the greatest possible number of users in that group. You're going to need to become aware of using terms that are more international. So you've got to design for the least common denominator.

Write at a common reading level. Newspapers have always attempted to write for the lowest common denominator audience. In many cases, this means that they write at the eighth-grade reading level. If your audience are all readers, this is a good idea for you as well. It is true that many Internet users tend to be well-educated professionals. On the other hand, many users may have a justifiable reason for needing material written for high school or below reading levels, namely, that they are still in high school.

Write to a reasonably low common denominator. Do not disenfranchise a significant portion of your audience. You can also add multiple hypertext paths for the differing knowledge levels to accommodate a wide variety in an audience.

Principle

Always create an LCD "lowest common denominator" page that meets the needs of the bottom 25 percent or more.

KEY POINTS

- Define and categorize your audience well
- Understand the expectations, needs and known desires of your users
- Your audience isn't everyone
- Novice users and experts have different requirements
- Different platforms, browsers, graphic capability, and e-mail capabilities influence the audience
- Develop for the least common denominator
- Consider the International audience

CHAPTER

5

Navigational Design

In cyberspace, each *page* (HTML) or *world* (VRML) is a unique location (URL). You, the user, move or *navigate* to the next page or world or location. The unit of measure of this motion is the *jump* or the *click*. Paths or sets of motion through this environment are called *clickstreams*.

This simple description does nothing to downplay the fear of being lost in cyberspace that the average user experiences every once in a while. And for good reason: Most sites do not have the structure and navigational capabilities to orient users and allow them to effectively control their movement. They do feel helpless clicking from page to page, like canoeists shooting the rapids of a whitewater river, being pulled by the will of the river instead of controlling their own movement.

The good designer will present the user with a structured site and good navigational controls to move within it.

In order to accomplish this, the designer must:

- Build an intuitive site structure.
- Make the structure visible to the user, even if the structure seems intuitive.
- Give users location information so they know where they are in relation to where they want to be.
- Present the user with clear, common navigational methods, and do not present the user with an overwhelming list of options.
- Accomplish all of this with a minimum number of clicks or jumps.

DOCUMENT SET STRUCTURES

For sites of 10–20 documents, structure can be fairly obvious. If nothing else, the user can visit every page at the site. Sites of hundreds or thousands of documents don't have the same option of being loose and free with structure.

Classical information structure defines four basic document structures, linear, web, hierarchical, and grid. Some of these document structures translate quite nicely to this medium. Some structures have limited use in this medium.

There are four basic structures that web pages can be linked in. The first step in designing a site is to determine which structure or combination of structures is needed.

It is best to start by understanding each type of structure. They are *linear, network, hierarchical,* and *grid*. Linear and network represent current ways of communicating. They both have their place in this world. However, the larger the site, the more structure is needed to keep the site comprehensible and coherent. For that reason, the hierarchical and grid, the third and fourth structures are the preferred structures for a large site.

In the future, even the hierarchical structure may not be sufficient to keep information at a tolerable level. The database-like grid structure stands to be the future of large scale web sites, even if it is made to appear hierarchical to the user.

■ LINEAR

Used for:

- Conversion of legacy linear documents.
- Timeliness – Linear document sets are used for all items that depend on sequence or a specific order. This includes step-by-step procedures, historical progressions, and following a proof or logical series of facts to a conclusion.
- Prioritized lists – Linear document sets are used for many types of lists where order is important, such as ranking or order of importance.
- Presentations - Archived versions of oral presentations tend to be one of the primary continuing uses.

Applicable Navigational Concepts

Linear documents imply that the user will start from the beginning and proceed until the end. This is a valid metaphor that should not be taken to extremes. It is important to provide both a navigational document to enable users to go directly to the point at which they want to start and navigational items on the control panel to jump from one chapter/section/page to the next or back to the previous.

Forward and **Back** have meaning in this limited structure, but since both are also a function of the browser, it is important to distinguish the document or contextual back from the navigational or last-place-visited **Back**, and the same for **Forward**. **Previous page** and **Next Page** tend to be less confusing than **Back** and **Forward**, but still more confusing than a contextual description.

Principle - If Back and Forward concepts must be used, use Previous and Next or preferably something more contextually descriptive, such as Back to Audience Considerations or Forward to Graphic Design. (Did you use different Principle format because of sentence length?)

■ WEB OR NETWORK STRUCTURE

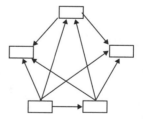

---

*The term web is used here because that is the classical name for this structure. Most web sites tend to reflect this disorganized link structure. However, this is **not** the perception of the web that should be perpetuated. Thus, for the rest of the discussion this structure is called network to separate it from the Web proper.*

Used For

A good analogy for this structure would be a rambling raconteur telling a story with the audience interrupting and going off on side-tracks. This tends to be interesting for a short period of time. Long term, however, users don't always know where they have been and end up retracing their steps.

When users are in an exploratory mood, this structure is adequate. When users are in a goal-oriented mood, this structure is worse than useless. It causes frustration and confusion. Use this structure only where a non-goal-oriented, rambling atmosphere should be created.

In the future, the use of this model for game-like VRML sites may experience something of a renaissance. It should be noted here that even games have structure. They have one or more doors to get on a level, one or more doors to get off of a level, regular characters, non-playing characters (NPCs), objects to act upon, and the structure of walls. Nothing of any scale ever successfully stays totally unstructured.

Applicable Navigational Concepts

None of the standard navigational concepts that can be embedded into a web page apply here. Some people believe that a Table of Contents or list of links is an appropriate model here. The problem with this model is the same problem with most lists of links—they lack structure and organization. Without some way for users to order the structure of the information, they doesn't know where they are going or where they have been.

■ HIERARCHICAL

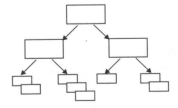

Used For

- Computer directories
- Taxonomy classification (i.e., going from the general to the specific)
- Just about everything

URLs were developed to reflect the hierarchical file structure of many of the more modern operating systems. This tends to make the majority of the Web tend toward a hierarchical mindset.

Hierarchies are a good way to break down a large set of ideas into related categories. Object-oriented programming is based upon a hierarchy of classes. Evolution offers hierarchical charts showing how complex mammals and even more complex primates evolved from a single, simple, wormlike creature.

By nature, the upper levels of a hierarchical structure are associated with general items, and the lower items with depth of specialization. It is this cognitive method of drilling down to obtain more depth on a particular topic that is the hallmark of most thinking. Our language is peppered with phrases reflecting this mental perspective.

Applicable Navigational Concepts

The concept of Up, meaning to go to the parent directory or the next, most general level of information is applicable here. The contents of each directory may have a structure within the directory. For example, a linear document set may reside in a directory. Thus, the linear concepts would also apply in that situation.

■ GRID

Data Elements

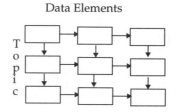

Used For

- Databases
- Multi-parent hierarchical models

The database is a fast-growing knowledge tool. It enables the user to get at the heart of the data in a very efficient manner. It can be used for information that resides in a structured form. For example, all products, from the most powerful computer to the simple bottle of shampoo, should have some sort of usage instructions.

A database can contain usage instructions for all items. Once the item in question is selected and the information about that item is requested, a specific block of information can be generated.

An example of multi-parent usage is companies. Some companies are organized by product line. Each product line has its own business unit of marketing, sales, and manufacturing staff.

In other companies, the company is organized functionally. In those cases, the sales department would contain information about all products. Thus, obtaining sales literature about a printer can be acquired by looking up a product and specifying sales literature or by looking up the sales document set and requesting information about a specific product.

Even if your company has one particular organizational structure, that doesn't mean this is the only way to display the information to the user. The client whose goal is to find out information about pop-can crushers from Acme shouldn't be forced to visit the Sales area for distributors, then backtrack to the Product info area to see the differences between a wall mount unit and a portable model.

Applicable Navigational Concepts

Without some form of reference, classical navigational concepts are invalid here. There would be a different parent to return Up or Back to depending on how the user arrived at the above sales literature page.

DECIDING DOCUMENT STRUCTURE

First things first, throw out the idea of using linear or network structures for web sites of any reasonable size. Since the hierarchical model is ingrained in the human brain, we might think that the best method for developing all web sites would be hierarchical.

Unfortunately, it isn't quite that simple. It is important to get the user to their destination in the fewest number of clicks possible. It is also important to present the user with a reasonably small number of options to choose from.

Given a site of 10,000 documents and a desire to get to any document within 4 clicks, there would need to be 10 options on the home page. Each of those 10 items would lead to a page of 10 more options. And again, each of those items would lead to yet one more set of pages with 10 document links on each page.

The real world isn't quite that structurally symmetrical. One branch of a hierarchy may have 1,000 documents in its domain. Another branch may only have 50 items in it. Both branches may have the same level of abstraction.

For a real-world example, consider a corporate site. The company may have 100 different products to go under the product button, but their corporate information may only have 10–20 documents at most.

■ LIMITING THE NUMBER OF CLICKS

How many hops should it take for users to obtain the information that they are searching for? A general rule of thumb is:

- Three hops are the maximum for important or commonly accessed information.
- Four to five hops should take users to 80 percent of the documents that they may want to view.
- Seven hops should take a user to any document on the site.

Limiting the number of hops means giving the user more options on each level. Bearing in mind the limitation that the user shouldn't have to scroll on a navigation-only page, this can be a rather sticky situation.

■ ADDING COHERENCE WITH FRAMES AND JAVASCRIPT

Netscape 2.0 offers the use of Frames and JavaScript. Stefan Raab used these tools to create an expandable/collapsible set of menus that doesn't require hopping from place to place. By clicking on the plus (+) buttons, the next level of links can be displayed. By clicking on the minus (-) button, the menu can be collapsed as needed.

With this method, users don't need to reorient themselves after each click. They can use the menu system to locate the item that they want and then click directly on the link itself to take them to that specific page. The fact that the entire menu structure is embedded within the web page also means that users don't have to wait for several conversations with a possibly slow server as well.

To see how this works, load the menu Frame (http://www.cuesys.com/outline.html) and view the source. JavaScript is embedded in the HTML.

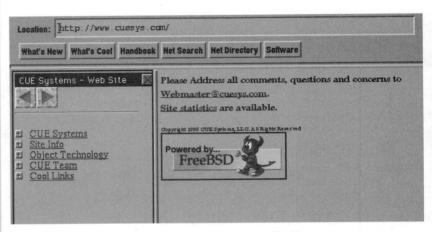

Figure 5.1 Cuesys with Menus Collapsed - http://www.cuesys.com

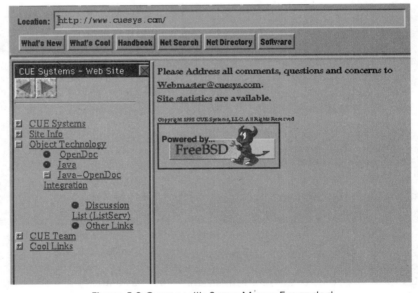

Figure 5.2 Cuesys with Some Menus Expanded

■ GOOD HIERARCHICAL FOUNDATIONS

Yahoo: Yahoo (http://www.yahoo.com/) has managed to limit its page to 14 main entries and the 3 most popular subentries for each entry. This method does double duty. It offers enough content at that level to expedite access to the critical items. It also makes understandable category distinctions for users to choose from if they want less common data.

At lower levels, Yahoo does warn the user when large quantities of items are coming up by placing the number of items in parenthesis after the topic name.

Point Communications. Point Communications (`http://www.pointcom.com`), on the other hand, offers limited choices at the upper levels. Once the category has been refined, Point Communications offers the listing in four different views, alphabetically, or based upon high marks in one of the three review classes.

Since this site is known for its reviews of sites, this is a reasonable classification. Either people are looking for a specific company or they are looking for the best in a class.

Sun Microsystems. Sun (`http://www.sun.com/`) is a site in the same quantity of pages/links category but isn't an index site. Looking at Sun, we find a similar mixture of main categories (Products & Solutions, Sales & Service, Technology & Developers, Corporate Overview, What's New) and quick jumps (the monthly articles, Sun on the Net, SunSite). Moving down into an area such as Products, again the most popular items get top billing and the long list of lesser-accessed products lies one more level down.

■ PITFALLS

Indiscriminately Adding Quick Access. One of the biggest problems with creating quick access to the most popular areas comes when that access is automatically generated and it makes more clicks rather than reducing them. For example, suppose your home page has links to links such as:

•Top 10 pointers on the site
•Products
•Service
•Corporate info

The first thing that you don't want to see on the top 10 list are the items that already appear on the home page. Why click to the top 10 and be offered the main Product page again?

Adding Too Much Trivia. Some developers might notice the success of adding quick links to upper-level pages and decide to structure their site based primarily upon popularity and secondarily upon logical classification structures.

This becomes a self-fulfilling prophecy. If most of what the users can find to get to are the popular links, they will be hard pressed to search several clicks beyond that to find additional things. A quick clicks list should assist users in finding common information efficiently, not supplant their logical mode of locating information. Thus, your latest or most popular press release may be a candidate for a top-level link for the next month or so. A link to the most politically important group of a department at the top level without having any user demand is not a good candidate.

■ GOING BEYOND HIERARCHIES

Even with the examples of Sun, Yahoo, and Point Communications, the strain of organizing so many different pointers and documents begins to show. The next level of document detail that you can offer a client comes from creating an information base and drawing out the elements that the user needs.

Instead of multiple clicks through a known list of categories, users can click through one or two navigation or interest refinement queries to isolate their preferences and then display pertinent information results from that. This is where the grid or database model comes in handy.

The most common uses of this right now are indexes and search engines. More complex information responses are possible. Some sites gather information about preferences and offer users a customized home page of their interests. The ultimate end to this strategy will be a customized newspaper aptly titled *"The Daily Me."* This is important to plan for because the trend is toward *mass customization*. Current web structures will not be able to provide that level of customization.

Even more sophisticated ideas are on the drawing board. However, realizing these goals of quickly presenting the user with refined information means that more structure must be added to the content to begin with.

■ MIXING HIERARCHY AND DATABASE

Adding meta-information, or information about information, to web pages and then indexing the meta-information is an obvious integration of databases and hierarchical web sites.

The alternative is also possible: placing the content in a database and giving the illusion of a hierarchical infrastructure through the use of relational database tables that reflect various levels of abstraction of the data. It is important to note here that a database alone is not sufficient to build the illusion of hierarchy from a a database. The database must also contain stored procedures that generate web pages based upon templates.

For example, the services page for Acme Design Inc., could be a template containing:

- Title
- Additional meta-information for the document via <META> tags and associated documents via <LINK> tags
- A listing or display of the main types of services that Acme offers, built on-the-fly from a Primary Service Type field in a table
- Footer information, including contact information drawn from the People table

Selecting a specific service could then generate a page of the following:

- Title
- Additional meta-information for the document via <META> tags and associated documents via <LINK> tags
- A listing or display of the secondary types of services that Acme offers, built on-the-fly from a Secondary Service Type field in a table.
- A listing of selected accounts that are used as a portfolio to demonstrate proficiency in the particular service, with appropriate copyright indications, drawn from a cross-reference of the specific secondary service type in the Client table and another-cross reference to a Permissions table for the copyright information
- Footer information, including contact information drawn from the People table

Unless the user is trying to refine specific qualities above and beyond general link hopping, these pages can also be generated frequently and stored as regular hierarchical web pages with the master content retained in the database for ease of reuse, redundancy, ease of customization, and, in some cases, version control.

The structure chosen as the primary storage method (hierarchical or grid/database) depends very much on whether the content is structured information or just a structured document, as the following discusses.

INFORMATION STRUCTURE

The level of organization of information determines the amount and variety of services that can be created to locate content quickly. The current tools, including search engines, are limited systems based upon raw data that still require the human brain to sift through the answers to find needed information.

When data is categorized into data elements like phone numbers or descriptions, the elements can be used to construct more complex data elements and, eventually, documents.

For example, a phone number data element, address data element, name data element, and e-mail data element can be combined into a contact element.

Another example might be combining a research statement element, one or more benefit statement elements, one or more risk statement elements, and a summary statement element into a risk analysis document. This risk analysis document can also incorporate contact elements from each of the contributing authors.

One benefit of this modular approach is the fact that it enhances the value and offers the inherent organization of creating the work in a collaborative fashion.

■ STRUCTURED INFORMATION

Structured information is information that can be grouped into specific data type elements for all topics of the document set. Structured information is best represented as a database, with each data type element being a specific field. Because structured information is computer generated or automated, documents or screens created from it are always structured.

This format offers organization and layout for creating scannable documents that can be subjected to automated information processing. It also offers significant categorization abilities for enhanced Content Locator services, discussed in depth in "Content Locator Services" on page 148.

■ UNSTRUCTURED INFORMATION

Unstructured information is information that will have varying or undefined data elements for each topic. A data element called *Body* may still be unstructured if the bulk of the information cannot be classified according to the type and function of the information.

The key difference between a structured document and structured information has to do with how well you could generate an answer to a query. If you can answer "What is the procedure for replacing toner in XYZ printer?" by looking up the printer, then procedures, then toner replacement, and receive a list of data elements that are the steps, in order, you most likely have this stored in a database and can generate other custom documents.

On the other hand, if you have a document created by a template that can use a format definition for a procedure header, and the document resides in a directory based upon the product name, and the document is named for the specific procedure, *but* the procedure itself may or may not be a set of steps, you come close to having structured information. If the main body of the document can still be in an unstructured form, it is a structured document—not structured information.

The best way to think about this is to ask yourself if the key data element types can be stored individually and assembled in different combinations to make different documents. If they can, they are structured information. If the document format revolves around the core content in a specific, unmodifiable organization, it is only a structured document. Again, this is a place where the company Information Mapping can enlighten writers on creating structured information as well as structured documents.

Unstructured information can still come in structured and unstructured documents.

Structured Documents. Just because the data elements aren't common across topics doesn't mean that documents can't be structured. Any document that is created with a template or standard style formats is a structured document. Ideally, any web document created with a template fits this model.

This format offers organization and layout for creating scannable documents that can be subjected to automated information processing. It can also offer categorization of data elements for enhanced Content Locator services. This option is limited to only common data elements.

Unstructured Documents. Unstructured information doesn't have identifiable, manipulatable elements. A hastily scribbled note fits into this category. So do most current web pages.

This format does not offer layout and organization capabilities and offers very limited manipulation by Content Locator services.

E-mail in a hypermail archive is a combination of structured (e-mail recipient and sender, date, subject...) and unstructured (e-mail body) elements. Since the bulk of the content is unstructured content, structuring these documents is limited.

CONTENT LOCATOR SERVICES

Standard services to locate content come in a few flavors. The most commonly used today are discussed below.

Table of Contents. This is a list of documents based upon title, author, publisher, citation, or other formal naming convention. This can be a hierarchical set of lists. A chapter can be part of a book. A book can be part of a series of books. A series of books can be one line of a publisher's catalog.

Taxonomy. A taxonomy can be roughly defined as a table of concepts. Like the table of contents, this can be hierarchical. For example, a taxonomy for a store or mall might start with Products and Services. Under Products might be Apparel, Jewelry, Hardware, and Furniture. Under Apparel might be Footwear, Hats, Dresses, Pants, Shirts and Blouses, and Suits or Outfits. Under Footwear could be Shoes and Socks. Under Shoes might be Sandals, Athletic Shoes, and so on. There can be a significant level of granularity in a general taxonomy tree as Yahoo (`http://www.yahoo.com`) demonstrates.

Vocabulary-Limited Indexes. When you turn to the index in the back of a book, there are a limited number of items that you can choose from. This type of index benefits the people that have something in mind, but they may not know the exact word to use in looking it up. This type of an index is finite and scannable.

Unlimited Vocabulary Indexes. The majority of web sites are based upon another type of index: free-text. In this case, all relevant information has been consumed and indexed by a computer. The user can then type in a word and receive a listing of places where this word occurs. This index is rarely available for scanning.

This type of index service can be very frustrating to many new users, as it is often very inflexible. For example, when searching for *book*, the search engine may not return entries containing the word *books*. The search engine doesn't always have the contextual knowledge to identify the difference between book—*a printed set of documents*—and book—*scheduling an event*.

It also makes finding a needle in the digital haystack quite easy only when you know the dimensions and composition of the needle as compared to the hay.

Without that preliminary knowledge, this type of index is of limited value. For example, finding an action item management system is much easier to find if you are look for a workflow process system. If you don't know that action item systems actually fall into the category of workflow, you may never find the right word to use in the text search.

Preference List. The above services depend on using the full text of the document or just the title. By indexing a descriptive subset of identification elements as described in Chapter 8, *Adding Meta-Information* users can define the subset of information that they want to see in a structured environment where they have a limited number of choices. This set of preferences can be generated on-the-fly as the user is creating a search request or stored and reused as needed. This is the basis of personal newspapers and targeted advertising.

■ LIMITING THE ELEMENTS OF A SEARCH

Each of these different Content Locating services can be used to search the full text of unstructured documents or can be limited to search only specific data elements common to all structured information or documents in a dataset, such as searching for title or author.

This is particularly beneficial when dealing with large datasets such as the major web sites that can contain 10,000 to 60,000 documents. In datasets this large, unstructured documents have little worth because many of the things that the user might search for are too common to give a limited response.

Going beyond a single web site to the Internet at large, AltaVista has been known to offer 10,000 web pages as the result of a search. This isn't uncommon on a search site that has indexed more than 16 million web pages.

Few users care to review 100 references to their search to find the information they want. Even fewer users are search-system literate enough to create a refined query of their own.

Offering people a limited number of items to choose from and creating forms to guide their search queries offers a much more user-friendly system than a blank text box and one to four (or more) paragraphs instructing the user on the use of commas, other delimiters, and the use of boolean devices.

SITE MAP

It doesn't matter how intuitive a site layout is, someone or many someones will get lost. Some people don't have the ability to visualize the organization of a site by moving through the pages. Some people need things spelled out, er, drawn out for them. The advent of GUI file management tools has created the need for visual maps.

To meet this need, sites should have a site map. It should also be an imagemap so that people can go directly to the page they find on the map. Large-scale sites may need to have something a little more complex than a single image with folders piled one on top of another, 10 and 20 deep.

This enhancement isn't widely available yet. One current pioneer in this area is Tenet Networks (`http://www.tenet.net/`) which offers the ability to switch between a VRML view of the site and the data itself.

LOCATION IDENTIFICATION

Another component of good web page navigation is the location identification. How can you get where you want to go if you don't know where you are now? This may seem to be optional because the URL is an absolute location mechanism. It is, however, necessary to assist the user in orientation. The problem with absolute location mechanisms is that they are computer-oriented, not human- or concept-oriented.

Yahoo effectively demonstrates how to tell where a user is by the page heading. Figure 5.3 shows that the user is on the currency exchange page and that the higher level categories are *Markets and Investments* and *Business and Economy*.

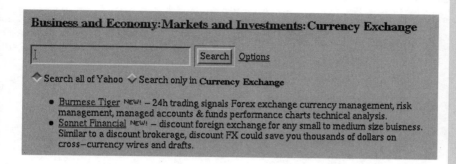

Figure 5.3 Yahoo Location Identification

One problem that crops up in hypertext is whether to display the path that the user came from or the fastest way to get from the home page to the current page (usually the directory structure listing).

Debates like these are best answered with an intelligent site map. Users should be able to identify from the information given, what site they are on, what topical area they are in, and what/where the current page is within that topical area. The full path is not necessary.

CREATE NAVIGATIONAL CONTROL

Navigation can come in many places in a document. It can reside in predefined places such as a navigation or control bar, listed in a block such as a hotlist or table of contents, or it can be embedded within the content itself. How navigation is used in a document can help the user understand what that link will lead to.

◼ EMBEDDED LINKS

Navigational links, embedded within text, should offer a description of the word or phrase cited, a contrasting viewpoint, or a tangentially related topic. Placing a link to the search engine with text may seem to be efficient for the user, but if the link citation is named differently than the navigation bar, the user may expect two separate destinations.

It is often wise to separate the general functional links such as Home and Search from content-specific links such as glossary entries or counterpoints. This embedded type of navigation is implemented in an unstructured fashion.

In Figure 5.4, all of the links are embedded tangential ideas. The body of the document is not a good place to put the common navigational items. For the user who does want more on the new InterNIC policy, however, the specific link is valuable.

What's In a Name

By *Mary E. S. Morris*

The number of Internet domain names has been growing at the rate of more than 10,000 per month. Since the InterNIC government contract did not provide the resources to deal with this kind of explosive expansion, on September 12, 1995, the InterNIC announced a policy of charging for initial domain name registration and yearly fees for updates and maintenance.

Note: Statistics on recent Internet domain growth rates:

- 1993 – 43%
- 1994 – 237%
- 1995 – 338%*

*Estimated for entire year. Domain growth for the first half of 1995 was 169%. If you don't want to figure out what those growth rates portend for the next few years, a few people on the Internet–Marketing list have taken stabs [1] [2] at prognosticating domain statistics.

Figure 5.4 Embedded Links to Tangential Ideas

■ INTRA-DOCUMENT LINKS

For long content documents such as chapters and What's New pages, position a TOC at the top of the document to access each main section. You can and should place return jumps at the end of each section.

It is important to note here that there are few documents that should be so large as to require links between parts of a single document. It is also good practice to make the links to sections far enough apart that the user will notice that the page has changed. Creating a link to something two lines down often confuses users who don't realize that their virtual position has changed.

All intra-document links should use only the <A HREF="#*{jump-point}*"> convention. If the full document name is specified, the entire document is reloaded and rendered again on many browsers.

■ CONTROL PANEL

Links provided in predefined places, such as a control bar, within a set of document should be used for major navigational or contextual transitions. Returning to the home page and terminating the current clickstream is one example. Executing a search or simply moving on to the next related topic in sequence are others.

Since each click takes time to move users from one place to another, it is important to minimize the number of clicks required for users to get where they are going.

The most important item here is to create a common navigational control panel of some sort on every page. This control panel takes users to common or standard locations. Some standard locations are universal, such as returning to the home page or going to a search page.

> **Principle**
>
> Create a navigational control panel for all HTML pages.

Most standard locations are dependent upon the structure of the site. By the same token, many navigational concepts are only valid in particular structures.

It is important to give users feedback about their navigational options. Offering them a navigation bar that includes a jump to a previous chapter or the first chapter can be confusing if they aren't aware of which chapter they are in. Offer a grayed-out or otherwise noticeably nonfunctional option on the navigation bar to determine location, or offer a content location marker next to the navigation bar that helps users identify where they are.

This graying-out is preferable to removing the item because one often-used user technique is to select navigation options based upon position rather than upon reading the name. Navigation items that change position depending on whether they are used or not can be disorienting to the user who leaves the mouse in the same place, expecting to click there to continue.

> **Principle**
>
> Items may change from page to page. Keep the items positionally constant.

■ CONTENT AND NAVIGATION PAGES

The types of navigational control offered on a page depend on the content of the page itself. Some pages are simply a list of links provided in blocks. These pages are best described as *navigation* pages. In contrast, pages that have significant amounts of content and embedded links are best described as content pages.

There can be hybrid pages with blocks of navigation and sections of content. This is *not* recommended because this usually implies a scrollable page. Scrollable pages may be tolerable for content, but they often leave unseen navigation items unclicked.

In a large site, there may be some main-level or site-wide navigational destinations such as the home page, table of contents or concepts, index, glossary, help, and human-usable meta-information.

The main table of contents is then broken into various subjects that may share many of the navigational destination elements. Subjects can be broken down in subsequent levels until one reaches topics, the lowest level of interdocument organization in the dataset.

Thus, the main areas of interest would be the site-wide services, subject-wide services, and topic-wide services. This is important to note even in the case of databases. Even a database will have some sort of taxonomy behind the scenes to reduce large bodies of data to a structure that isn't overwhelming to humans.

Different types of pages will have different navigational elements.

Navigation pages should have verbose, topic-wide navigation. Yahoo, show in Figure 5.5, is a good example of a navigation page. The user has the option of returning up the topical area, to *Business and Economy*, going down to any of the subtopical areas such as *Currency Exchange* or *Stocks*, or visiting specific links, such as Dead*man's Island*, at this topical level.

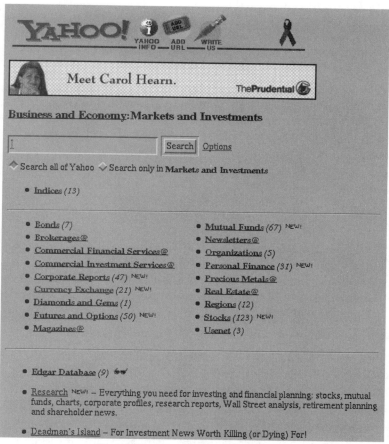

Figure 5.5 Yahoo Navigation Options

Content pages should have intra-document navigation, if the length of the document warrants it, and concise, topic-wide navigation. Figure 5.4, is a good example of a content page.

All pages should have concise site-wide and subject-wide navigation elements and location identification.

> **Principle**
>
> Provide TOCs at top of page for long content pages.

NAVIGATION IN VRML

VRML browsers, like HTML browsers offer rudimentary generic navigation pertinent to the medium. The closest metaphor for navigation in this experiential medium is games.

Games usually offer a long-distance jump capability via an out-of-sight, control panel. They also offer the ability to switch modes from an *in the thick of things* mode to a *bird's eye view* mode. These different jump and perspective capabilities should be built into your world.

Above and beyond offering mode changes and enhanced control panel teleporting for out-of-sight destinations, the medium is still too new to offer more.

CLOSURE

Until now, the Web and hypertext have been used by embedding a significant portion of the links within the text. Referencing a tangential work is an important feature of hypertext, but for large bodies of documents, structured navigation is a requirement.

A web site isn't just a home page, it is a set of data. When given structure, this data can be elevated in value to information.

By nature, the HTML web tends towards hierarchical models for structure. Each site has a defined home page or starting point. The home page is, more often than not, also a navigation page.

Thus, structured navigation, structured information or documents, and the effective use of either a real hierarchical or database infrastructure can increase the quantity of easily accessible information.

KEY POINTS

- To develop good navigation, start with a good structure.
- Simple structures such as linear or network style structures aren't effective for large sites.
- Because of the amount of information available, unstructured documents will have a short life span.
- The good designer will move toward structured documents, using templates and eventually structured information, to be able to order and organize information sufficiently for the user.
- In addition to a structure for the site and the documents themselves. core navigation elements are needed. They are:

    -Content Locator Services

    -Location Identification

    -Common Navigation

CHAPTER

6

Layout

Layout is the biggest area of contention in the web authoring community. Netscape has single-handedly added more layout or presentation aspects to HTML in use than any other vendor or organization. But—HTML wasn't designed for presentation control.

HTML Philosophy

HTML was designed as content markup language, not a presentation language. A content markup language is a set of designations that define the parts of a document, e.g., title, heading, and body paragraphs. Sometimes words need to have *emphasis* added. Sometimes they need to stand out **strongly**. HTML 2.0 and even HTML 1.0 provided this capability.

Each web browser developer was not expected to determine what the best display method was for a title or a heading or just plain body paragraphs. The ultimate control was supposed to be placed in the hands of the user.

Writing has gone beyond the standard 11-sentence paragraph and 5-paragraph composition. Information is often more comprehensible if we use a variety of display tools to organize the concepts on a page. Tables, footnotes, figure, and bulleted lists are just a few of the tools used to create a more coherent document. HTML 2.0 and 3.0 have created content markup to accommodate these additional compositional elements.

The need to convey information more and more coherently leads writers and publishers to find even more techniques to organize information. Font control, colored text, and text line width and justification have been used from the dawn of the desktop publishing era to

159

compress still more information into the same visual space. Netscape HTML additions were created to add these publishing features to the web publishing medium.

Unfortunately, the original HTML philosophy declares many of these additions to be *presentation* markup, not *content* markup. This causes many problems because there isn't a single, standard display medium. Presentation control means a move away from the heterogeneity of the Internet.

There are valid cognitive reasons for controlling presentation. Ideally, designers are more aware of the cognitive impact of their layout than the average reader is, making the reader's life easier.

This is often untrue with most web page authors. Too often they create compositions that are cool, which is to say, visual works of art, including flashy graphics, enhanced typography, and lots of activity. More often than not, they are also works of cognitive chaos.

"Cool" web pages aren't necessarily good web pages

Good layout design can be used to create effective web pages or good works of art. There are very few that fall into both categories. It is important to remember this. This chapter addresses good cognitive layout.

PUBLISHING HISTORY

When books were first created, there was text. Text was written in sentences and paragraphs. Chapters had titles and often an initial capital letter was *illuminated*, or graphically enhanced. Because paper was a scarce commodity, it was used fully. Books didn't have large margins or lots of space between lines. In many older books, new chapters didn't even begin on a new page.

Publishers recognized that some of these elements needed remodeling to assist the reader. Lines of text were shortened to make it easier to return to the beginning of the next line. Chapters started on a new page. Footnotes were added in a visually distinct manner. Bulleted lists were recognized as a new and improved communication technique. Chapters began to have headings and subheadings. Page headers were added that told not only the page number but the chapter and often the section heading being discussed on that page.

Currently, the advent of desktop publishing and other enhanced layout advances have added pull quotes, sidebars, controllable margins, gutters, leading, Dingbats to enhance bulleted lists, and the imaginary grid used by other design professionals.

HTML did not go back to the very beginning of print history when creating this new medium. Because of the limited nature of many original systems, however, HTML did take layout back to the dark ages. Gone were many of the capabilities introduced by desktop publishing.

Since many of the designers worked primarily in scientific and technical publishing where visual layout still isn't as important as content, the design capabilities were not valued as highly as the homogeneous system capabilities.

HTML 2.0 is roughly equivalent to current scientific and technical publishing standards. Pick up a scientific book from a university press and examine it. This is the level of capabilities that are available in HTML 2.0.

HTML 3.0, stylesheets, and Netscape 1.1N+ will reintroduce the enhancements known and loved by desktop publishing and other design folks. These enhancements are roughly equivalent to publishing capabilities used by popular and trade print publication now. Netscape 2.0 adds advanced hypertext capabilities such as segregating display space.

LAYOUT PRIMER

Layout is still layout, regardless of the medium. Layout philosophy doesn't change just because the tools differ. There are some generalities to follow regardless of the design. The nature of HTML is such that some of these guidelines cannot be directly implemented yet. That doesn't mean that designers can't work towards a goal, even if that goal isn't yet feasible.

■ MAKE THE PAGE READABLE

Short Lines

Keep lines short. A good rule of thumb here is 40–60 characters or about 11 words per line. Most magazines follow this dictum right now. Newspapers tend to take this concept to the extreme of shortening text to about 5 words per line. This admonishment, like many others, is good in moderation but not good in extreme. Shortening lines to the 5-word length can make readers work harder again, because they must jump to a new line and reorient themselves at the start of a new line.

This is one of the features that cannot be directly implemented in HTML yet. Workarounds can be done with tables and Frames. Attempting to implement this can cause more problems than it solves. For example, forcing line breaks at specific points can backfire when the user has a thinner screen or larger font than the designer intended, as Figure 6.2 below demonstrates.

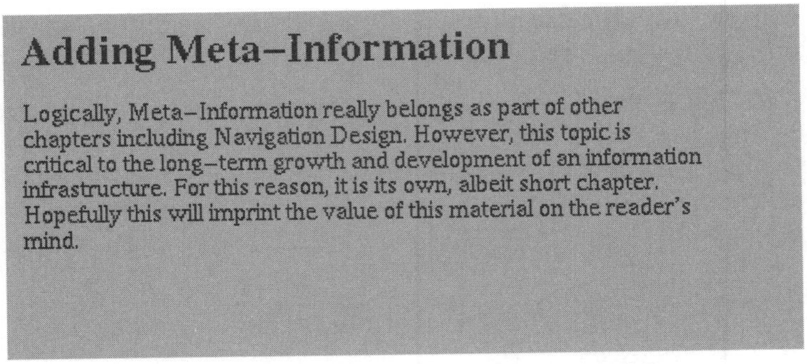

Adding Meta–Information

Logically, Meta–Information really belongs as part of other chapters including Navigation Design. However, this topic is critical to the long–term growth and development of an information infrastructure. For this reason, it is its own, albeit short chapter. Hopefully this will imprint the value of this material on the reader's mind.

Figure 6.1 Short Lines Created by <BR> on Most Screens

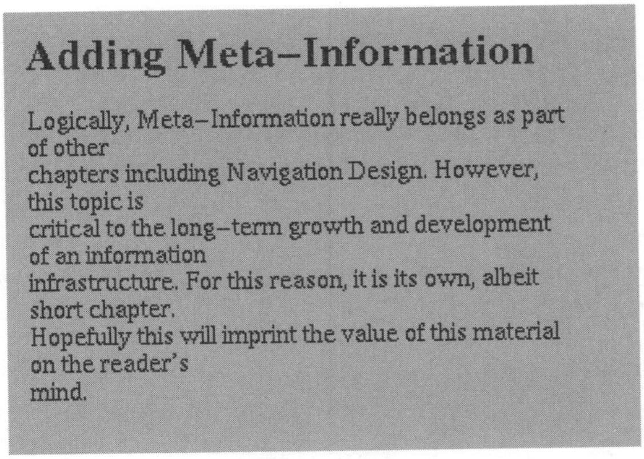

Adding Meta–Information

Logically, Meta–Information really belongs as part of other chapters including Navigation Design. However, this topic is critical to the long–term growth and development of an information infrastructure. For this reason, it is its own, albeit short chapter. Hopefully this will imprint the value of this material on the reader's mind.

Figure 6.2 Short Lines Created by
 When the User Adjusts Font Size or Window Size

Short Paragraphs

Keep paragraphs to four to eight lines. The longer the paragraph, the more monotonous the visual stimulation. If you can't make a point in about eight lines, the point is too complex. Break it down into more manageable bites.

Margins

Web pages should be scannable. This equates to *lite* reading. Wider margins tend to add the visual contrast necessary to make the reading easier, thus lighter. Placing text close to the margin makes for denser text, thus *heavier* reading. There are several techniques to implement this in the various HTML variations, including pouring text into tables without visible borders and stylesheets.

Mix Thoughts

Short thoughts are usually headlines, bullets, pull quotes, and sometimes sidebars. Short thoughts can be considered foreground. They are most likely to be read by all users. Long thoughts are more like paragraphs or the explanatory text after the bullet heading.

Short thoughts should be there for people to scan. Long thoughts should be there to expound on the short thoughts. People should not have to click to another page to see the one paragraph continuation of a short thought.

Contrast

Short thoughts are usually darker or brighter (higher contrast) than long thoughts. By making distinct contrast changes, you make it easier for the user to scan the highlights of a page.

High-contrast text is equated with the Internet concept of shouting. Shouting can be bold text just as easily as it is all caps. More than a line of high-contrast text gives the impression of shouting or at least strong emphasis. Conceptually, if you have to shout about everything, the content may not be good enough to stand without the nonverbal emphasis.

Principle

Limit paragraph size.

Principle

Use wide margins.

Principle

Mix short and long thoughts.

Principle

Make distinct contrast changes.

Principle

Keep high-contrast text short.

■ CREATE VISUAL VARIETY

Mono-brightness pages are boring. Looking at books printed a hundred years ago; it is difficult to understand how people managed to read from start to finish. Part of this problem is the stimulation level that is common now. TV, magazines, and most trade books now cater to the information-saturated consumer by offering high contrast *Cliff Notes* versions of things. As a society of learners, we are conditioned to use contrast as a nonverbal cue for locating and organizing information.

Visual Block

It is important here to realize just exactly what mono-brightness is. To understand this concept, take a look at a page, but don't pay attention to the text itself. As the text blurs together, the page takes on the appearance of blocks of gray in various shades.

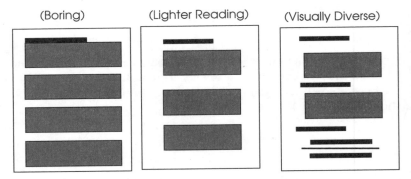

Figure 6.3 Stepping Back from the Text to See the Contrast

A paragraph followed by a blank line and another paragraph is nice repetition for a short while, but if the entire page is like that, the brain doesn't find any elements that stand out, requiring immediate attention. A page requires elements of different levels of importance.

Principle

Create different visual blocks.

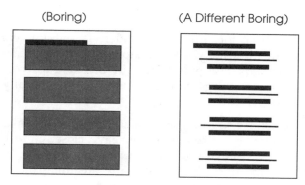

(Boring) (A Different Boring)

Figure 6.4 A Different Shade of Boring

Many people have tried the alternative of creating single text lines that are separated by horizontal rules as in Figure 6.4. Again, one or two of these are good, but composing an entire page of these is monotonous, repetitious, and visually boring.

Brightness

Brightness is a relative thing. A medium-gray text block against the standard gray browser background stands out somewhat. A dark heading or bolded line next to a dense paragraph stands out somewhat as well.

However, a dark heading surrounded by whitespace has a much higher contrast and thus stands out better. It is important to remember here that *some* contrast is built into the layout of most HTML browsers.

Headings by nature have more whitespace around them than plain bold text. Thus, in many cases, headings are used to create a dark region surrounded by whitespace, even if the text doesn't fit into the heading category. This is a very debatable (and hotly debated) practice. There are better ways to create the same effect in some of the more advanced versions of HTML. Basic HTML 2.0 should be used as specified on the label for the most part.

Principle

Punctuate a page with 30 percent brightness changes.

Principle

Use a grid.

Principle

Framing text blocks can be good or bad.

▪ CREATE BLOCKS

The grid is the basis for virtually all modern layout. Photographers have used this method for years. Desktop publishing breaks pages into columns, sidebars, and pull quotes. By breaking a screen into a grid and laying out the page, you can create an aesthetically varied and appealing page.

Framing a block of text can draw the user's eye to the text. Unfortunately, framing text can also give it the heavy, closed-in feeling that a small framed piece should not have. Gutters and margins must also be maintained in the framed area to ensure breathing room for the text. One alternative is to create mock reverse-video frames with whitespace.

In Figure 6.5, The first example has a reverse video frame created by sufficient whitespace. The second item could be created by using tables and adding borders. In the second one, it is easier to find the pull quote, but harder to read the small text next to it.

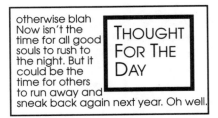

Figure 6.5 Framing: Good and Bad.

■ DEFINE FOCAL POINT(S) OF A PAGE

The brain needs to know what to attend to first. You, the designer, know the message that you want users to get from your page. It is up to you to guide them through the page and ensure that the most important message is where they focus their attention first.

High contrast is focal point(s). Motion ranks as the number one focal point for a page. Images rank number two. After this, comes large, high-contrast text. In some cases, large, colored text can actually get the user's attention before a graphic does.

Undefined focal point becomes natural reading. Natural reading starts at the top or the upper left for English. This starting point varies from language to language. If a focal point is not created by other methods, it becomes the start of the natural reading cycle.

LAYOUT FORMULAS

There are a few simple items to remember when creating web pages.

Common Look and Feel. People should be able to recognize the pages of a given site. When a new user is greeted with web pages from a site, the pages shouldn't be a candidate for Sesame Street's *"Which One is Not Like the Others?"* game.

Common Elements. These elements can be incorporated into a common template to work from, filling in the specific page identification and content.

Navigation bar – Unless this is a web site of one page, the site needs a common method for navigation. Since the most common navigational metaphor is that of a control panel or bar, the term navigation bar is used here.

Placement of the navigation bar at the top or the bottom of the page depends on the page. In cases where the web page will exceed a single screen, it is good practice to place the navigation bar within the visible screen, thus, at the top of the page. If the user must scroll more than a few screens, it is a good idea to repeat the navigation at the bottom of the screen.

Placing a navigation bar only at the bottom of the page to force users to scroll down to go somewhere is a good recipe for encouraging the user to press the Back button and avoid the hassle.

Principle

Give all the pages a common look and feel.

Principle

Give the pages common elements.

The Netscape 2.0 Frames enhancement and HTML 3.0 <BANNER> tag can both be used to keep a navigation bar on the screen regardless of the size of the web page.

Identification – Site and page identification occur at the top of the page on about 95 percent of all web sites. Unless a more visually active focal point occurs somewhere else on the page, this is the starting point for the user's attention.

It would be interesting to see someone break this mold. The few sites that do break this monotonous mold tend to be the advertising design firms that place the site identification at the bottom but leave the page identification at the top. The universe doesn't have to be this rote. Magazine advertising has proven this, but the experience has yet to sink into the web community.

Common cognitive cues – Colored bullets or links that have a consistent meaning are very good cognitive cues to use. Qbullets mentioned in Chapter 7, *Designing Graphical Elements* are an excellent example of this. Placing the miniature envelope next to a link is a good way to indicate that the link will mail to someone rather than go to another page. When the link itself doesn't give any clue about the e-mail nature of the link, some people can be surprised.

Common header elements – Page identification is still done at the top of the page virtually all of the time. As long as we read from top to bottom, this will probably be the case. This puts the main page identification element in the list of common header elements.

Common footer elements – The footer of a document usually includes the copyright notice and the address of the developer or designated contact person. On longer pages, the navigation bar may be repeated here as well.

Common graphics style – One of the most discordant things about web pages is the use of graphics of different styles. Using an almost photographic quality image, with shiny, well-rendered colored balls works well. Using good-quality images side by side with cartoon style images looks tacky and potentially represents the design work of a committee.

Unify graphics sizing – Having rectangular bullet icons for some elements and square icons for others breaks the visual flow. So does having visual elements of different sizes. In cases where the graphics are related to one another, the graphics should all be the same size.

Grid. Break the screen or window into regions and put the same information in the same regions. Creating an invisible table is a good way to ensure the use of the grid. This becomes even more important when Netscape Frames are used.

Margins. Try to give things more space when you can.

Horizontal Layout Control. Under strict HTML 2.0, the right side of a web page usually suffers from large blocks of whitespace. This can be reduced by using a table to define the grid. Centering more than a few lines, aligning text on the right, or justifying text completely are not answers to this problem. Each of these has its own inherent flaws.

Principle

Define a standard size for your margins and implement it.

Review

The above prescription resembles the definition for templates. It is. Style guidelines and templates are common in the writing profession for good reason. It gives books and manuals the same ease of use and recognizability that we are trying to create on the Web.

LAYOUT FOR MULTIPLE AUDIENCES

If you are designing a web for an intranet or private corporate network, you have the advantage of having a fairly homogeneous audience. Unfortunately, the Internet isn't as uniform.

There are several possible approaches to dealing with a widely diverse audience.

■ LOWEST COMMON DENOMINATOR

The first option is to write only for the lowest common denominator, which in this case is HTML 2.0. This means that you will meet the display needs of all your audience. However, enhanced web pages can offer significant layout control, equating to additional cognitive assistance that is vitally needed. To choose the LCD option means to offer a significant reduction in coherence on the pages.

■ ENHANCED AUDIENCE

Another option is writing for the majority of the audience, using enhancements that augment the message. Writing for the Netscape enhanced audience is a good strategy. Netscape usually offers the best up-and-coming layout control and enhanced coherence on web pages.

However, the strategy of writing only enhanced pages disenfranchises in many cases up to 20 percent of your audience, making this an unacceptable alternative.

■ TWO SETS OF WEB PAGES

By far the most strategically intelligent option is to create two sets of web pages, one for the lowest common denominator, one for the enhanced audience. However, the method of delivery of those enhancements to the appropriate audience has alternatives of its own.

Audience Choice

Letting the audience choose which method they want by offering options on the home page is one alternative. It forces the user to make a decision. Often, to the new user, this choice is between two sets of jargon, where their best response is to flip a coin to make the choice.

Offering the user the choice of heavy graphics and light graphics is not an equivalent choice.

> Remember, having a Netscape browser does not automatically mean that the user wants larger graphics. In fact, a Netscape-enhanced page can take advantage of the fact that lossy images take up less space in JPG format than in the default GIF, thus offering the user a shorter wait time along with enhanced layout.

Using the Server to Decide

Using browser identification technology on the server to decide which web pages to serve is another alternative. It is a valid one for some small sites that have CPU power to spare. However, this option requires rewriting the server identification routines every time a new browser or version of a browser comes out. This is very time consuming and CPU intensive.

Letting the Browser Choose

Letting the browser itself load the enhancements if it can is a third option. This option is superior in that the choice doesn't need to be made by the neophyte user or the overworked server. Basic pages can be loaded and rendered, and enhancements can be loaded if and only if the browser understands the enhancements.

This has been done for quite a while with client-pull offerings by placing the following line in the basic web page head:

```
<!-- Load Enhanced Page -->
<META HTTP-EQUIV="Refresh" CONTENT="1;URL={enhanced-page-url">
```

A new option has arrived with Netscape 2.0, that of using Frames. To accomplish this, the basic web page is placed between <NOFRAME> start and stop tags. The enhanced pages are loaded via <FRAME SRC="{enhanced web page}"> tags. It is important to note here that you don't need to create a multiple frame environment to display a Frame. This method is recommended.

LAYOUT IN BASIC HTML 2.0

HTML 2.0 offers very limited layout capabilities. This doesn't mean that HTML 2.0 documents should be exempt from designed common elements, a common look and feel, and templates to achieve these goals.

Navigation Bar. One alternative to the navigation offered in the template example below would be to separate the navigation items into individual elements. As long as the ALT text reflects the description, two separate navigation items are not required.

Horizontal and Vertical Layout Control and Margins. Horizontal layout control is officially limited to the use of the <PRE> tag to define preformatted text that should be rendered with whitespace intact in a monospace font. This isn't often done, since the monospaced font doesn't always look as appealing as the proportional font.

Some less than official appropriate alternatives do exist. The <BLOCKQUOTE> tag does indent text on many browsers. Other alternatives include creating a list <UL> but not creating any list items.

Sample template

```
<HTML> <HEAD>
<TITLE> Title Goes Here </TITLE>

<FRAMESET COLS="*">
<FRAME SRC="enhanced.html" SCROLLING="auto">
</FRAMESET>
```

```
<!-- Initial Meta-Information -->
<META HTTP-EQUIV="Keywords" CONTENT="item1 item2 item3">
<META HTTP-EQUIV="Abstract" CONTENT="Description">
<META HTTP-EQUIV="Subject" CONTENT="Description">
<META HTTP-EQUIV="Author" CONTENT="Name here">
<META HTTP-EQUIV="Contact" CONTENT="webmaster@blah.com">
<META HTTP-EQUIV="Expires" CONTENT="Mon, 08 Dec 1995
12:00:00 GMT">
```

The URLs listed below are listed as absolute but local URLs, (i.e., they reference documents in relation to the root of the document structure, but the server is assumed to be the same system as the page that is referring it). This technique is useful for developing and testing web pages on a staging server and then pushing or publishing them to the formal web site as needed.

```
<!-- Relationship Identifications -->
<LINK REL="Home" HREF="/Welcome.html">
<LINK REL="Index" HREF="/search.html">
<LINK REL="copyright" HREF="/cpyrt.html">
<LINK REL="Up" HREF="/parent.html">
</HEAD>

<!-- Common Header Items including graphic navigation -->
<!-- and site identification-->
<BODY>
<IMG SRC="/images/logo.gif" ALT="Acme Company Logo - We do
things better !">
<IMG SRC="/images/navbar.gif" ALT="Navigation Imagemap -
Use Navigation Links at the bottom of the page for text
navigation" ISMAP>
<H1>Page Identifier Goes Here</H1>
... {Document goes here} ...
<!-- Common Text Navigation -->
<HR>
<A HREF="/Welcome.html">Home</A> ||
<A HREF="/search.html">Index</A> ||
<A HREF="/cpyrt.html">Copyright</A> ||
<A HREF="/parent.html">Up to {insert topic here}</A> ||
<A HREF="/comment.html">Comments</A> <P>
<HR>
```

Principle

Use visually identifiable delimiters between links.

The double vertical bars function as delimiters between the various links. They are small but visibly identifiable. It is recommended that some sort of noticeable visual delimiter be used between links.

> *Also note that there aren't any spaces between the anchor tag, the anchored text, and the closing anchor page. This prevents underlining of leading and trailing blank spaces. Leading or trailing underlines can be less than aesthetic on some browsers.*

```
<!-- Common Footer -->
<ADDRESS>
<A HREF="mailto:webmaster@blah.com">webmaster@blah.com</A>
Blah Products<BR>
Metropolis</ADDRESS>
</BODY></HTML>
```

LAYOUT WITH TABLES

With tables, full screen layout is available. No more of the wasted real estate on the right side of the screen.

Navigation Bar. Tables offer the ability to match the text navigation description with the image version when an imagemap is used. Since the ALT tag can still be an effective method of providing text for individual images, the table option may seem redundant there. If the navigation bar is a single imagemap, the use of a table to position the text version is recommended.

Margins. One thing to remember about margins is that they differ from browser to browser. On Netscape 2.0 for Microsoft Windows, the text will almost butt up against the right side of the window frame. On Netscape for UNIX, the right margin almost seems reasonable as is.

When defining margins with a table, test them on lots of browsers and platforms to find an optimal solution that doesn't look poor on a specific platform.

Horizontal Layout Control. Tables offer the ability to make shorter lines of text by boxing text into smaller cells. As with margins, your mileage will vary from browser to browser. It will vary even more when the user resizes the font. Don't try to make a perfect 11 words per line, just find a happy medium.

Vertical Layout Control. Vertical layout control is possible with tables. However, the height of a browser varies more than the width. Vertical layout is effective for aligning lead-in text with an associated paragraph. Vertical layout is not effective for positioning elements at the absolute bottom of the screen.

> **Principle**
>
> Use tables to create adequate margins.

LAYOUT IN NETSCAPE 1.1 HTML

Netscape 1.1 adds more HTML 3.0 capabilities than just tables. It also offers some nonstandard enhancements. One of the most widely used features is the ability to alter the background and text coloring. Aligning text is a close second for most implemented feature. Last, the ability to resize the height and width of images also adds significant value to this release of Netscape.

■ BACKGROUNDS

A background can add significantly to a web page. It can also destroy the page. The key to having an effective background is to remember that a background is just that, *background*. It adds by highlighting and featuring foreground elements. When a background becomes a foreground element itself, the effect fails.

Finely textured backgrounds look great on a high-resolution, high-color monitor. They degrade significantly on a low-end system. This degradation can cause the text to become unreadable.

It is important to provide the following things when modifying the background, either by a background image, or setting the background color.

Always set the colors for *all* text. An example of when this would be important is would be when the user reverses the default colors, making the background black and text white. If you set the background to white to make things *more readable* and don't set the text colors, you have white text on a white background.

Dark red on a dark blue background is not very readable. Neither are some combinations of the same color. Blue is the most notable culprit here. There are fewer blue color receptors in the center of the eye than other color receptors. Blue color variations are harder to distinguish and require a more dramatic difference. Another factor contributing to this problem is the fact that monitors have some variation in how they display a color.

Netscape didn't augment general text coloring until 2.0. But the Netscape 1.1-compatible browser, Internet Explorer 2.0, does offer this enhancement.

Ideally, there is a distinguishable contrast between background and plain text. You may have reasons to color-code link text differently. For example, color variations may highlight which links are glossary entries and which are tangential trains of thought. Followed links

Principle

A plain-colored background is a superior choice when the audience's technical capabilities are unknown.

Principle

Always set the colors of all text—not just what you want changed.

Principle

Create sufficient contrast between text and background.

Principle

Don't make too many color changes.

Principle

If you need a legend to explain your text color meanings, you have gone too far.

usually have still a different color. That is four colors without a single image. Adding one more color should be all of the text variation you will use.

Remember, the brain has a ability to remember a finite amount of things.

A background can still be used very effectively to highlight text. A two-color background, as shown in Color Plate 1-3, can lead the eye down the left edge of the page.

Background images should always use the same colormap as the images on the page. Colormap slots aren't always an endless resource.

■ ALIGNMENT

Alignment can be a good thing or a bad thing depending on how it is implemented. Netscape created the <CENTER> tag to meet the alignment desires of the web authoring community. This has become a bad thing, primarily because it is a nonstandard way of doing things.

The HTML 3.0 standards indicate that alignment should only be implemented as an attribute of standard tags such as <P ALIGN=CENTER>, and <H1 ALIGN=CENTER>, not as a tag itself. Netscape 1.1 does implement this method of tagging. Unfortunately, the old <CENTER> tag method was not removed for backward compatibility reasons. Use the standard method instead of the Netscape variation.

Above and beyond the technical issues, there is the age-old battle between aesthetics and readability. Left-justifying text makes it easy to read. Centering text makes it more difficult to read. Centering is often used for headlines and pull quotes, where the single line of text is important enough to slow the reader down.

On the Web, centering has been used indiscriminately. This leads to web pages that are difficult to assimilate. If text takes 3 lines (classical 11-word lines) or more to deliver the message, the message should *not* be centered.

Principle

Use mixed color background images.

Principle

Background images should always use the same colormap as the images on the page

Principle

Backgrounds should usually have no more than 3–4 colors.

Principle

Use standard HTML as opposed to browser-specific tags whenever and wherever possible.

Principle

Limit the amount of text to center.

▪ IMAGE SIZING

Netscape offered the ability to declare the size of an image in pixels and allow the browser to render the page without waiting for the full image to load before continuing. This is a good thing and should be used regularly.

This sizing capability has other uses as well. The most noticeable image problem on the Internet today is horizontal rules that scroll off the right side of the screen. As long as the image can be stretched or compressed without losing value, the sizing feature can be used to declare that the custom horizontal rule image will be sized to fit within the browser screen by addition of the attribute WIDTH=100%.

This is only good for images that can be stretched or compressed some. If your custom horizontal rule cannot be stretched to 130 percent of its normal width without degradation, don't use the WIDTH attribute.

Another approach is iconizing an image to use for a bullet. For example, you can use a simple logo at the top of the page and then repeat it as bullets without loading additional image files by adjusting the HEIGHT and WIDTH attributes.

Loading a large image and using it only as a bullet is not recommended. If you don't have a use for the large-size image, load a small image.

Last, the HEIGHT and WIDTH attributes can be used to massage similar but not quite the same pixel size images to a single displayed size. Having fewer visual breaks and changes adds simplicity to a page.

LAYOUT IN NETSCAPE 2.0 EXTENSIONS — FRAMES

Netscape 2.0 offers some small HTML additions such as superscript and subscript options for fonts. It also implements client-side imagemap, and Java and JavaScript to remove some load from the server. The most striking enhancement is the creation of *Frames* or windows within windows.

Each frame in a browser window can now act independently, scroll independently, have different background colors or images, and be addressed individually. This is a great boon for the developer who wants to have fixed components such as the site identification and navigation bar. It also offers the opportunity to display the main train of thought and a sidetrack such as a glossary definition at the same time.

The biggest problem with Frames is that Netscape did not implement an efficient navigation method within each frame in 2.0. Netscape revises very frequently, so this problem may be resolved in the next release. However, when using Frames, it is a good idea to offer a "Back in Frame" button or link on every page. This can be implemented with a JavaScript program.

Frames are not immune to design extremism. As everywhere else, some Frames are good, more are not necessarily better. The key items to remember with Frames are discussed below.

Limit Frames. Limit the number of Frames that are used in a window. After a certain number, you will end up with Frames that are too small to display anything reasonably well. The scrolling principles apply here as well. Your navigation frames shouldn't need to scroll significantly, and the most important text should still be visible without scrolling. Adding Frames does not motivate users to scroll any more than they previously would have.

> **Principle**
>
> Limit the number of Frames.

Common Template. A common Frame template complete with standard sizing is just as important to look and feel as basic layout. Use common Frame templates across the site. Frames are an important part of look and feel.

> **Principle**
>
> Define a common Frame template.

Define specific functionality of each Frame, e.g., a navigation Frame, a body content Frame, a local Table of Contents Frame, a definition Frame, or a notice Frame for Copyright and disclaimer information.

> **Principle**
>
> Define each Frame functionally.

Making a Frame where words must split across lines on any standard browser configuration is poor design.

> **Principle**
>
> Don't make Frames too small.

Gutters. The gutter size varies from platform to platform when implementing Frames. Create a large enough Frame to enclose an image without requiring scrolling.

> **Principle**
>
> Allow sufficient gutters around images.

Test this layout on all platforms.

Principle

Create one main Frame.

Primary Frame. Make all other Frames support one main Frame. One exception to this guideline would be to create one main text Frame, one main graphical or otherwise experiential Frame, and make the rest of the Frames supporting.

LAYOUT IN STYLESHEETS

Stylesheets represent the standardization of document formatting seen on most large-scale publishing projects. By creating templates, you have taken the first step towards this organization. However, even the logical markup defined in HTML falls short of the standard publishing stylesheet by a large margin.

Many technical writing style guidelines define different Level 2 headings for a text discussion and step-by-step procedure. There are several special information types such as Note, Warning, Pullquote, and Caution. In order to customize the look and feel for a specific audience or organization, the standard HTML layout may not be desirable.

Stylesheets offer the ability to encapsulate layout enhancements and to use them without affecting the base document. This keeps a document viewable for the HTML 2.0 audience and adds significant value for the enabled browsers. Stylesheets also offer significant layout control, including complete font definitions, leading, and alignment.

> *Stylesheets, when available, offer a superior method of creating layout because they offer the ability to segregate layout, which is usually browser specific, from content, which is generic.*

Stylesheets also have their drawbacks. They are currently manually created, which can be as time consuming as writing basic HTML. They are currently only implemented on Arena, the W3 Consortium reference browser, and a few, not widely used browsers. Netscape is committed to supporting HTML specifications and they may be waiting for stylesheets to become a standard before implementing them. Netscape has not implemented them as of Netscape 2.0.

The important design items to remember about stylesheets are discussed below.

<LINK> vs. <STYLE>. The <LINK> tag will point to a URL containing a stylesheet. The <STYLE> tag will define style information within a document. The use of the <LINK> tag is preferable because it allows the stylesheet to be updated without revisiting multiple documents, which ensures consistency. In addition, some older web browsers have attempted to render some of the multiline <STYLE> information as regular text. Ideally, this shouldn't happen, but in the real world, sometimes it does.

Define element color completely. Stylesheets are a way to completely control layout. Text color is changed often. The white text on a white background problem noted earlier can occur here as well.

Use cascading stylesheets. Stylesheets can be cascaded. Cascading means a stylesheet with general, site-wide formatting can be called from a stylesheet that implements product-specific formatting. This is again a good thing to do for maintenance reasons.

LAYOUT IN HTML 3.0

HTML 3.0 is still in the discussion stages. Browser developers are adding enhancements as they become stable. Most browsers will probably have implemented some subset of HTML 3.0 long before it becomes a declared standard. However, most of the 3.0 enhancements have been discussed in the previous sections. This section deals primarily with theory. Visit http://www.w3.org/pub/WWW/Markup/ for new activities in this area.

HTML 3.0 adheres to the design philosophy that a web page should not be a layout- or presentation-based markup language. The stylesheets addition and Subsidiary Windows addition (aka Netscape Frames) will evolve to meet the layout needs for formal HTML 3.0.

HTML 3.0 proposes adding the following enhancements.

Banners. Banners are a fixed set of items that will not move when the page is scrolled. Netscape Frames have eclipsed this feature. As long as Netscape holds a predominant market share, banners aren't much use.

<FIG> Tag. The <IMG> tag has some limitations. The <FIG> tag has been proposed to alleviate those limitations. The <FIG> tag will allow people to overlay a base image with another image to save bandwidth.

Some people claim that the <FIG> tag will become obsolete early because of the <EMBED> tag. The <EMBED> tag is proposed as a way to incorporate different types of media, not just images. Some hypothetical enhancements would lead to the use of the <EMBED> tag for embedding Java applets and other programs.

Don't expect to use the <FIG> tag on most mainstream browsers in the short term. Watch the <EMBED> tag developments closely.

LAYOUT IN VRML

So far, this chapter has dealt exclusively with the text-based web. That doesn't mean that layout doesn't add value to VRML. As always, visit your local computer game player to learn how layout, spacial relationships, and control panels are used.

In an experiential environment, users don't start to assimilate a scene with the upper left-hand corner (assuming English or similar language); they start in the center and work their way out. Place the most important item in the center of the screen.

Foreground is no longer blinking text. It is now movement and detail. Backgrounds can now be textured walls as long as the user will not be required to distinguish a small item on the wall.

Items that are in the foreground and middleground usually have more detail and definition than the background does. The brain perceives less-defined items as being farther away and thus *in the background*.

Control panels, navigation bars, and the like are best placed on the periphery of the screen. The action is best placed at the center of the screen.

KEY POINTS

- Layout can be used to add cognitive coherence to the Web.
- Define standard layout and develop templates to reflect this.
- Layout techniques vary according to the enhancements used.

CHAPTER

7

Designing
Graphical
Elements

The ability to include inline graphics in a page was the critical factor that catapulted Mosaic to the head of the browser race and put the Web out in front of other distributed information technologies such as gopher. The graphical ability has been both blessing and bane to the web community, primarily because of the philosophy, *if some is good, more is better*. Ice cream is good—three gallons of ice cream per day is *not* better. The same is true for graphics.

ELEMENT PROPERTIES

Graphics can add significantly to a page, or they can be the biggest detractor. There are several graphical design characteristics that can enhance or degrade a web page. Sizing the elements of a design is just as important to the designer as sizing the server is to the Webmaster or System Administrator. Good size means good performance, which means happy users.

■ PIXEL SIZE

The screens that web pages are displayed upon vary widely. A laptop may only have a 640 x 480 pixel screen in which to display the web page and surrounding browser. On the other extreme, a user may have a 1600 x 1200 pixel monitor and expand the browser to fill the screen.

The advent of the Internet PC also throws a curve here. Internet PCs that use a television for the display device are often at a distinct disadvantage because of the low resolution of the television. TVs were originally designed to display about 320 x 200 pixels. The magic of modern gaming systems has increased the apparent resolution by sacrificing some color quality. Nonetheless, there is only so much compensation that can be done for this device.

Another curve thrown into this game are application defaults. Most browsers have a default size screen that they come up in. They user may resize the window, but more often than not, the user will not resize the screen until a seriously compelling reason comes along. Unfortunately, most images are not that compelling.

Horizontal Size

Bear in mind that the designer should work within the visible screen area to capture and keep the user's attention. As little as the user reaches for the scrollbar to move the page up and down, the horizontal scrollbar is far more ignored.

Subtracting the application border, scroll bar, and gutters around the edge of a document, leaves roughly 540 pixels of viewable width on the majority of browsers at startup. Macintosh browsers tend to be slightly smaller at about 480 pixels.

When designing graphics that extend from one side of the screen to the other, such as custom horizontal rules and button bars, take these sizes into account. If a considerable portion of your audience is Macintosh, err on the lower side.

...Netscapism"

Netscape HTML offers a method of adjusting the size of the image to fit the screen. To do this, set the WIDTH attribute of the IMG tag to 100%. For example,

```
<IMG SRC="blah.gif" WIDTH="100%">
```

This resizes the image to extend completely across the window regardless of the original size of the image. The standard HTML horizontal rule automatically resizes itself when the window size is changed. Horizontal rules are a good visual cue to indicate content separation.

It is important to note here that this is *not* SGML compliant and thus may not be adopted into the HTML 3.0 standard. Percent signs are not used to denote size in SGML. A future permutation of this might be to use a decimal number as stylesheets use. For example 0.8 would be 80 percent of the screen and 1.0 would be 100 percent.

As with text, it benefits the designer to use all available space. This can't always be accomplished when designing to strict HTML 2.0 standards. Nonetheless, when possible, space on the right side of the page should be considered equally valuable for placing images.

Vertical Size

The vertical size of a page is important in creating navigation pages where the user shouldn't be forced to scroll. Most navigation pages are predominantly text, and there is no guarantee about what font and size will be used. This means that there is little control. Build navigation pages to fit within the screen when the browser is set to application defaults.

Vertical size is important for images when an image is expected to take up a full page or images in a set should all appear on the page. Screen size varies widely here. Laptops usually have about half the display area that a desktop system does. Vertical size also varies somewhat between browsers and platforms.

Principle

Put the most important content in the first 300 vertical pixels of a page.

A logo or other site identifier has a certain importance. That importance does not extend to being the dominant element on the page. This is a key point on the Internet. Classical marketing places a high value on the visibility of the corporate emblem. On the Internet, a logo is valuable when readable, annoying when overwhelming.

An analogy can be made here to shouting at a person. Many people raise the volume of their voice instead of rephrasing the words when they aren't understood. More often than not, saying something louder doesn't add one iota to the communication. Neither does doubling the size of an already readable logo.

Put the next most important information (hopefully all the rest of the information on a navigation page) in the next 260 pixels. This number may seem a little short to the UNIX and Macintosh worlds, which both run longer than this. PC browsers tend to run a little bit shorter than the others. PC-based browsers tend to dominate the Internet surfing community and should be a significant factor in determining page sizing.

Principle

Put important information in the next 260 pixels of vertical space.

■ BYTE SIZE

The byte size of each image is very important, both individually and as the total of all images on the page. Some general rules of thumb are:

Background Images. Background images should always be very small. Many older browsers will not render the page until the background is loaded. Thus, a fancy 30-Kbyte background on a 9600 baud line will delay the displaying of a 2-Kbyte web page for 20–40 seconds. A good size for a background image is no more than 4 Kbytes.

Site Logo. Ideally, a site logo will be reproduced on each page as the site identifier. In this case, the image will probably be cached by the browser, and loading additional pages will be much faster. However, do not neglect the first impression. It is important that the user is motivated enough after loading the home page to go on and explore the site. Keep this image to about 12K.

Imagemap. An imagemap usually needs to have a set of clearly defined visual elements. This tends to make an imagemap larger than individual images. Regardless of how important a imagemap may be to the page, some people will not wait forever for the centerpiece.

- If the imagemap is the entire page as in the magazine issues of http://www.sun.com/ , the size of the imagemap can be as large as the entire page would be.

- However, when the imagemap is only a portion of the page, it is important to limit the size of the imagemap.

The best way to keep imagemaps, and indeed all images, to a reasonable size is to limit the number of color blends. This is discussed in detail in *Colormap Size* on page 189. Keep this image below 60K for a full page imagemap and below 30K for a page with other items.

Main Image. If the main image on a page is not the imagemap, this image should be kept small or convey a lot of information. Adding a large main image just to give a page *feeling* is more appropriate for an experiential site. Keep this image to 30 Kbytes or less, or generate it on-the-fly with a technology such as Java.

Make sure that the Java applet or embedded world is smaller than the image that it replaces or this change isn't worth implementing.

With the advent of tools to embed any type of information will come the ability to embed static virtual worlds into a web page. This would be a good thing in that it will allow detailed images to be created faster than they can be downloaded.

Generic Bullets. Generic bullets such as colored balls should be really tiny. There isn't much reason to devote more than 2 Kbytes to any generic bullet. Also, remember to reuse your generic bullets. It saves transfer time, and color-coding your information can add another level of coherence.

Custom Icons. Custom icons have a lot more to say than a generic bullet. They usually contain an image that requires good-quality definition. However, bytes can add up quickly when you use several custom icons. Ten kilobytes per image is a good figure here.

Custom Horizontal Rules. Keep custom horizontal rules to 5-10 Kbytes. The lower the better.

Banners and Navigation Bars. Banners and navigation bars (aka button bars) are usually carried from page to page. There are a few different strategies.

- *Individual Buttons/Special Images* — Many years ago, someone dreamed up the concept that you should not give a person the ability to do things that can't or shouldn't be done. In order to block this effect, grayed-out menus and buttons evolved. This is a very good thing in the web world where the confusing situation of a user clicking on a button and being returned to the same page can occur. Removing the button entirely can confuse the user who depends on placement cues. Thus, a grayed-out button is a good user cue.

- *Individual Buttons/Standard Images* — This option adds value over a single button bar in that the user can see the different URLs on the status line. It shouldn't add value over the Individual Buttons/Special Images approach. If your buttons are so large that loading a big button bar becomes a time constraint in amusing the user, redesign the buttons. Don't gloss over this problem by breaking up the buttons into separate images.

- *Single Button Bar/Image Grayed-Out on Current Page* — The big detriment here is the constant reloading of a new bar for every page. On low bandwidth clients, this is not a trivial concern.

- *Single Button Bar/ No Visual Cues* — This is the most-bandwidth, cost-effective solution available. It is also the most cognitivly disorienting solution. Use at your own risk. Cognitive-enhancing new technology such as client-side imagemaps, the Java-enhanced imagemap applet, and HTML 3.0 figure overlays can make this a viable solution.

Photos. Photos are a touchy thing on the Web in its current state. They tend to be large, colormap-intensive things that are better rendered in something other than the default image format, GIF. If you can keep the photo to 30K, you are doing well. In general, however, it is best to make photos an optional thing for the user to load and then warn the user about the size of the file when offering the choice. Also, wherever possible, use JPG or another lossy format for photos.

Page Byte Sizes

In addition to watching the size of each image, watch the size of the entire composition. It's not going to do you any good if each image is within size but the whole composition turns out to be 120 Kbytes and your audience are primarily home users on slow lines.

Another time problem is caused by having too many images in a page. Each time the browser must obtain an image, it must make a new connection to the server. In many cases, this connection can be achieved in a matter of milliseconds, but if the server is overloaded or there are network bottlenecks along the route, the connection make take one more second before the data starts flowing. Thus, 12 different images on a single connection browser might add 15–25 seconds to the transfer time.

Newer browsers are overcoming the problems inherent in loading multiple images by a process of creating multiple connections. This is configurable under some newer browsers. it alleviates some problems—but not all.

Add up the size of all images on the page, and figure out how long it will transfer that page to:

- Your slowest users (probably 9600 baud, or 14.4k baud)
- An average user

Ask yourself how long in seconds you would wait to see the page. Ask this question of the people reviewing the page. Adjust the images on the page according to the answers.

Just because your clientele can receive web traffic via an ISDN or a T-1 line doesn't mean that you should design to this level as a minimum. The Internet is always an experiment-in-progress. It doesn't yet guarantee bandwidth speeds from point A to point B. There are places where the Internet or the local provider's site is so saturated that web data transfers at 1 Kbyte regardless of the size of the pipes. In corporate environments, there are additional hurdles for web traffic to negotiate, including firewalls and proxy servers. Even if the clientele have a T-1, don't assume any better than 3–5 Kbytes per second performance for the majority of the corporate users.

One last thing to remember here is that with GIF images, the direction of color gradations can make a big difference in the size of an image. If you must used a graduated color change, make it a vertical color change. For example, Color Plate 1-9 is three times as large as Color Plate 1-10 when they are rendered as GIF images.

■ COLORMAP SIZE

The size of the colormap is another hotly debated item. The short history of the graphical web is littered with the anguished cries of the developers whose image degraded with the release of a new version of a browser.

Colormap Control. You the developer have little control over the user's colormap. On well-behaved systems, your page may be able to grab up to 80 percent of the screen's available colormap. On more color-possessive systems, you may have fewer than 50 color slots to define as you will, regardless of the color capabilities of the video.

Dithering. Dithering colors is another debatable area. Conceivably, to get around colormap problems, the creator can dither down an image to give it a smaller colormap. Sometimes this works—when the image can control sufficient colormap slots on the client's system.

One example of problems with this was when Netscape decided to allocate about 240 colors roughly equidistant from one another in one version of their browser and use this as the base colormap for Netscape 1.1 browsers. Dithered images were then redithered to fit this new colormap and ugly duckling images occurred. A sample of this colormap can be found at `http://www.phoenix.net/~jacobson/rgb.html`.

Platform Dependency. The next graphics obstacle to overcome is platform-dependency problems. More graphics are created on Macintosh systems than on any other platform. The Mac offers a wonderful-

Principle

Don't dither an image just to reduce the number of colors.

ly crisp, color-laden environment to create print images, color separations, and to work easily with photorealistic images. It is not the ideal platform to develop platform-independent, screen-viewable images.

There are significant color variations between most Mac monitors and PC and UNIX monitors. What looks right on a Mac appears dark and muddy on a PC. This is due to the gamma variations between PC and Mac monitors. Adjusting the gamma value of an image can correct many of these problems, especially for scanned images.

Another problem is the 30+ million colors that come standard on a Mac display system. This encourages wonderful shading effects that add considerable bulk to a colormap with all of those subtle color changes. Shading is a neat effect that can backfire when transferred to many low colormap systems where dithering can be cruel.

> **TIP — In order to compensate for the shortfalls of a wide audience of disparate video systems do the following.**

Limit dithered and undithered colormaps. Create images of 256 undithered colors or 64 dithered colors for all GIF images. This compensates for the large body of low-end graphics systems available currently on most PCs. The best way to keep colormaps small is to go for cartoon or line art as opposed to photorealistic art. Using flat color reduces colormap size significantly.

Home user systems tend to have better graphics capabilities than corporate systems. Don't assume that just because you have a corporate audience you can get away with more. The best-endowed systems are the home users that are dedicated to gaming. Few systems surpass the multimedia capabilities of these dedicated users.

Use Netscape default colormap. Whenever possible use the Netscape 1.1 default colormap as the basis for creating your colormaps. Netscape did some careful thinking when they came up with this. It prevents designers from filling a colormap with 200 variations on the color blue for a shaded background and then running out of slots to put the yellow, red, and other general foreground image colors.

Principle

Design to a 50-color colormap whenever possible, and 256 colors max.

Tune your colormap. If you use your own colormap, make sure that the slight-variation colors are at the end of the colormap list, so that they can be created via dithering if the colormap slots become full before the entire colormap is loaded.

In Color Plate 1-8, the colormap on the left has all of the large-scale color changes at the start of the color table, whereas the bad colormap lets them fall where they may.

Merge colormaps. Combine the colormaps from the various images on a page. All images on a page have to share the same colormap anyway. This can be done with Debabelizer and Photoshop.

Visit `http://www.cis.ohio-state.edu/hypertext/` `faq/usenet/graphics/colorspace-faq/faq.html` for more color information.

■ NUMBER OF POLYGONS

VRML presents new challenges to the web designer. This is a world in which text must be imported as a graphic or rendered locally, taking a big bite out of the page-drawing time.

The unit of measure of complexity in VRML is the polygon count. Most non-CAD based systems are poor at drawing polygons. Polygon-accelerated video cards have been "just on the horizon" for almost a year and will take considerable time to propagate to a majority of the population. Thus, it is wise to limit worlds to 500,000 polygons for the measurable future.

Try This!

ALT ATTRIBUTE USAGE FOR LIMITED GRAPHICS

HTML 2.0 was designed to accommodate all types of browsers, including browsers that didn't display inline images. The ALT attribute of the <IMG> tag was created to give a text description of the image that the user was missing.

Originally, the ALT attribute was only important on a few browsers such as Lynx. Users that could load images, but deliberately chose not to, were left in the dark. Many browsers have now expanded the use of the ALT attribute to users that deliberately choose to turn off images. This is important since there is a significant portion, often as high as 20–30 percent, of the audience that chooses to load images selectively, if at all. Since the only information they will receive comes from the ALT text, it must be used wisely.

Graphics should augment a page. Thus, when people turn off image loading, they run the risk of missing something. Of course, if they don't miss anything, it may be an indication that the graphics are superfluous and should be reduced.

◼ CREATE LITERAL REPLACEMENTS

The ALT attribute was created as an alternative identifier for the image that it replaces. ALT should tell the user something about the image that is there. [Image] or [Image Here] doesn't add to the user's knowledge at all. Text should always convey the information that the graphic was to impart. This often means that the ALT description should be a figurative description, not a literal account of the image. This is to say that [Search] is superior to [spyglass] as a description of an icon often used to indicate the index or search engine of a site.

◼ MAKE LOGOS EXPLICIT

The corporate logo or site identifier at the top of each page is a good example of literal replacement. The logo is there to identify the site to people that may not know which site they are on. Placing [Logo] in the ALT description, does nothing to orient users. Placing [NoClue Direction Services Logo] assists users in determining where they are.

◼ MAKE HORIZONTAL RULE ALTs COMPENSATE FOR LAYOUT

In cases when a custom horizontal rule was used, the image usually stretches across the screen instead of taking up only a small portion of the left side of the screen. When using ALT to compensate for a custom horizontal rule or other layout and spacing device, make sure that the ALT tag description takes up similar space or add formatting that will achieve the same goal without disrupting the flow when images are used.

Thus,

```
<IMG SRC="blah.gif"
ALT="========================================">
```

or
```
<IMG SRC="blah.gif" ALT="==="><BR>
```

is superior to

```
<IMG SRC="blah.gif" ALT="===">
```

Behind the Scenes

IMAGEMAPS

An imagemap is a clickable image where several different URLs can be loaded, depending on where the user clicks. It is more popular than several separate images because, due to connection overhead, a single image usually loads faster than several smaller images that add up to the same number of bytes.

■ IMAGEMAPS CREATE AMBIGUITY

One of the biggest problems an imagemap creates is ambiguity. Users aren't given as many clues as to what is clickable and where it will take them. When the cursor is placed on an image or an imagemap, a single URL is displayed on the status line of most browsers. The only indication of change is the changing x and y coordinate numbers, which tell the user next to nothing. That status line doesn't change when the cursor is moved from one section of the image to the other.

When several, small, separate images are grouped, each has its own URL to cue the user into the different destinations offered. Thus, it is important to add clarity to an imagemap. This can be accomplished by good graphical design and the use of the new technologies.

■ ELEMENTS IN AN IMAGEMAP

Imagemaps are usually navigation tools, not concepts to be assimilated. Thus, the 5   1 r ule doesn't explicitly apply here. This doesn't mean that 30-element imagemaps are all good. Each section of an image must still be a visually distinct image, thought, and concept.

This brings us to the concept of how the user determines what is clickable. The novice user requires very explicit cues. The user who hails from the fantasy, role-playing game world is likely to click on everything once, even the ripples in the textured background.

Distinct Elements

Imagemaps are not the place to add extraneous background noise for the sake of appearance. Each element must be visually distinct. The example below demonstrates this clarity.

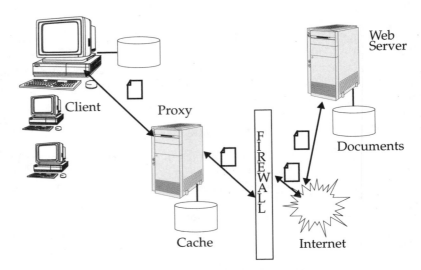

Figure 7.1 Sample Network Structure

In Figure 7.1, there are 18 distinct elements. They are:

- Main Client System
- Disk for Client System
- Secondary Client System
- Secondary Client System
- Proxy Server
- Cache Disk
- Firewall
- Internet Cloud

- Connection from Client to Proxy
- Document travelling from Client to Proxy
- Connection from Proxy to Firewall
- Document travelling from Proxy to Firewall
- Connection from Firewall to Internet
- Document travelling from Firewall to Internet
- Connection from Internet to Web Server
- Document travelling from Internet to Web Server

- Web Server
- Document Disk

This list can be reduced considerably.

- If you aren't going to say anything about the page at each stage of the transfer, don't put pages there. The pages are redundant with the network connections.
- If you don't have some contrast between the main client system and the secondary client systems, take out the secondary systems.
- If there isn't anything to say about the client's disk, take it off,

Color Plate 1-1
Golfweb's Home Page - http://www.golfweb.com/

Color Plate 1-2
Sun Microsystems' Home Page - http://www.sun.com

Virtual Society on the Web

 Home

 Japanese

V I R T U A L   S O C I E T Y ...

Surfin' the Web like Zappin' the TV,
Chat On–line like talkin' by phone
Shopping in a virtual city...

The place where all this comes together is
in our fast expanding Virtual Society

Breakfast on Fifth Avenue,
Lunch in the Ginza,
Tea at Piccadilly Circus,
Dinner at St. Germain,
And a cappuccino at the Galleria.
Make yourself at home wherever you like.

The streets are filled with neat
music and the signs are flicking as
you float breezily around the city,
or stroll along the roof tops.

Color Plate 1-3
Virtual Society on the Web - http://sonypic.com/vs/

Color Plate 1-4
Time Warner's Experiential Site

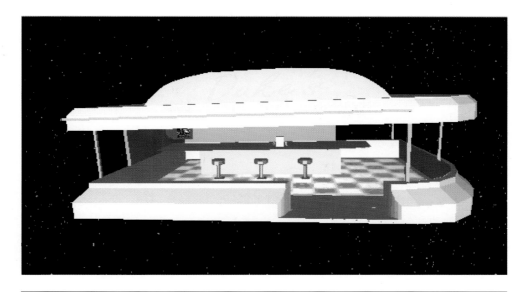

Color Plate 1-5
Virtual Reality Cafe - http://www.marketcentral.com/vrml/duke.wrz

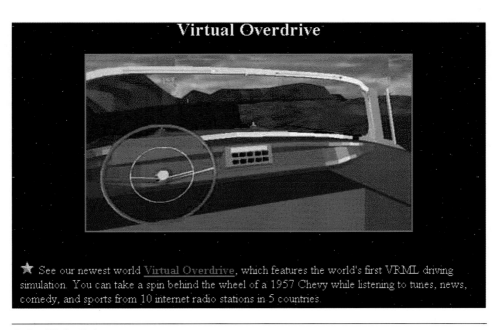

★ See our newest world Virtual Overdrive, which features the world's first VRML driving simulation. You can take a spin behind the wheel of a 1957 Chevy while listening to tunes, news, comedy, and sports from 10 internet radio stations in 5 countries.

Color Plate 1-6
Virtual Overdrive, 3-D Color Virtual Reality

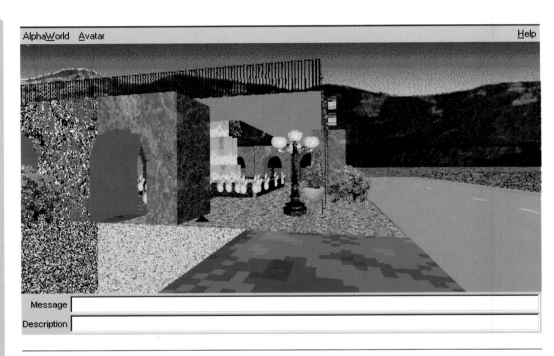

Color Plate 1-7
Alphaworld

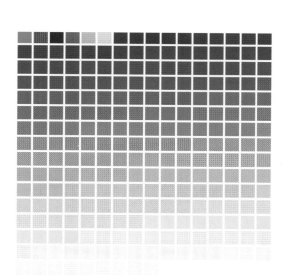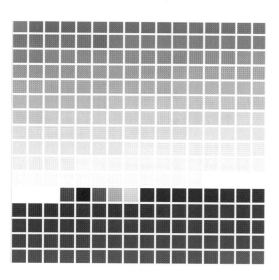

Color Plate 1-8
Samples of a Good Colormap (left) and a Bad Colormap (right)

Color Plate 1-9
Sample of Horizontal Color Graduation - Gif file is approximately 83K

Color Plate 1-10
Sample of Vertical Color Graduation - Gif file is approximately 26K

- If you don't have anything to say about each stopping point in the web traffic connections, don't put end points there. Make one continuous flow from end to end.
- If you don't need to point out that the disk is local to the web server, take it off.
- To add even more clarity, you can remove the mouse and keyboard on the client, unless you need to specifically talk about them.

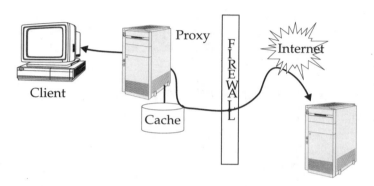

Figure 7.2 Reduced Network Structure

The new reduced image has only seven elements. Users will receive a unique discussion about each element in the image. They will not be constantly returning to the imagemap, feeling they are missing something and yet receiving the same discussion when they click on a new item.

▓ IMAGEMAPS WITH FIGURE OVERLAYS

Eventually, many browsers will be able to implement the `<fig>` tag and overlay sections of images with updates. This will enable designers to gray out buttons without the current impact of downloading a new button bar.

Figure overlays are a proposed addition to the HTML 3.0 specification, but not yet widely implemented. They can be accomplished very effectively in Java, now. Given the current availability of Java and Shockwave and their enhancements beyond overlays, it may be a more appropriate design technique to do everything in them instead of using the figure overlay.

■ CLIENT-SIDE IMAGEMAPS

Netscape 2.0 implements the W3 consortium draft standards for client-side imagemaps. Client-side imagemaps were proposed to take the load off a server. They fulfill this function well, but the other tools currently available go beyond client-side imagemaps.

Client-side imagemaps enable the user to see the URL for each individual element. They give the user the same amount of feedback as would individual images. Client-side imagemaps are also eclipsed by the features offered by current Java applets and Shockwave files. As long as Java and Shockwave are available, they will remain a superior solution for many situations.

■ IMAGEMAPS ENHANCED WITH JAVA

In the Java Developer's Kit (JDK), there is a demo applet directory called `ImageMap`. This directory contains the main ImageMap class and several supporting classes. The applet that these classes create offers an entirely new level of presentation cues for the user.

The ImageMap applet works in a fashion similar to regular imagemaps in that you define a region of activity. However, classical imagemaps are limited to loading a URL after a region has been clicked.

The Java ImageMap applet offers the designer the flexibility to:

- Load a URL when a region is clicked, just like classical URLs.
- Brighten the region when the cursor is inside to demonstrate what the region encompasses.
- Play a sound when the cursor is placed in the region.
- Display a message in the browser's status area.
- Any combination or all of the above.

A quick look at an HTML sample implementing these features looks like:

```
<applet code=ImageMap.class width=500 height=400>
```

This declares the applet to run with the `code` attribute and defines the size of the image that will be used.

```
<param name=img value="computers.gif">
```

This passes the URL of the image to be used in the imagemap.

```
<param name=highlight value="brighter30">
```

This defines how bright to make the highlighting.

```
<param name=area1s
value="SoundArea,200,100,120,60,audio/bigdog.au">
```

Each action must have a name. The value area lists the type of action that is to be performed (in this case, play a sound when in the region), the size of the region, and the value of the action (in this case, the URL for the sound).

```
<param name=area1m value="NameArea,200,100,120,60,Big
Computer!">
```

Here, a message will be displayed on the status line when the cursor is in the region. The value of the action in this case is the message to display.

```
<param name=area1c
value="HrefButtonArea,200,100,120,60,spec-sheet.html">
```

Clicking in the region results in the loading of the URL listed as the value of this action.

```
</applet>
```

The applet is complete.

Any HTML author can incorporate this applet. No Java programming is required. The HTML author must place all `*.class` files in a directory called `classes` where the HTML file resides. This imagemap can give the user more clues about what to expect from clicking on each item in the imagemap. It is this additional hint feature that makes Java a superior choice.

The enhancement in understanding must be contrasted with the additional bandwidth impact of downloading the applet itself.

USING GRAPHICS

It is often assumed that the designer must always use graphics when designing for the Web. This isn't true. There are quite a few very successful pages that don't depend on graphics.

Nonetheless, graphics do add something to pages that would otherwise put the user to sleep. Graphics should always be used judiciously.

■ WHEN TO USE GRAPHICS?

Graphics add value by

•Giving more information about a link.

Qbullets are a wonderful example of adding value with graphics. They are small and convey information well, like icons do. Refer to http://www.matterform.com/mf/qbullets/aboutqbullets.htm for a quick sample. Probably the best thing that they add is knowledge about what will happen when the user clicks a link. Will it download a large file or bring up a mail window? Qbullets answer these questions effectively.

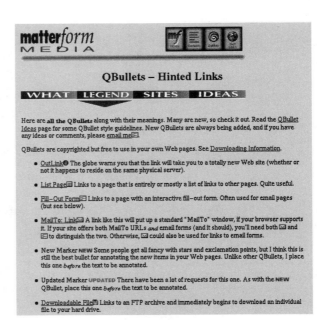

Figure 7.3 Qbullets
http://www.matterform.com/mf/qbullets/aboutqbullets.html

- Drawing the browser's eye to a particular place on the screen and thus controlling how the screen is viewed,
- Bringing some area into foreground that might otherwise be middleground, e.g., the new Note and warning areas in HTML 3.0.
- Giving "the big picture," i.e., demonstrating various areas and their relationship to one another. This is especially important in imagemaps.

■ WHEN NOT TO USE GRAPHICS?

- Graphics slow down absorption of a page. If the page should be primarily scannable, fewer images should be used.
- Graphics tend to take up large portions of real estate on most pages. This means that there is proportionally less space to convey a message in text. If the page needs to scroll, look for graphics to remove.
- Photographic-quality graphics look poor on lower-resolution monitors. Use photographic-quality images when the audience capabilities are known to be able to display them without degradation.
- Bandwidth requirements should affect graphics usage heavily. Limit the use of graphics for the low bandwidth audience.
- May lead user to look at them and miss the message in the text by being more foreground than the message. Use only graphics that don't dilute or detract from the message.

Graphics should convey the same message as the text. If the graphics have a different agenda than the text, there is conflict and the user is likely to absorb only one message or sit, confused, trying to integrate the different messages.

■ DETERMINING GRAPHICS USAGE

When determining the graphical requirements of your pages, test them on content-novices. Show the novices graphics-less (and ALT textless) pages and ask them to tell you the message they are receiving. Add a few images and repeat. Once you know which images augment the message and which images degrade the message, prune your page accordingly.

> *Change content-novice users very frequently, as they lose their innocence and begin to understand more than a new user of the page should know on first encounter.*

KEY POINTS

- Graphical elements need to be designed with more than just the aesthetic appeal in mind.
- Graphics need to be designed so that they won't degrade performance, and vewiability on low-end systems.
- Graphic elements need to be distinct to be useful in imagemaps.
- Use graphics when they add value; don't use them gratuitously.

CHAPTER

8

Adding Meta-Information

L ogically, meta-information really belongs as part of other chapters. However, this topic is critical to the long-term growth and development of an information infrastructure. For this reason, it is its own, albeit short, chapter to imprint the value of this material on you.

Meta-information is not the contents of a document. It is the information *about* the document. This information is used to index the site more efficiently, keep documents timely, provide filtering where content may be inappropriate for some audiences, and provide appropriate bibliographic information about each document for distributed reference.

THE NEED FOR META-INFORMATION

A single web site of 1–20 documents stands alone. It may require some simple navigation and good content structuring, but for the most part, information can be located and assimilated without significant effort.

A single web site of 10,000 documents is another story. So is a web of thousands of 1–20 document sites, such as the Internet is now. Software was originally simple as well. There was a time when people could not conceive of software that would require more than 64 Kbytes of memory, either.

The complexity of the Internet and its vast seas of content have grown just as the complexity of software grew. It isn't uncommon now for an operating system to devote as much as 10 percent of its processing to overhead. The time is ripe for planning and implementing similar overhead management hooks in web design as well.

Automating the production and delivery of information is not enough. At present, there is no single indexing standard that all web creators adhere to. Indexing is done by brute compute force and offers overwhelmingly numerous results for the inexperienced searcher.

At the time of this writing, Yahoo (http://www.yahoo.com/) is the only Internet index site to offer a comprehensive, human-organized structure that all skill levels can use effectively. This is accomplished by circumventing compute force with the human knowledge of the context of content. Thus, *book*ing a flight falls under travel and a *book* can be found under publishing.

Yahoo has become a large, people-intensive undertaking. In order to move beyond the human requirements for adding significant structure, we must embed this information into each and every document. This will make the information available to agents such as web robots or spiders that visit sites across the Internet or on corporate webs.

When only the pertinent information is presented for cataloging instead of a cacophony of raw data, not only are incredible human labor savings offered to the indexing bodies of the Internet, but better, more-targeted visibility is created for the audience and a designer's clientele.

Looking toward the future, in order to realize the vision of an agent searching for concert tickets, we must create more than just a bibliographic reference. We must standardize and format a wide variety of information such that these automated agents can locate a product, event, or service, compare and contrast the offerings, and even make decisions about purchasing without human intervention.

Creating information that is understandable and actionable by a web agent is not a trivial prospect, but one that we must anticipate and prepare for.

Visit http://www.scit.wlv.ac.uk/wwlib/position.html for more discussion on this topic.

Try This!

INFORMATION ABOUT THE DOCUMENT

Information about a document's contents is placed within the HEAD of a document (i.e., between the <HEAD> and </HEAD> tags). There are several elements of information that are important to include on most documents. These elements are inserted with the use of the <TITLE> and <META> tags.

■ TAGS

<TITLE> Tag

The <TITLE> tag is one of the most basic types of meta-information. It is already used when document information is stored in hotlists and bookmarks. It is already gathered by Lycos and some other web robots.

One of the biggest problems with a title is the fact that some people use the title as a fancy attention-getting name for the document, and others use the literal description of the contents for the title. This doesn't make for uniform indexing. Thus, there is a need to create more information elements than just the title.

<META> Tag

The <META> tag has become the main tag used to add all other types of intra-document information. This is reasonable since there is no guarantee that other information elements will apply to all documents. This use allows for a very extensible environment.

The <META> tag also offers the use of the HTTP-EQUIV attribute for returning this information to a web agent without retrieving the entire file on many web servers. The HTTP-EQUIV attribute also names the type of information that it is returning, such as *keywords* or *author*.

The two remaining attributes for the <META> tag are NAME and CONTENT. The NAME attribute can and often is the same as the HTTP-EQUIV attribute and thus is optional. The value of the information named in HTTP-EQUIV or NAME is stored in the CONTENT attribute.

There are numerous formal classification schemes for organizing documents. For most publications, the Dewey Decimal system, the Library of Congress classification, the USMARC and the TEI systems are all being considered. It is recommended that the classification scheme that is used be both defined in the meta-information and be explicitly noted. The recommended method of doing this is to add an additional <META> tag entry defining the scheme of the information element. See Code 8.1 for examples of this.

Most of the meta-information techniques are still being debated and the merits of each strategy considered. As with most of the rest of the web technology, a standard will probably not emerge until six months to a year after everyone is using it. The following suggestions are classified as (+) fairly likely to be used, (*) discussed heavily but not the only option, and (-) the personal recommendation of the author, Mary E. S. Morris.

■ IDENTIFYING AND QUANTIFYING CONTENT

(+) Title. The title is the one element that has been a part of HTML from the beginning. It is usually a string of words naming the document as uniquely as possible in the near infinite sea of documents.

(+) Subject. The subject of a document is usually a little more mundane than the title. There are several classification systems to place subjects within a structured hierarchy, such as the Library of Congress classification.

Some web malls may choose to create their own (or develop a common) taxonomy to accommodate product and service classifications. In the future, new interactive media, such as hypermail listings and MUDs (Multi-User Dungeons), may require classification systems as yet undreamed of. Thus, defining the classification scheme is important and recommended if a recognized structure is used.

(+) Abstract. There are times when the title, subject, and keywords are still not enough to refine the list of interesting documents to a manageable level. This is actually quite common in the medical and legal publication areas. Thus, a short summary or abstract of the document is an added feature.

(+) Keywords. Keywords are important for web documents that may range over a wide variety of topics that can't be slotted into a single subject classification. Keywords like Subject can be freeform, or they can be classifications in a recognized taxonomy. Thus, adding scheme information is appropriate here.

■ IDENTIFYING ASSOCIATED PARTIES

Parties can be identified for purposes of searching for all material created, edited, or published by someone. Parties can also be referred to as the contact person for more information or reproduction permissions.

Thus, the content may vary between formal names, e-mail addresses, and other contact methods. Use the TYPE extension in the same manner as the SCHEME extension is used to define the type of contact information that is included here.

(+) Author. The author is an important key to indexing documents. There are times when searching for materials based upon author is valuable service. Computer Literacy Bookshops (`http://www.clbooks.com/`) is an example of this.

(+) Publisher. Publisher is a rather open field. It can refer to the person or organization responsible for the current web site. It can refer to the person or organization responsible for the content in all of its varied media.

(-) Contact. There are times when the author and the publisher may not the best choice of people to contact concerning a document.

One example of this is the web site at Sun Microsystems. (`http://www.sun.com`). There are almost 10,000 documents on the site at the time of this writing. Few publishers are going to be intimately familiar with this quantity of material. On the other hand, the author may move on to other things and no longer be the responsible party for a document.

At Sun, this contact void is filled by the role of a gatekeeper, a person responsible for a manageable chunk of related documents. The gatekeeper can delegate update responsibilities to a new person, keeping the document timely and responding intelligently to user feedback.

People change positions frequently these days, making it difficult to assign a person's name to hundreds of documents every time a new person is hired or placed in a position. Therefore, it is preferable to make the authoritative contact be a title or alias to the current responsible person, instead of hardcoding a name in each document.

(*) Other Agent. Publications may need to identify other people responsible for editing, illustrating, or translating a document. These parties can be identified here.

(*/-) **Distributor.** The distributor party can have multiple meanings. In the case of web pages as purchasable intellectual property, distributor can refer to the agency that distributes the document in other media formats. In the case of web pages that describe product or service web pages, distributor can refer to the place to contact to obtain the product or service mentioned in the web page.

Distributor can also be referenced as a meta-information link to a list of distributors. Listing multiple distributors or maintaining quickly changing distributor entries would not be recommended within a document itself. This function is better performed in a single referenced document.

■ IDENTIFYING DOCUMENT PROPERTIES

(*) **ObjectType.** This field is used for identifying the web page document type. Some examples might be novel, poem, FAQ, RFC, or glossary. The Internet contributes several new types of documents, and it is important not to be limited to the document types found only in the print world.

(+) **Form.** This is a classical mime type definition for the document. Ideally, each server knows the mime type of the document from the document extension. However, this method of reference does not extend to other data forms, such as documents generated from a database. Thus, embedding this information element into the meta-information is recommended.

Looking toward the future: Much of this meta-information will be moved or reproduced in Universal Resource Catalogs (URCs). This element will gain importance when that step happens.

(+) **Identifier.** There is a good motive for having some unique identifier for a web page or its topic. In the publishing world, ISBN and ISSN numbers often meet this criterion. In the commercial site, a product number is the rough equivalent.

(+) **Language.** English is not the only language used on the Web or in the world. Defining the language of the document saves time and frustration for the user.

(*/-) **Order Process.** This is a mildly discussed item that would be useful for the web agents looking to purchase those mythical concert tickets. By defining the process required to order or obtain something, this step can also be automated. Of course, this does assume that some standard ordering methods will be implemented, perhaps by EDI, maybe?

■ DATING AND TIMELINESS INFORMATION

Expiration. The most important information about a document is when the document is no longer valid. This is just as beneficial for IETF proposed standards as it is for Acme's Christmas Sale.

Last Modification Date. This date is usually generated by the server for regular web pages. Like the *form* information element, it has merit for database-generated documents.

■ EXAMPLES OF USAGE

A simple subject definition might look like:

Code 8.1 Simple Example

```
<META HTTP-EQUIV="Subject" CONTENT="Trains>
```

A subject definition based upon one or more categorization systems would be more likely to look like:

```
<META HTTP-EQUIV="Subject.DDS.scheme" CONTENT="Dewey
Decimal System">
<META HTTP-EQUIV="Subject.DDS" CONTENT="004.64">
<META HTTP-EQUIV="Subject.SOS.scheme" CONTENT="Some other
system">
<META HTTP-EQUIV="Subject.SOS" CONTENT="Model Trains">
```

A more complex example might look like:

```
<TITLE> Web Page Design: A Different Multimedia </TITLE>
<META HTTP-EQUIV="Subject.DDS.scheme" CONTENT="Dewey
Decimal System">
<META HTTP-EQUIV="Subject.DDS" CONTENT="004.64">
<META HTTP-EQUIV="Author.Type" CONTENT="email">
<META HTTP-EQUIV="Author" CONTENT="maryment@best.com">
<META HTTP-EQUIV="Identifier.Scheme" CONTENT="ISBN">
<META HTTP-EQUIV="Identifier" CONTENT="0-13-239880-X">
<META HTTP-EQUIV="Distributor.Type" CONTENT="email">
<META HTTP-EQUIV="Distributor"
CONTENT="sunsoftpress@sun.com">
```

INFORMATION ABOUT RELATIONSHIPS

Just as the information in a document is important for cataloging, so is the information about the web page's relationship to other pages. Most of these relationship information elements are the same thing that you will find in a standard navigation bar or banner, so none of this should come as a real surprise.

Within the HTML 3.0 draft standards and hopefully built into most future browsers, the <LINK> tag will define these relationships and even build navigational tools such as a banner. Since some browsers use some components of this now, it is a good idea to implement this now to save rework later.

<LINK> Tag. The <LINK> tag is the main tag used to define document relationships. Since it does reference other documents, the HREF attribute is a necessary component.

The <LINK> tag is primarily used with the REL attribute, where REL stands for *relationship*. There are several predefined relationships that are in standard use. Inserting

```
<LINK REL=Home HREF="http://www.blah.com/">
```

indicates that http://www.blah.com/ is the home page for the current document.

The <LINK> tag can also define reverse relationships with the REV attribute. This option isn't often used, since most pages have a single home page, but a home page is the home location for many documents. The many-to-one relationship is not rendered as easily.

■ STANDARD NAVIGATIONAL RELATIONSHIPS

Home/TOC. In most cases, home and TOC tend to mean the same thing, since the de facto definition of a home page is the main list of contents for the site. In cases where the home page and the TOC are different pages, both items can and should be listed.

In large sites where there is a site home page/TOC and a topical home page/TOC, it is recommended that Home be used for the site home page and TOC be used for the topical home page/TOC.

Index. Index refers to the search mechanism used for the site. If both a vocabulary limited and unlimited (i.e., free-text search) option exist, use the URL for the unlimited option and create a specialty entry under Bookmark for the vocabulary-limited option. The reasoning behind this is that on the Web, *index* refers to free text search more often than the book meaning of a vocabulary-limited search.

Glossary. The glossary is the list of definitions for terms that require explaining. A glossary should have a named anchor for each entry and glossary links within the content should point directly to the related entry. However, the main relationship identification should point to the document in general, not to any specific entry.

Bookmark. Bookmark is used for other important relationships not defined by the customary list of relationships. To accomplish this goal, bookmark has an additional attribute, TITLE.

Previously, we noted that Distributor should not be used as a meta-information element if it referred to a list of distributors. Instead, the list can be placed into a file and the bookmark relationship can be used. The relationship is defined in the TITLE attribute.

Copyright. Every document should be labeled with appropriate copyright information, including contact information for reprinting or reproducing the content in other media. Since this is usually an unwieldy block of information, it usually gets a page of its own.

Up. In a hierarchical document set, this value would be the parent document for this topic area.

Next/Previous. In the context of a linear document set, Next and Previous would define the documents before and after this document in the document set.

■ EXAMPLE OF USAGE

An example of the use of the <LINK> tag to define relationships might look like:

Code 8.2 Using Link Tags

```
<LINK REL="HOME" HREF="http://www.prenhall.com/">
<LINK REL="INDEX" HREF="http://www.prenhall.com/">
<LINK REL="Copyright"
HREF="http://www.prenhall.com/mischtm/legal.html">
<LINK REL="Bookmark" TITLE="Distributor"
HREF="http://www.prenhall.com/~ray/mischtm/magnet.html">
```

USES

Meta-information has many uses. Since meta-information is not currently widely used, these services are not yet available. This becomes something of the chicken and the egg problem: *Why implement something that isn't in use yet* vs. *why use something that is so sporadically implemented.*

The Web evolved because people took chances and invested in things that weren't yet standards. The Web will continue this evolution. Design well now, and you won't have to go back and do a lot of rework later to keep up with the Jones' and the Acme's of the web world. Many benefits will arise from using meta-information.

■ ENHANCED WEB ROBOTS À LA YAHOO

As soon as there is a critical amount of documents with meta-information embedded within them, a new breed of web spider will spring up to catalog this information and offer something close to the search quality available on Yahoo and the work load of a Lycos or AltaVista setup.

Users that now place a great value on the quality of information found at Yahoo will no longer need to choose between a search service that locates and indexes most documents and one that offers intelligent and useful categorization. Web sites themselves will benefit from targeting their audience much more specifically.

■ URCS (UNIVERSAL RESOURCE CATALOGS)

While it is nice to be able to have this information about each document embedded in each document, eventually it will also be nice to have all of the meta-information in one single place to use for

- Searching for specific keywords or authors
- Identifying the same content in different forms and returning a form that is appropriate for the user, such as a PostScript® version for one user and a plain text version for someone with out PostScript capability.
- Identifying the closest copy of a mirrored resource to save bandwidth on the backbone of the Internet.

URCs are the proposed method of placing this information in a common location. Much of the proposed meta-information content is the same between URCs and intra-document meta-information. If documents are created with a complete set of embedded meta-information, the task of copying that information from them and placing it in a common URC will be trivial.

■ PICS RATING SYSTEM

The PICS rating system is the proposed standard for rating materials that might not be suitable for some audiences (such as preventing children from experiencing violent or otherwise overly explicit materials).

Similar rating systems exist in the U.S. for movies, magazines, and even recently for computer games. Due to pressure by some special interest groups, this type of rating system is being recommended for web sites as well.

PICS appears to be the shoo-in candidate for a long-term web rating system. The short term solution is downloading a list of inappropriate sites and denying access to those sites. Since this is a site-by-site solution, a site having both materials for the general public and materials that should have restricted access is the loser.

Most current browsers do not have the capability to use the PICS ratings attached to pages. However, browsers evolve very fast, and as soon as the standard is fairly stable, browsers that filter via PICS ratings should become available. Based upon the current PICS draft standard, a PICS label in a <META> tag should look like the following:

Code 8.3 PICS rating system

```
<META HTTP-EQUIV="PICS-label"
 CONTENT="(PICS-1.0 "{URL here} 1 ratings (suds 0.4 density 0
 color/hue 2)">
```

Details about the items in a PICS label can be found at http://www.w3.org/hypertext/WWW/PICS/labels.html. Visit this site to learn the latest about this technology.

KEY POINTS

- The best way to manage the infoglut is to add a higher order of structure to all web pages and, eventually, all documents.
- At present, the method used to add this additional information is by adding meta-information to the head of the document with <META> and <LINK> tags.
- This concept is being expanded to include content rating systems and to develop shopping catalogs and offers enough information for intelligent indexing.

9

Interactivity
Design

Interactivity is one of the most vaunted features of the Web, second only to the multimedia capabilities. Interactivity means many things to many people.

To some, merely having the multiple choices of a hypertext document means that the reader can interactively choose a unique course through a site. Interactivity of this type is dealt with in Chapter 5, *Navigational Design*. To others, the ability to fill out forms and *talk back* makes the Web interactive.

To yet a third group, interactivity is the ability to create custom content for each user, based upon the preferences recorded when that user talked back.

FORMS STUFF

Forms design has been an evolving science for many years. By now, most of the guidelines seem obvious.

■ SUBMIT BUTTON

The submit button is the final act in completing a form. Logically, the final act should be at the bottom of all other stuff. Putting the submit button in the middle or at the top of a page does not ensure that the user will scroll when needed beyond the visible screen to complete the rest of the information or read the fine print of a license agreement. Someone reading Figure 9.1 may miss the Tuesday cutoff listed in Figure 9.2.

Principle

Always put the Submit
button at the bottom of all
information—nowhere
else.

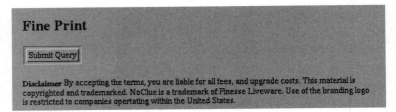

Figure 9.1 Bad Positioning of Submit Button

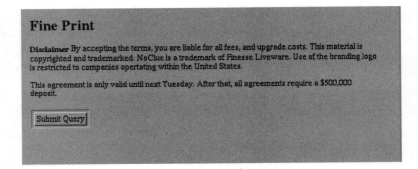

Figure 9.2 Good Positioning of Submit Button

■ SIZE TEXT BOXES

Principle

Size the input field to
reflect the expected size of
the information.

Text boxes create expectation. Seeing a long text box leads users to believe that they can fill up all visible space. The other side of this coin is also true. Offering a 10-character text box will lead users to a more terse response. The text box should reflect the size of the information required.

In Figure 9.3, users will be confused when they try to enter a full name in the State field, which accepts only a two-character entry. Figure 9.4 manages the user's expectations for the sizing of the State and Zip fields.

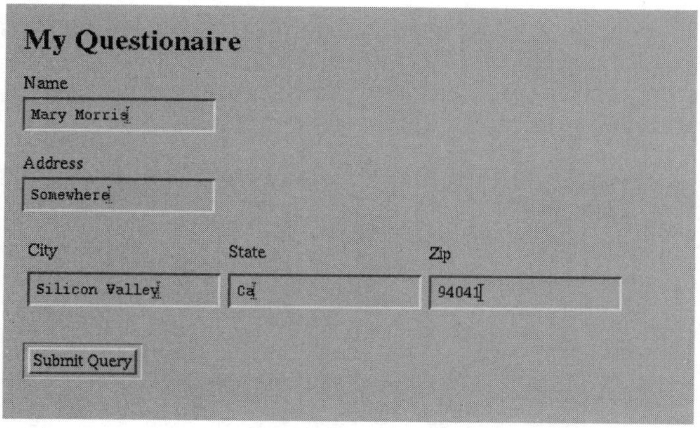

Figure 9.3 Large State and Zip Fields

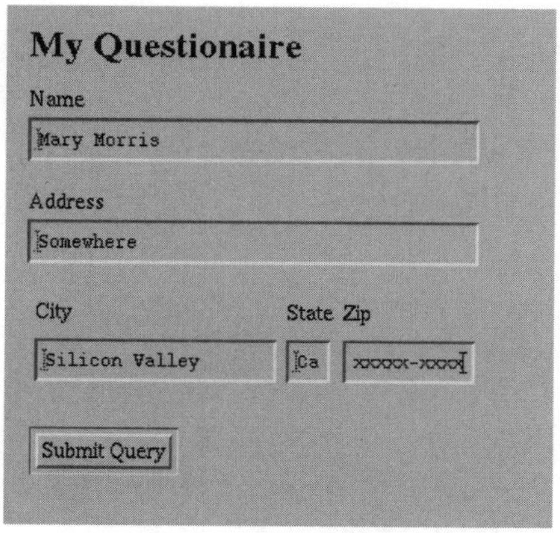

Figure 9.4 Appropriate Sizing of Fields

Additionally, put a template of the expected field format in the field. This can be done by declaring the VALUE of the form element. With JavaScript, this template can be refreshed and the field can be validated before submission as well.

Principle

Keep input fields on the screen (i.e., no more than about 70 characters) wide.

■ KEEP FIELDS VISIBLE

If you need a field longer than average screen width, make it a <TEXTAREA> instead of a single text line. Horizontal scrolling is very disorienting for the user, and not all browsers scroll the screen when the user reaches the end of the visible text line.

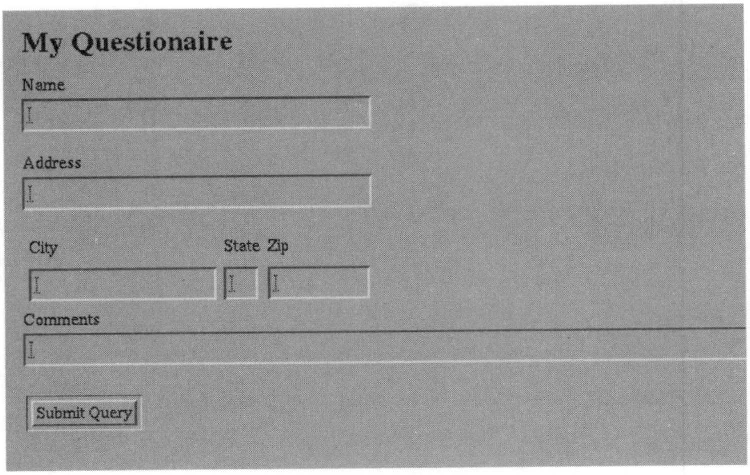

Figure 9.5 Text Line Too Long

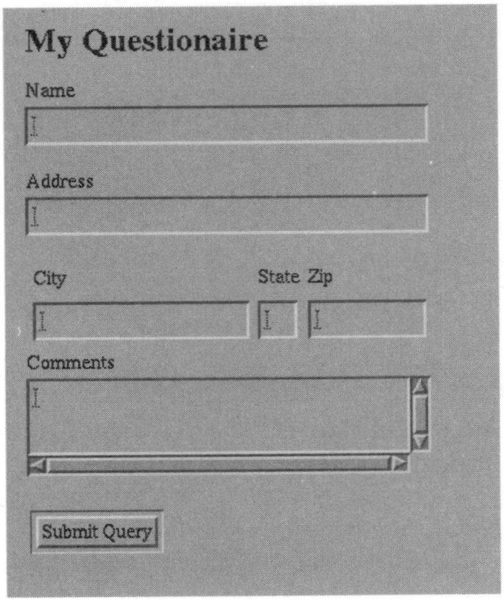

Figure 9.6 Textarea Used Instead of a Single Line

■ CONSISTENTLY POSITION LABELS

Be consistent about where labels and headers are placed. Users expect to see a pattern. In addition, place labels so that they follow the flow of reading. Some examples are:

Principle

Put the input field comments in the same place for all data items, i.e., to the right, left or above. Don't mix right and left.

- If you have a pull-down list or scrollable list, place the label above.
- If you have several radio buttons that will be listed on a line, place the header label to the left.
- If the radio buttons are to be listed vertically, place the label header above.

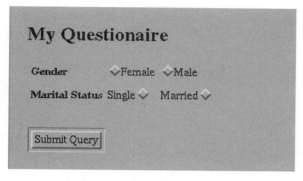

Figure 9.7 Inconsistent Label Placement

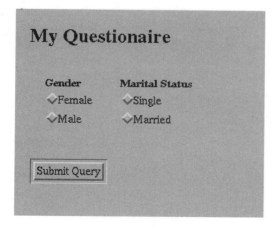

Figure 9.8 Consistent Label Placement

Principle

Group related fields
together.

■ GROUP FIELDS

Just as in designing content layout, grouping fields together has value. Offering a user a long set of text boxes, buttons, and lists can seem like one really long run-on paragraph. Grouping related elements together and adding some breaks with whitespace or horizontal rules assists with the overwhelmed feeling.

In Figure 9.9, the query about Favorite Color doesn't relate to the other items. Separate groupings, as shown in Figure 9.8, are preferable. Labeling the groupings gives the reader an added bonus.

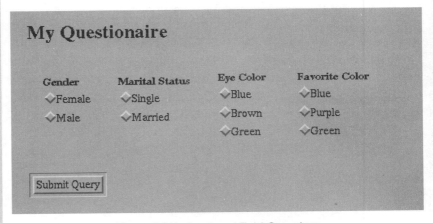

Figure 9.9 Unstructured Field Groupings

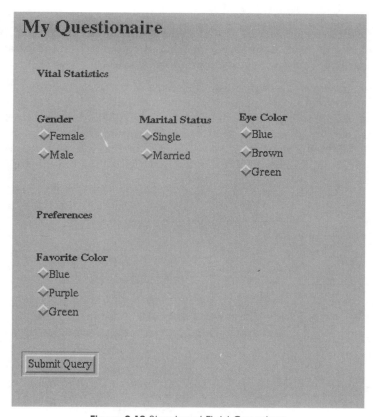

Figure 9.10 Structured Field Groupings

BUILDING CUSTOM PAGES ON-THE-FLY

The ideal goal is a program that could respond to requests by processing natural language, converting that to a set of commands that will achieve the goal, running those commands, and altering them as dead-ends are encountered or more optimal paths are discovered.

People view a shopping or information-finding agent locating specific products or information as the epitome of interactivity. Not only can it, theoretically, interpret and communicate human-style requests and responses, but it can move in an unknown information space with an ease most humans cannot equal. Until clients can create their own agents to customize information, the wise developer will offer customizing options.

■ LIMIT USER CHOICES

In order to respond to human requests, you should have a finite number of requests defined. Servicing unbounded requests created by the user is beyond most software available today.

This means not only limiting the scope of things that users can ask for, but presenting the options that they do have in a logical manner. One example is the Saqqara database engine. The database presents the user with a set of options for the product in question. In the ThinkPad™ example, in Figure 9.11, when the user chooses the projection panel option, the display is refreshed, displaying only the options that are still open.

Select your options, one at a time, by order of their importance to you. You can click any pre–selected option at anytime to UNDO it.

ℹ️ *Processor Type:*	Intel Pentium I Intel 486DX4 I Intel 486DX2 I Intel 486SX I PowerPC 603e
ℹ️ *Processor Speed (MHz):*	33 MHz I 50 MHz I 75 MHz I 90 MHz I 100 MHz I 120 MHz
ℹ️ *Standard Memory:*	4 MB I 8 MB I 16 MB I 32 MB
ℹ️ *Hard Disk Size:*	No Hard Disk I 105 MB PCMCIA I 170 MB I 260 MB PCMCIA I 340 MB I 360 MB I 540 MB I 720 MB I 810 MB I 1.2 GB
ℹ️ *Internal CD–ROM:*	Yes I No
ℹ️ *Internal Modem:*	Yes I No
ℹ️ *Display Type:*	Active–matrix TFT I Black Matrix TFT I Monochrome STN I Passive–matrix dual–scan STN
ℹ️ *Display Size:*	8.4" I 9.5" I 10.4" I 12.1"
ℹ️ *No. of Colors:*	65,536 at 800x600 I 65,536 at 640x480 I 256 at 640x480 I 64 Gray Scales 640x480 I 16 Gray Scales 640x480
ℹ️ *Projection Panel Display:*	Yes I No
ℹ️ *TrackWrite Expanding Keyboard:*	Yes I No
ℹ️ *Infrared Communications:*	Yes I No

Figure 9.11 Saqqara Database http://www.saqqara.com/

Once you have identified what the user wants to know, a response is required. This means developing common information blocks and an information structure to support and deliver responses as needed. Using the techniques mentioned in Chapter 8, *Adding Meta-Information* will help identify the blocks.

FUTURE DESIGNING

Creating information blocks to respond to guided user queries is only the intermediate step in creating an automated response system. Eventually, the user will send out that agent, and it will interrogate your database. The human element will be gone from many data searching activities. Future designing means planning for this.

Most agent-to-agent or agent-to-system communications are now being developed in an object-oriented style. Not only will your book object have title, author, and abstract properties, the book object will also have a built-in purchase method.

The object-oriented world is pioneering these processes by encapsulating both data and the methods to manipulate that data in one unit. By marrying this with distributed populations of information that will eventually interact with common methods as well as our beloved TCP/IP network does now, we can create the infrastructure.

- Develop standard information messages
- Embed these methods into all objects
- Create meta-information
- Standardize on a core set of method/data, message/response (s).

For example keywords, expires, and author or contact are a good starting point.

KEY POINTS

- Design forms to customize and lay out text coherently
- Plan for the next generation of mass customization by creating knowledge spaces and databases that can provide real answers.
- Plan for the generation after next by preparing for agent-only or agent-to-agent communications.

CHAPTER

10

Designing
for Time

Content, like everything else, is rarely immortal. There may be a few documents that will remain infinitely available, but even those documents will evolve with current content and new media. Since a web site is an ongoing publishing device, procedures need to be put in place to manage the time factors.

EXPANDABLE STRUCTURE

Developing an expandable structure for navigation and document set organization is mandatory. It is very unlikely that a site will stay its original size. Even with a moderate amount of content creation, a site can double or even quadruple in size every year. Any structure that you design should be able to weather the growth without complete restructuring every six months.

OWNERSHIP

It is important to create the role of *document owner* and keep it separate from the role of document creator. Creators often move on to other projects and are not available for maintenance work.

At a small site, the ownership role can be placed upon the Webmaster. However, a single person is not the best solution for a large site of 1,000 pages or more. A single person cannot give adequate attention to thousands of documents.

It is important to define ownership as a role, not a person, to allow for personnel transitions. E-mail and other aliases can then be updated in a single location to accommodate the change of ownership.

It is also important to segregate ownership. A site will grow in document quantity. It is important to be able to segregate documents efficiently when the responsibilities grow from one to many people.

An example of this would be to draw a line in the sand and say that each owner should manage about 1,000 documents. Project the growth of the web site for about three years down the road. If you expect to have 10,000 documents at that time, figure out a way to break up those expected 10,000 documents into separate areas and declare an owner for each group.

A corporate site may have one owner for product pages, another owner for sales pages, and yet a third owner for corporate information. Since there are currently only 500 documents, one owner is sufficient for the moment. This person, however, should respond to role of Product owner, Sales owner and Corporate Info owner. In time, a new person can take over the role of Corporate Info owner without a significant hassle in updating documents.

CHANGE NOTIFICATION

Some things will change over the lifetime of a site. Under Construction signs are just one symptom of poor communication when it comes to notifying users of these changes.

■ CONSTRUCTION ZONES

The best way to handle construction zones is to block off the area by disabling the link, rather than let people wander through them. If you have a page that you are building, add a note on the parent page with a *coming soon* icon, but don't link to a less than polished page.

Sneak peeks or *beta* access can be offered to pages that require review, but those links should be clearly marked at the link source with something akin to *enter at your own risk, beta page ahead.*

Beta pages should always have feedback links established and have content worth visiting. A page with two lines of text and a hard hat does not constitute a beta quality site.

■ SINGLE LANDMARK CHANGES

Change notification goes beyond more sophisticated construction marking. People get used to a specific look and feel. If you move the furniture around in a blind person's house, you are going to confuse that person.

Users aren't much better than blind people. They get used to landmarks and depend on those landmarks being there. When those landmarks go away, the user becomes confused. It is important to notify the user of all landmark changes.

The more important changes should be so significant that users are stopped in their tracks and forced to acknowledge that a change has taken place or will shortly take place.

For example, suppose you start offering separate search pages for different areas, create new icons, navigation bar items, or links but leave the original there. When people click on the search option that they have always known and loved, you should bring up an interim page that notifies them that things are changing and how to determine which option they should choose now.

> Do **NOT** take away an interim page until the hit rate on that page becomes negligible (i.e., one hit every couple of months or so). If you make it take longer to get to a page by going through an explanation page, users will take the most efficient route possible.

■ FULL PAGE CHANGES

Ripping the carpet out from under a user should be done sparingly and with support and understanding of the learning process the user must go through again, unless of course you don't want repeat traffic.

When a significant page changes its entire look and feel, it is important to offer users both a legend or instructional guide to navigating the new page *and* access to the old page. By watching who accesses the old page and where they go from there, you can learn which parts of the new page are confusing to users and adapt the page accordingly.

It is nice to also offer the user notification on the main home page of these broad and sweeping changes. However, not all users enter the site by the home page, and not all users read everything on a page, so don't expect to use this method as the only way to notify users.

■ LOCATION CHANGES

When a page is moved to a new directory or location, it is a good idea to offer redirection services to the new page. The Webmaster should be proactive in situations like this, by recording the referring page and notifying the owner of every referring page of the location change.

Principle

Leave interim pages in place until the hit rate is negligible.

Principle

The Webmaster should be proactive in notifying upstream sites of URL changes.

AUTOMATING MAINTENANCE PROCEDURES

No human being should be responsible for knowing when every document expires, what should be done with each document, which documents were orphaned by other changes, and which documents will be affected by changes to a current document.

Compute power is a much more cost-effective resource for accomplishing these goals than a human being is. However, a computer requires scripts or programs to be accomplish these goals, and a document catalog, or in the short term, meta-information in each document to help the programs accomplish their goals.

It would be nice to be able to print sources of these tools. Unfortunately, because of the lack of meta-information use to date, these tools do not currently exist. Meta-information has to start somewhere, and here is as good of a place as any to start it. Refer to Chapter 8, *Adding Meta-Information* for more information on using meta-information.

■ DEFINING TIME FACTORS

There are four key time factors for a document:

- Estimated active life-span or rate of change
- Party responsible for change
- Status or state of a document
- End of life processing (EOL)

It is important to define these items *before or while* each document is created and to incorporate this information into the document meta-information or document catalog.

Expiration. The document should be appropriately marked with an expiration date via information placed in the <META> tag, information, prepended by the server on the document, or both methods.

Rate of Change. Some documents may never really *expire*. For example, the home page of a web site is a traditional entry point. Just because the document seems for all intents and purposes immortal doesn't mean the document stays the same.

Thus, a rate of change can be used in addition to the expiration date. For current purposes, all documents should have an expiration date even if they have a rate of change, because current standards recognize only an expiration date.

Status. Status or the state of a document should be included for all documents. Pertinent status types might be `active`, `archive`, and `update pending`. The best place currently to place this information is in the `<META>` tag. Ideally, this will be incorporated into some sort of URC (Universal Resource Catalog) later to accommodate more than just HTML.

However, this information may be important to the user, especially the `archive` or `update pending` states. Consider also adding visible status information where appropriate.

Action at EOL. When a document has expired, some action needs to happen. This action could be the evaluation of how current the document is, conversion of the document to an archive status, complete removal of the document, or revision or upgrade of the document. Defining the action at EOL is important because it facilitates automation and carries information from one owner to the next.

Even if the document is converted to an archive status, a new expiration timer should be provided. Knowing that a document is an archived version is one thing. Knowing when that the document will no longer be available is yet another.

The advent of magazine-style sites that offer back issues is an example of this. Many would like to believe that disk space is cheap and that old articles should be retained in perpetuity. However, as publishing evolves, old media types and less structured documents will become less and less popular.

There will come a point in the foreseeable future when all unstructured documents (and possibly all unstructured information) will be next to worthless. It will be more work to find the information in the vast sea of data than the information is worth. The quality content will have already been upgraded to appropriate structured formats. Thus, even archived documents should be evaluated periodically and either revised or removed.

Progeny or Direct Descendants. If the document becomes an archived document and a new document replaces it, a pointer should be created to reference the current version.

This pointer can be placed in the `<LINK>` tag or eventually incorporated into a URC. The link should also be made visible to the user if the HTML 3.0 `<BANNER>` isn't used to create a navigation bar from the `<LINK>` tags.

Owner. Documents are much like children. They can't do everything for themselves yet, so they need an owner to take action for them when action is required. This owner is responsible for responding to reported problems, evaluating a document and changing its status when it expires and, most importantly, managing the content creation and revision process.

At a small site, the owner may also be the document creator. At a larger site or a site that uses diverse types of media, the owner may simply oversee this process in the role of an editor or content integrator.

ANTICIPATE NEXT GENERATION WEB TECHNOLOGIES

One of the biggest parts of designing for time is the relentless onslaught of new software, tools, protocols, standards, and media types to create new content. There is no way to keep up with all of it. Trying to keep up with everything will cause serious future shock. That doesn't mean that you should stick your head in the sand and only use what is available today.

Integrate the parts that attain critical mass, but don't go out and try to be everything to everyone. The key issues for 1996 and the short-term future are:

- Database usage for various uses, including creating structured information sites
- Using meta-information for more intelligent catalogs
- New graphics formats
- Java
- VRML.

■ DATABASE USAGE

Databases have a long history in the corporate world. They often are the source of legacy data that the company still runs on. There is a movement toward making that legacy data available via the Web for both Internet and Intranet use.

The use that will take more adapting to is the use of the database for storing and serving web documents. The unstructured document is a lame duck in the evolving world of the Internet. The industrial disease, Information Overload, overwhelms many users now, and the problem is growing. Structuring documents and information and storing them in databases is the way of the future.

■ CATALOGING AND THE <META> TAG

Regardless of whether databases are used to store and serve structured information, there is still a significant need to present the user with more targeted information with less work on the part of the user. Use of meta-information is vital for creating the next-generation catalogs. If you don't offer good meta-information, you and your product or service will be a lot harder to find by the intelligent-catalog-enabled users.

■ GRAPHICS CHANGES

GIF, the default graphics format of the Web, is no longer alone. The majority of Internet web users can now view images created in JPG format. This one change will affect the quality of image usage significantly in the near term.

■ JAVA

Java is the most significant interactivity booster available on the Web today. Java development tools are growing at a phenomenal rate. Books such as *Instant Java* will be available for those unwilling to learn the low-level tricks needed to accomplish effective sites.

It is important to look beyond the current use of Java to create gratuitous animations. Java has far more potential than just mindless amusement the first time around and abiding annoyance in future experiences.

Java and its scripting sidekick, JavaScript, enables the browser to take over the processing load, freeing the server from heavy loading, and giving faster feedback to the user when interacting with databases.

■ VRML

VRML is a significant divergence from the classical web world. Its experiential aspects make it the best tool for creating sites that users can immerse themselves in. With the advent of behaviors in an upcoming version of the VRML standard, VRML will be useful as a non-textual interface to service sites like banks, travel agents, and community gather sites. The book, *Snowcrash*, eloquently foreshadows this phenomenon.

KEY POINTS

- Establish procedures to manage documents.
- Automate maintenance.
- Keep abreast of change and implement judiciously.

CHAPTER

11

Experiential Design

M aybe you've spent some time playing Nintendo or Sega games. Or you've ordered airline reservations in America OnLine (AOL). Maybe, you've played with King's Quest™ or Myst™ on a personal computer. Maybe you've even played with a MUD (Multi-User Dimensional Sites) on the Internet. If so, you've been playing with experiential sites.

Paper Design Only. On the World Wide Web, the design environment has imitated and been limited by paper design. That is, because the vast amount of data on the Web resides in paper form, the Web has replicated the document look. It is textual, two-dimensional, and uses book metaphors for navigation (tables of contents, indexes, alphabetical tabs). Not anymore.

Beyond Paper. Users are demanding more interactive experiences on-line. They are clamoring for virtual reality, on-line banking, and interactive collaboration to take place. The user wants to actively participate in a site, not just read and click. VRML (Virtual Reality Modeling Language) is one of the technologies that will allow users to participate more fully in on-line interaction. Java is another. While the implementation of these new technologies is somewhat primitive in relation to the 3-D games that are on the market today, new standards are being defined that will bring both the VRML worlds and Java applications into the forefront of on-line interaction.

Warning – Not everything that you do on-line is appropriate for a virtual reality site. 3-D games, like environments, are great for experience-oriented interfaces but are generally cumbersome for navigating large bodies of information.

WHAT IS EXPERIENTIAL DESIGN?

Experiential design is concerned with what users want to do at a web site. It focuses on designing an environment that the user can interact with to perform a task, be entertained, or experience whatever is there.

In an experiential world, the major design issues concern creating an environment in which the user can have an experience. The experience can be reserving airline tickets, configuring the components of a computer system, playing a game with others, or banking on-line.

The difference between most web sites and an experiential web site is that in a regular web site, users are simply recalling information. They read, click on graphics to read more, and surf through volumes of marketing and advertising information. In an experiential web site, the user is doing something either with the information at the site or with information he wishes to put into the site. There is an interaction where both the user and the site are communicating messages back and forth.

Primitive Experiential Sites. Ordering a product is a primitive example of an experiential site. The user is taking information gained at the web site and filling out a form to order a product. In some sites, electronic transactions take place, sophisticating the experience. At the minimum, the customer is able to order a product, get information mailed back to him, or receive something in the mail.

Presently, web designers are using tables (as in Netscape) and forms to create primitive, interactive experiential sites for users. Take a look at Saqqara Systems Inc. in Figure 11.1. Saqqara provides intelligent on-line catalogs for Internet commerce, allowing you to find the right computer system by filling in items in a table.

IBM - ThinkPads

| Home Page | General Info | Step Search Help |

Select your options, one at a time, by order of their importance to you. You can click any pre-selected option at anytime to UNDO it.

ℹ	*Processor Type:*	Intel Pentium | Intel 486DX4 | Intel 486DX2 | Intel 486SX | PowerPC 603e
ℹ	*Processor Speed (MHz):*	33 MHz | 50 MHz | 75 MHz | 90 MHz | 100 MHz | 120 MHz
ℹ	*Standard Memory:*	4 MB | 8 MB | 16 MB | 32 MB
ℹ	*Hard Disk Size:*	No Hard Disk | 105 MB PCMCIA | 170 MB | 260 MB PCMCIA | 340 MB | 360 MB | 540 MB | 720 MB | 810 MB | 1.2 GB

Figure 11.1 Experiencing Laptops to Fit Your Needs. - http://www.saqqara.com/

Current Experiential Sites. On-line financial service, as the Internet Society uses in Figure 11.2, simulates the experience of paying for goods. In this case, the good is Internet Society membership. Because secure transactions on-line are the focus of Internet Commerce, this site uses CyberCash, First Virtual, direct pay with credit cards over secure servers, and even mail-in payment for those hard to convince. This is a more elaborate experiential site. It allows users to simulate using their transaction cards directly from the web site. The user is involved in a "paying" experience.

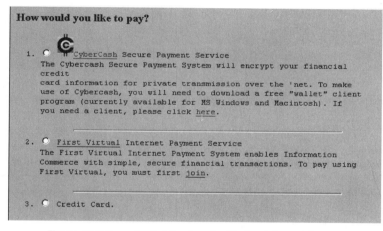

Figure 11.2 Experiential Payment with the Internet Society

Virtual Reality Experiential Sites. The experiential sites with 3-D environments allow a user to manipulate objects in or build a world to participate in. Take a look at AlphaWorld. It is a 3-D virtual reality environment in which you can build your own property, see Figure 11.3 and Color Plate 1-7. But imagine you are trying to represent a firewall behind which lies the information you are looking for. Because fire has properties and behaviors that we are all familiar with, this kind of representation heightens the user's experience into believing that the passage through the firewall is impossible. These are the worlds of future commerce, where users will be able to enter and move around as in a mall or a marketplace. They'll be able to assign behavioral properties to the objects in this world and will be able to communicate directly on-line with others in this world.

Figure 11.3 AlphaWorld - Virtual Reality Experiential Site

AlphaWorld is a virtual place populated by real people where you become one of its citizens and help to shape it. You acquire and develop property, assume an on-line persona, and interact in and with a living, breathing, multiuser community.

CyberPassage™, Sony's new Experiential world, shown in Figure 11.4, enables you to walk around the 3-D space and is also equipped with the enhanced functions for manipulating moving images, movies, and sound.

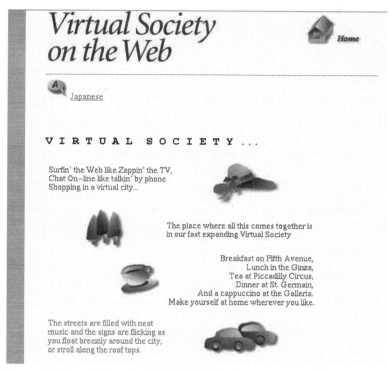

Figure 11.4 Sony's Experiential World - http://vs.sony.co.jp/VS-E/vstop.html

Time-Warner in Figure 11.5 has joined the foray of experiential sites with the Palace, which encourages users to design their own worlds. It is an Internet-based multimedia chat architecture, akin to an IRC (Internet Relay Chatting environment) and hypercard. You can author and run your own social on-line environment on your server, and visit other people's servers. Color Plate 1-4 shows what the inside looks like.

Figure 11.5 Time Warner's Experiential site - http://www.thepalace.com

Java. Java from Sun Microsystems is a simple, object-oriented, distributed, programming language that creates experiential environments. Java supports programming for the Internet in the form of platform-independent Java applets.

Sun has Java applets that can be included in an HTML page, much like an image can be included. When you use a Java-compatible browser to view a page that contains a Java applet, the applet's code is transferred to your system and executed by the browser. The browser then provides an experience in which you can manipulate graphics on the screen. The interplay of objects and ideas provides a user with an ability to discover. The site is interactive.

A clever applet written in Java teaches Ohm's law (see Figure 11.6). Users learn it not by a definition, but by a hands-on experience. They are challenged to ignite a light bulb, adding resistors to a battery. The light bulb will break, light, or not light depending upon the amount of resistance they apply dragging graphic resistors onto the wire. The experience allows users to simulate working with electricity. The user walks away having learned Ohm's law by example, not by definition.

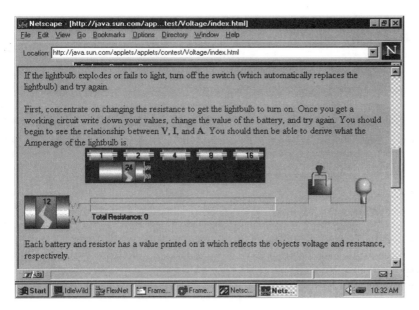

Figure 11.6 Experiential Java
http://java.sun.com/applets/applets/contest/Voltage/index.html

■ HTML IS NOT AN EXPERIENTIAL LANGUAGE; IT IS AN INTELLECTUAL ONE

Most people, when they read the word intellectual or see a lot of text, think "boring." Or perhaps they think "time consuming."

VRML (Virtual Reality Markup Language) may add a new dimension to the Web, but it will in no way replace content-based communication such as HTML. There are people that consider word-based pages to be dry and boring. Words have often been linked with a dry cerebral experience. Used properly, words can convey information much more succinctly, even in the case where words create an image in the mind. Words are the essence of intellect.

We communicate in symbols, and many who have deeply entrenched meaning in words as symbols will require some form of written language. Written language contains semantic cues that belong to historical development and global consciousness. What we need to do is combine the wisdom of the past with future visions.

■ OTHER WEB TECHNOLOGIES MEET THE EXPERIENTIAL NEEDS

HTML provided users with the ability to create home pages. On a home page, a user could reference the wide range of documents, fewer graphics, minimal audio experiences, and nary an MPEG movie or two. You hyperlinked around, following word trails, semantic families. But your experiences were chaotic, spontaneous, random, and unrelated. Information continuity depended upon your ability to navigate a web site. In an experiential site, users are pulled into the environment as though it were a system where all the interrelated parts belonged to the entire site.

There is now a wide range of Internet multimedia products and plug-ins to stimulate the senses and add a more fully integrated experience with information. At present, the big technologies that make this happen are VRML, Shockwave, and Java, with other emerging technologies on the way.

Java: Java is cursor sensitive. You can place your cursor over an area within a Java-enhanced site, and a reaction happens. Sometimes, the graphic is animated, sometimes an audio sequence is played. Java allows you to have interactive environments in which one graphical image responds to another graphical image's input and creates a response. It's as though you could make your images come alive. Instead of images simply being clickable and hyperlinking to another document, you can make relationships among images.

Java applets will take off and build the Internet into an experiential environment. Where procedures were taught with numbered line items, the experiential flavor of Java will allow one procedure to start, while you decide which to choose next. You can imagine a personalized image of yourself and the clothes you have to wear. You can change one shirt for another and watch the color and style of your pants automatically change.

You could conceivably have one set of graphics representing information flow throughout your organization, and another set of graphics representing client/server Internet solutions within your business.

The client/server icon is introduced into the flow of your organization, and suddenly you see immediate results in financials, processes, or behaviors.

VRML: With VRML, you are presented with environments in which the rules are not apparent. The tools enable you to manipulate the environment in 3-D, allowing you to identify patterns and take on views that you might not otherwise examine. Imagine shopping online for houses and being able to walk through the design and detail of any nook or cranny. You can develop decorating ideas for your house as you enter the room from different angles.

In HTML patterns, we describe moving through the pages, linking to sites, as though we were going from point A to point B. We choose to use movement terminology when we talk in HTML format. Web servers have a similar structure. VRML can make that structure visible through 3-D movement and catapult a user into inquisitive mode. After a few hours investigating the site, users will have a thorough understanding of how it works, as though they had been playing with it for real.

VRML 2.0, or Moving Worlds, will give Web-based applications plenty of new power for the World Wide Web. The technology will include powerful 3-D enhancements that let users visualize database information in real time. Graphics generated from complex spreadsheet data will be monitored in real time. Users will be able to shop in virtual electronic malls, walking around showrooms. They'll be able to play in multiplayer virtual reality games. And, they'll increase their experience by socializing in multimedia chat rooms. The integration of socializing and collaborative experiences will make VRML 2.0 a winning design tool in the future.

VRML is scalable, so it can move easily across networks. With this increased capability, many of the bandwidth issues will be solved for some platforms.

Marques. Marques (Microsoft) are different from VRML. They provide less visual freedom than VRML. Marques scroll words around on the screen. This capability can be found in Java, as well.

Marques that use logos or other images (Java) add more value to the experience that graphics communicate quickly. For example, a logo is a complete thought in one piece. It is recognized as a whole. Thus, these types of marques save valuable real estate (i.e., the visible screen) and can heighten the experience.

DESIGN ISSUES

In order to develop an understanding of how you might be designing in the experiential environment, let's explore some of the design issues.

- Design for sensory dominance.
- Include the user as the center of attention.
- Design the experience to look as it does in the real world.
- Include language as an audio experience.
- Include tools.
- Design for discovery.
- Apply the principles of foreground/background.
- Design for problem solving.
- Use motivational techniques.
- Design for play.

■ DESIGN FOR SENSORY DOMINANCE

Neurolinguists have determined that people are dominated by one sense over the others. In essence, some people are visual. They must see something to experience it fully. Others are aural, needing foremost to hear things to enrich new experiences. Some individuals are tactile, needing to touch things, turn them around in their hands in order to pick up subtle information about an object, and so on. The senses for smelling, tasting, and touching seem a bit out of the bounds of today's technology.

Design for differences. On the Web, when you design for the experiential environment, you must consider that users are going to be sensory dominant. You cannot develop only a graphical environment, inasmuch as you'd attract only visual users. You need to provide a full sound experience to accommodate hearing dominance. Additionally, you'll need to design an environment in which users feel as though they could manipulate objects. Use a combination of graphics, sound, and text. You may even consider buttons that identify each variation. Keep in mind that the differences in information processing must be attended to.

■ INCLUDE THE USER AS THE CENTER OF ATTENTION

The whole purpose of an experiential site is to include the user as the center of attention. Users will become more engaged and involved in anything that is focusing on serving them. They need the freedom to choose.

Users like to read and view graphics, undoubtedly. But the activity is fairly passive. Users get more excited when they can e-mail, manipulate objects, cause unforeseen reactions, receive information spontaneously, and adapt to various environments. Take a good look at what arcade games are being played. The best ones make the user the car driver, the warrior, the adventurer, the one with all the tools.

■ DESIGN REAL EXPERIENCES

Make the experiential site look as much as it can like the real world. If you're a real estate site, make the environment look like a real estate office. If you're providing a shopping experience, provide the user with shopping carts or 3-D movable objects that can be manipulated.

The site must resemble the store front, or the service counter, or the vending machine, or whatever environment you are replicating. Users will navigate the site faster as a result. They'll also be able to use any tools you provide for them more readily, because they'll recognize them and use them as needed.

Although it is just a virtual reality game, Duke's Diner in Color Plate 1-5 is designed to look like a diner. It may be futuristic, but you can see the bar stools, the salt and pepper shakers, the trash bin in the back, the neon sign, the fan turning and the television playing the Apollo moon landing. Users will respond favorably to a realistic-looking site, even if it's in VR. They will certainly be able to manage and navigate the environment faster as a result, because they know what to expect in an environment like this. Imagine a virtual showroom, or office, or classroom.

■ INCLUDE LANGUAGE AS AN AUDIO EXPERIENCE

Adding sound to the experiential site makes it more realistic. In simulating the real world, sound must accompany experiential sites. Whether it is the sound of money clinking from a virtual slot machine or a voice explaining a procedure, language is integral to the Web. Presently, the tools are limited, and in some cases they don't yet exist. However, vigorous efforts to produce them are under way. Start planning the design to include sound.

■ INCLUDE TOOLS

Whenever you are designing a real environment, you must include the tools of the trade of the experience you are building. In banking for example, use a checkbook tool, as Quicken™ does as a tool for inputting information.

If the technology permits, in virtual worlds where objects are manipulated, provide a pick-up tool, so a user knows how to pick something up without instructions. Turn the cursor into a hand, for example. Again, the web technology may be a bit slower in developing the authoring tools to create tools in the environment, but start planning for them now, as the tools will become available soon.

■ DESIGN FOR DISCOVERY

Whatever tools are provided for a user as an individual moving around the Web, the user is in discovery mode. He is figuring out an environment that is only partially known. He is constantly in a state of discovering information. How do I find something? Where's the next place to go? What do I click on first? What's the purpose of this object?

Simplicity First. Design so that the experiences users have at first are relatively simple. Make sure, for example, that they understand the concept of navigation. Since you're developing in a nontextual world, you will have to devise tools or on-screen devices that will assist users in understanding navigation. Include textual information about how to use the site, hints to use the site, or whatever is required to help users maneuver in this new environment.

Many of the arcade games are designed in levels. At the first level, the user has a one-to-one interaction with the environment. He may be walking, then jumping over things. After the user accustoms himself to moving in the environment, suddenly a character with unpredictable behavior begins to interact with the user. The user must respond, by walking or jumping. Next, the user begins to discover and use tools. This cycle occurs until, at the top level, the user is manipulating every possible resource available. Finally, the user is solving problems and devising creative alternatives.

Nontextual Clues. Devise some way of introducing clues or cues to users to help them make discoveries. In some programs, a dialogue bubble, as you see in comic strips, appears when you pass your cursor over a unique spot on the screen. The bubble indicates what your next step should be. If you take the suggested path, you are rewarded with immediate feedback that you've gone in the right direction. Nontextual cues are becoming the norm on the Web.

Principle

Don't forget, your users need feedback in VRML as well.

Principle

Introduce simple experiences, like navigation, first.

■ APPLY THE PRINCIPLES OF FOREGROUND AND MIDDLEGROUND

In any experiential site, there are elements in the foreground. These elements are things you can touch and that have reactions when you touch them. You can use complex tools to perform certain activities within the new world. Anything that has action is considered in the foreground.

Develop all of your tools in the foreground. Develop the cues and clues you want the user to pick up for navigation in the foreground. Design navigational items in the foreground. Design passageways, doorways, or direction passageways for users in the foreground.

Middleground. Design help into the middleground; that is in the area where the greatest amount of text lies but is hidden from the VR view.

Backgrounds. The background is reserved for all the inert objects. The background is nonvirtual. That is, if you click on it, nothing happens. Users are used to background spaces on the Web. To them, if it doesn't do anything, move on. This inert activity or functionality of a geometric location may seem odd to you, because in the real world there is a reaction to every action. If you feel something, it has a particular feel. If you look at it, you understand its inherent qualities or characteristics. In the virtual world, it's just there and has no functionality.

> **Principle**
>
> Design nonessential information in the background.

In the background in an experiential site, you are signaling to the user that background information is not relevant in their pursuit of more knowledge. It is a virtual shorthand to distinguish the essential from the nonessential.

■ PROBLEM SOLVING

Many people turn to the World Wide Web to solve a knowledge problem. In short, they need to know something to help them do something else. The Web calls for increasingly sophisticated problem-solving skills and for the retrieval, sorting, and application of large amounts of information. In HTML, there is little guidance for problem solving. Most of the activity is reading and passively viewing.

> **Principle**
>
> Create collaborative environments.

Collaborative Relationships. In experiential design, problem-solving skills will be coordinated in a collaborative environment. The user can team up with a leader or act as the expert in any particular environment. Together, they will collaborate with others on-line in an attempt to figure out how to get to the bottom of a problem.

Collaborators can integrate their skill sets, analyze the cause-and-effect relationships they encounter in the virtual world, and help draw conclusions about the underlying deep structures of the problem. A designer's task will be to create a collaborative environment.

■ MOTIVATION

Experiential sites motivate users to engage more thoroughly in the content of the site. Because the user is capable of moving around in a 3-D environment, he is presented with more opportunities to use information. Problems occur more quickly, solutions are needed more often, tasks have to be performed, decisions have to be made. Because of the need to solve problems, users rush to find information to help them go into action.

Excelling in the Environment. In an experiential site on the Web, the experience is user-centered and motivational. Whether for entertainment or for education, the user needs to become a part of the site. It is the user's nature to attempt to survive and perform superiorly in the site. He needs to master the cyberenvironment, departing either well entertained or educated. Realize that your user needs to excel.

Make sure there are different levels of expertise. Provide various tools that help individuals survive in any particular environment, but don't give them everything at once. They will need the right tool for the right job. Make sure that the tools are available, but let the user figure out which one is right for the job. The better he does using the tool, the more he'll feel as though he's excelling.

Reward and Recognition. To ensure excelling, make sure that you provide some form of reward or acknowledgment that the users are succeeding. Usually, moving from level to level, or world to world, is a form of success for many VR surfers. Design reward and recognition: Provide free software, show more exciting Virtual Sites, offer free gifts and contests to encourage their participation. Users feel as though "more" is a reward in itself.

Fear or Punishment. Another form of motivation, and certainly a part of the real world, is fear and punishment (the kind that can be imposed in a simulated sense, of course). Fear of losing, being last, not being part of an information set increase the user's need to excel in the environment. In the Nintendo and Sega games, losing to an opponent in a fight is a form of punishment. Users want to move through the environment, discover it, excel, and win. Any challenger or opponent provides a creative tension that the user must interact with. Time is one of the greatest opponents.

Principle

Amply reward users to motivate them to press on.

Principle

Provide tools for excelling in the environment.

■ DESIGN FOR PLAY

Many experiential sites are game oriented. Technically, a game must have four critical characteristics: conflict, control, closure, and contrivance. The *conflict* in a game is the competition between the user and the virtual opponent. Any obstacle that prevents the user from reaching his goal is considered conflict. *Control* appears in the form of the rules, what navigation is required to move through the site, and what consequences occur. *Closure* is special event signaling the end of the experience. In Sega games, you reach the top level and destroy the opponent. Finally, *contrivance* is what the designer used to prohibit the most efficient solution to reach the goal.

Experiential sites can be as gamelike as you desire. Games can be motivational and highly reward oriented. They can be equally instructional, teaching more than just how to win the game. In fact, many games carry with them a message. Monopoly teaches real estate marketing; SimCity teaches urban planning.

Games that simulate environments, like the Sim series (SimCity, SimEarth, etc.) are excellent examples of experiential environments that will affect the design of web sites. Unfortunately, today, the programming languages are not robust enough on the Internet to produce similar environments. With the advent of Java, however, we may see the appearance of more gamelike environments on the Web.

DESIGN TOOLS

Designing in the experiential world on the Web is evolving past HTML and CGI scripting in PERL. Now, more robust design tools are required. VRML, Virtual Reality Modeling Language, JavaScript, and Java are the forerunners for this environment.

■ VIRTUAL REALITY

First there was TCP/IP, a protocol that would allow networks to communicate with one another. Then, there were HTML and URLs, which provided users the ability to share files in identifiable, easy-to-use locations. Now, virtual reality has taken shape to allow users to become included in the site, as though they were actually there.

You are inside. VR's claim to fame is that it immerses you in the environment. Immersion causes accelerated learning, because the user has to react more quickly and more often in a VR environment. Users have to access knowledge and apply it instantaneously in order to perform in the virtual environment.

Movement. Virtual reality provides a sense of movement. You enter a 3-D space and look for items to click on or fly through. You look up, down, sideways, and behind. You have a location and can be perceived by others. As you move through the environment, you pick up clues about what you can do next. In essence, you are experiencing a new world, a virtual world. You might open doors, go through passageways, or fly over other 3-D objects.

Virtual environments abound in 3DO, Sega, and Nintendo games, and VR arcades like Virtual World. Take a look at them as soon as possible. They will become one of the major interfaces for designers to work with.

■ VRML

The Virtual Reality Modeling Language (VRML) is a language for describing multiparticipant interactive simulations. It permits you to program virtual worlds that are networked via the Internet and hyperlinked to the World Wide Web. VRML concerns itself with geometry, spheres, polygons, cylinders, etc. It resembles animation and offers a unique form of navigation, as though you were flying through space. It also uses lighting and cameralike effects to provide a simulated real world.

■ VRML DESIGN ISSUES

The key design issue for VRML is to design a useful site that engages the user by allowing him to have multiple experiences.

Use about 1/2 million polygons per world. Most users' systems are not yet equipped with 3-D accelerators and their system will slow down quickly.

Text created from polygons use inordinate amounts of polygons; stay clear of them. Users would be sitting around for twenty minutes while the text is rendered.

If you do decide to use text in your virtual experience, you may want to consider limiting it even more. Graphical 3-D images that you can move around quickly are generations ahead of text and graphics because they communicate more quickly.

Users have developed an ability to navigate through two-dimensional space on the Web fairly well; they have learned to handle the cognitive requirements for doing so. In the VRML world, link your objects to other hyperlinks and let the user make the associations.

Principle

Use low polygon art.

Principle

Design text as gifs, not as polygons.

Principle

Minimize the use of text.

Principle

Design objects to hyperlink.

■ VRML Sites

A few sites you can visit include the following. Remember, you have to have a VRML viewer, and it must be configured properly.

- Virtual Vegas
  `http://www.virtualvegas.com/vrml/vrml.html`

- WaxWeb http://bug.village.virginia.edu

- World Chat
  `http://www.worlds.net/products/wchat/index.html`

- Cool Worlds
  `http://www.paperinc.com/wrls.html`

KEY POINTS

- We must design beyond the paper, 2-D environment. Otherwise, we can but replicate only what paper can do.
- Experiential design allows users to perform some kind of activity on the Web. This activity goes beyond forms, e-mail, and electronic polls.
- Experiential design activates discovery learning and allows the user to experience a simulated environment.
- Experiential sites exist in primitive forms, like choosing a product to fit your needs in tables.
- Experiential designs exist in on-line banking and other on-line services where the user is involved in activities that he might in reality be involved in.
- Virtual Reality is a great start for creating an experiential site.
- Java will encourage designers to develop experiential worlds.
- Design to engage and self-motivate the user; he must be the center of attention and experience a world that is as close to reality as his own.
- Use low polygon art, and design text as gifs.

CHAPTER

12
Testing the Design

Testing is one of the most important things any designer can do. There are too many variables to assume that you have everything right. Testing *won't* guarantee that everything is 100 percent. Testing *will* expose the most glaring problems that aren't obvious to the person who is too close to the work.

Some of the facets of testing can be automated. Some require a human being. The ones that can be automated should be done routinely, even for small changes. Invest early in automation. It will save time and money in the long run.

BEFORE YOU GO ON-LINE

The bulk of testing can and should be done before the site is exposed to the public. You don't want to give users a bad first impression. There are too many sites available on the Internet for users to remember to come back to one silly site that couldn't check the work before releasing it.

■ COPYEDIT

One of the most preventible errors with any web site is web pages that have spelling errors, punctuation errors, or grammatical problems. The web site often gives a person the first view of your company, organization, product, or yourself. That impression can be marred by careless distribution of web pages without apparent concern for their professional appearance.

- **Check Spelling** — Spelling errors tend to be the most flagrant violations, since virtually every computer has a spelling checker somewhere. When all else fails, it is possible to load your web pages into a word processor, spell check them, and then save them as text files.
- **Check Punctuation** — Punctuation errors such as using a comma instead of a period, or vice versa, are often undetectable on small screens. The most effective way to verify punctuation is to print out the web page and examine the paper copy or use the browser to enlarge all fonts to a distinguishable size.
- **Check Grammar** — Grammar is probably the hardest of the three to check, at least in English. It is important to use proper language, but it is also important to retain a conversational style. If the text is made grammatically perfect at the expense of building a rapport with reader, the design suffers. Also make sure sentences are simple. A young person without a complete vocabulary or a person who doesn't speak your language as a native shouldn't get lost in the linguistic complexity.
- **Check Layout** — Do the pages meet the layout and style guidelines developed for the site? Do they have the common items required on all pages?

■ JARGON CHECK

Checking for jargon is the most important thing for virtually any web page. Often the designer and subject matter experts are too close to the material to determine which are valid terms and which are jargon.

Jargon builds walls. This is a matter of critical importance. It gives the illusion of some elite group that already *knows* what these terms mean. Too often the potential clients go to some other place where they don't feel like an idiot.

Try This!

For a really eye-opening experience, gather a group of your casual customers. Don't use the militantly devoted evangelists that already eat, sleep, and breathe your products. Take the wishy-washy, middle-of-the-road folks that could stand to be upgraded to high-quality customers, and perform a test.

1. **Make a list of all potential jargon. Put these terms on index cards, one term per card.**

   - Brand names
   - Trademarks
   - Servicemarks
   - Acronyms
   - Standards and specifications terminology
   - Other words not contained in a standard dictionary

2. **Ask the casual customers to separate out the terms that they recognize from the ones that they don't.**

3. **Then ask them to define the ones that they recognize.**

You are likely to find that your most cherished brand names and trademarks are unknown to a third (or more) of this audience. Confusing and alienating a third of any audience is a bad thing, but doing so to a third of the audience that can be upgraded is unforgivable.

Review for Jargon

The simplest technique for screening out jargon is to get a third party to review the documents, provided, of course, that the third party is sufficiently detached from the material to give an objective opinion. This option isn't always available, and it can be very time consuming.

In general, use the spell checker. Most spell checkers have a larger vocabulary than the average person for average words, but they can efficiently expose glaring *jargonitis* much more easily than a human can.

Remember to disable your custom dictionary before using the spell checker for this function.

- Review every word that starts with a capital letter but isn't the start of a sentence. If it is jargon, add a glossary entry.
- Review every word that doesn't occur in a standard dictionary. If it is jargon, add a glossary entry.
- Get a third party to review the documents for jargon.

Deal With the Jargon

When you encounter jargon, rewrite the content to explain the term locally or drop the jargon. Explaining everything locally can be redundant, and there may be cases where marketing wants the brand name or trademark exposure everywhere. In those cases, supplement the page with links to a glossary. This is most effective when coupled with a glossary or message frame by means of Netscape Frames.

Principle

Always define jargon.

- Explain or offer a glossary entry for every acronym in the documents.
- Explain or offer a glossary entry for every trademark, servicemark, or product name in the documents.

Remember to make the glossary links similar to the regular text color. Using several different colors for links can make a page too colorful to be readable. People can get used to the slight variation of underlining only to indicate that a definition is available.

■ READABILITY AND USABILITY CHECK

A web page can be syntactically correct and still be unreadable. This is a good place to use a wide range of people representative of your expected audience, from those unfamiliar with your topic or product line to your most savvy admirers.

Offer these people an opportunity to test drive your web site. Make a note of their reactions. Don't just write down their comments. People don't always say everything that is on their mind, and many of them will not indicate confusion after they have figured something out. It is important to note where they are confused initially and remedy these problems, even if they eventually figured things out for themselves.

- Are they confused?
- Do they get frustrated?
- Do things seem to flow for them?

Give these people various scenarios.

- **Scavenger Hunt** – Can they find various pieces of information that are commonly asked? How many wrong turns did they take before they found the right place?
- **Exploration** – When allowed to explore the site, where do they go?
- **Graphics Limited** – Turn off graphics loading and see how they respond to your site. How much does the confusion level rise?
- **Afterward** –When they are done viewing the site, test their comprehension. Did they get the message you wanted them to get? Did they have any problems? Is there anything that they would like you to explain to them?

■ VALIDATE HTML

There are dozens of browsers and dozens of platforms and versions of most browsers. The number of unique browser identifier strings is well over 800. With that many variations, it is impossible to test them all. When faced with such overwhelming odds, fall back to the standards. There are validation programs available for local use or via a web site to verify the syntactical correctness of HTML. They include:

- **HALSoft Validation Site** – Offers validation of HTML 2.0 pages, Mozilla, aka Netscape, pages, and HotJava pages. They can validate pages or snippets of code, or you can download the HTML Check Toolkit.

  Webpage:http://www.halsoft.com/html-val-svc/
  Toolkit:http://www.halsoft.com/html-tk/index.html

- **Weblint** – Offers validation of HTML 2.0 and Mozilla pages. Weblint is available for the MS-DOS PCs. Weblint is an effective site-management tool that does more than just check syntax.

  Webpage:`http://www.khoros.unm.edu/staff/neilb/weblint.html`
  Script:`ftp://ftp.khoral.com/pub/perl/www/{weblint.zip or weblint-1.011.tar.gz}`

- **College of Computing Validation Service** – Offers validation of HTML 2.0 and *Mozilla-flavored* HTML. They can validate the page for you, or you can download the scripts and do it yourself.

  Webpage:.`http://www.cc.gatech.edu/grads/j/Kipp.Jones/HaLidation/validation-form.html`
  Script:`ftp://ftp.cc.gatech.edu/pub/people/kipp/check-html.tar.Z`

- **VRMLlint** – Offers validation of VRML worlds. This comes bundled into the WebSpace™ product.

  Webpage:.`http://webspace.sgi.com/`

All of the pages that are intended for general consumption should pass HTML 2.0 validation. This will ensure that there will be few problems with older or less swiftly evolving browsers. Pages with Netscape and HTML 3.0 enhancements, should be validated by the appropriate program.

■ VERIFY LINKS

Ensuring that the web page can be rendered adequately on a standards-based browser is one thing. Verifying that other errors don't occur is another. The most common error message is *file not found*. This happens frequently on design projects with many content providers. The Webmaster, or whoever wears the On-line Editor hat, should check that the pieces come together properly.

Link-checking programs aren't really state of the art yet. New ways of referencing URLs such as in stylesheets and Java-enhanced or Netscape Frame-enhanced pages take a while to be incorporated. Keep on top of link-checking updates.

Link checking ideally should also include checking for orphans. Orphans are files that don't have any web pages pointing to them. When web pages are removed, it is important to know which pages they point to and deal with these downstream, orphaned pages.

Principle

Always validate HTML syntax. [Moved from start of bullets]

Principle

Always check links.

Principle

Check for orphans.

- **EIT's Webtest Toolkit** - This is a customizable link checker. It offers many nice features like incremental checking.

  Webpage:`http://www.eit.com/wsk/dist/doc/admin/webtest/verify_links.html`
  Toolkit:`ftp://ftp.eit.com/pub/wsk/doc/webtestdoc.tar`

- **Webxref-** A perl program.

  Webpage:`http://www.sara.nl/cgi-bin/rick_acc_webxref`
  Program:`http://www.sara.nl/Rick.Jansen/Web/webxref/`

- **HTMLchek** - This offers both syntax checking and link checking.

  Webpage:`http://uts.cc.utexas.edu/~churchh/htmlchek.html`

■ BROWSER AND PLATFORM CHECK

Validating HTML doesn't ensure that everything is perfect. It is just a shotgun approach to take care of many nonobvious problems. Now comes the human element. Set up a group of systems with various browsers and have people load the pages and look at them. Your testing hardware should always be low-end systems. Don't use the top-of-the-line systems here; they will warp your perspective.

Hardware and OS

- A laptop with Microsoft Windows 3.11 or Microsoft Windows for Workgroups. Microsoft Windows 95 is *not* an equal substitute. This is a good test platform because it exposes problems with low graphics systems. Most laptops are limited to a 640 x 480 pixel resolution. With the older Microsoft Windows products, the colormap can be limited to 256 colors quite easily. Do this. This platform will expose problems with pages where the logo is overpowering, the graphics become too grainy, and colormap problems occur.
- Macintosh with small screen – Don't get a 17" monitor for the Mac; use a small screen. Macintosh browsers open the smallest windows and tend to display things smaller than anyone else. This platform will expose problems with image width and other sizing problems. **Don't resize the browsers!** Leave them at the default size. Also, compare the colors to the laptop. If your colors seem to wash out or get too dark from platform to platform, massage your images, by altering the gamma values, to look reasonably good on both.

- **Monochrome X-terminal served by a UNIX system** – The $600-$800 X-terminals are the choice of many companies for their employees' home use. Some companies even put these on the desktop. Using a monochrome monitor is a good way to make sure both that the monochrome users aren't too washed out and that your color-blind users don't have too much problem. Color-blind people can still distinguish saturation and brightness, even if they do have some problems identifying the hue.

Rendering HTML may seem straightforward enough that it should be platform independent. Graphics aren't always the same from platform to platform. Other multimedia types definitely vary between platforms. With the addition of VRML and, in a few rare cases, Java, a little more checking is always in order.

Software

It is good to test on a variety of browsers, but it isn't always practical. Always test on browsers that make up more than 5 percent of the audience. Browsers here refer to a certain company, version, and platform. UNIX browsers can be lumped together, but don't lump PC or Mac browsers together. Check with the main browser statistics sites to learn the latest browser statistics.

If you have an Internet audience, always include at least two of the main commercial on-line services such as CompuServe, AOL, or Prodigy. The main on-line sites don't always have accurate numbers in the browser statistics areas, and they do include a larger percentage of novice users than full service Internet service providers.

- **Yahoo's List of Browser Statistics sites-**

> **Webpage:**http://www.yahoo.com/Computers_and_Inter
> net/Internet/World_Wide_Web/Browsers/Browser_Us
> age_Statistics/

■ SPEED CHECK

Always verify the speed of your pages. If you don't, others might do so, and tell the public—not just you. Below is a real world example (names were deleted to protect those still learning).

After Melanie's post (29 June) I decided to visit some sites. I'm not a developer (yet) but I am a communicator learning about this medium. Here is the woman-on-the-net's viewpoint, ok? (and I have a 28.8 modem & 7100 Power Mac, by-the-by)
- (*site name deleted*) : Don't know about content because my first "click" took so d--n long to load that I aborted. Too many separate trips between my computer & host.
- (*site name deleted*): Same complaint. I waited 60, count-em, 60 seconds and it still hadn't finished loading! Abort time, particularly since at that time I had not a clue what the page was going to look like.
So ... REMEMBER!!!! We real-world folks don't have a lot of patience. The coolest graphics won't mean anything if we abort before they load! (in fact, I usually load with graphics OFF, but made an exception for this experiment)

The importance of speed **cannot** be overemphasized. Speed (and byte size) is very important outside the United States. Some countries, like many ISPs (Internet Service Providers) in New Zealand, actually charge for traffic. Most European countries have more expensive telecommunications, thus lower average bandwidth. Speed is also important to the users on commercial on-line services where by-the-hour charges are incurred. Most importantly, speed is critical to the novice user who gets confused and frustrated easily and thus requires a faster response.

To test for speed, test in the real world.

- If the site will go on the Internet, test from a remote spot on the Internet, not from the same Internet service provider. Ask your System Administrator to verify that your test site is at least eight hops from your web server.
- For U.S. sites, test during the peak time, usually 11 a.m. to 2 p.m. Pacific time.
- If even 20 percent of your audience will be home or nomadic users, test with a 14.4K or 28.8K modem.
- Make sure your pages load in less than a minute maximum, less than 30 seconds ideally.

AFTER THE SITE GOES ON-LINE

After the site goes on-line, your job is not complete. There is no test that can replace real-life usage. Your pool of testers has now grown to encompass your entire audience community.

■ FEEDBACK – COMMENTS FROM USERS

Feedback from your customers is important for many reasons. Part of the perception of interactivity is the response from the Webmaster when communicating problems.

User comments are valuable in that they give insight into areas that the design team may be oblivious to because they are too close to the material and the design.

Take user comments with a grain of salt. It takes all kinds to make up the Internet and there is always one person with a really skewed perspective. If the complaint or comment seems unreasonable, wait until more than one person comments on it before taking action.

However, it should take only one complaint about a page having too noisy a background, being too heavy on graphics, or suffering from other design detriments listed in this book before you take action.

■ LOGFILE ANALYSIS

Logfiles are gold mines of information. Always review the error log. This is the first place to find problems. Problems are neatly recorded here for you. Investigate these errors.

- `File not found` errors can indicate that a link checker needs to run. It can also indicate that you are listed improperly in a web index somewhere. Your web doesn't end at the boundary of your server. All links coming and leaving your server also need to be maintained.
- `Server not available` errors indicate that the server is overloaded. Hardware upgrades may be needed, and it is important when these appear to rerun your speed tests. Start monitoring system resources at the first occurrence of this error message, if you aren't monitoring already.
- `Invalid METHOD` or `Invalid request` errors can indicate that network bandwidth problems are mangling requests. This can be on your side of the Internet or on the client's side. Make sure that you know which side it is on.
- Research all other errors that occur regularly.

The activity logs tell the story of where people do go and where they don't go.

- Obtain a list of web pages that are expected to be requested regularly. When they aren't requested routinely, find out why. Has the link been removed, leaving the web page an orphan?
- Check the commonly accessed pages. Are they three clicks or less from the home page?
- Check to see if images are loaded when their pages are loaded. Rule out the images that are stored in proxies. The remaining pages represent the percentage of your audience that is running without graphics. Are you adequately meeting the needs of the graphics-less population?
- Check times; some log files list start and end transfer times for each request. This is a very valuable resource to make sure that your pages, including images, will transfer in the recommended 30-second timeframe.

TEST AFTER UPGRADE

Static sites aren't very popular. Thus, change is often occurring on your web site. You don't need to go through a full-blown test for every little change.

Copyedit, validate HTML, and run the link checker after every update. If you are a creative hacker, create an orphan checker. This is the one significant automation tool lacking from a complete webmaster toolkit. Run these automated tests after every update.

After every significant publishing cycle, whether it be weekly, monthly, or just every time a new product is added, run a full-blown test on all new material including all human-intensive testing.

Test all new potential jargon with a sample of your middle-of-the-roaders.

FINAL NOTE

Testing isn't always seen as a part of design in most media. In many media, it doesn't need to be. On the Web, testing is a vital function. The Web is half aesthetic creation, half technical creation. The technical half does require an investment in quality similar to any software project.

An intelligent design shop will dedicate 5–10 percent of resources for this activity.

KEY POINTS

• Testing allows you to find errors before the user can, which is cause for some embarrassment.
• Testing has many phases including:

> -*Copy Editing*
>
> -*Jargon Check*
>
> -*HTML Syntax Check*
>
> -*Link Check*
>
> -*Browse/Platform Check*
>
> -*Speed Check*

• Testing doesn't stop when the site goes on-line.

PART
two
case
studies

- The case studies in this section were chosen to represent examples of "good design."

- There are more than enough examples of what to do wrong on the Web. These examples are here to demonstrate how someone did it right.

Sun and Java

URL: http://www.sun.com/

Purpose: Provide information about Sun's products and services

Audience: Current and potential Sun customers

BACKGROUND

Sun Microsystems' motto has been *the network is the computer*™. They have been large contributors to the Internet community. In 1994, they provided the World Cup soccer news often sooner than did conventional news sources.

The current Sun web site has been pushing the envelope all along. This site currently holds more than 10,000 documents and provides:

- A catalog of the thousands of products sold through SunExpress,
- Information on 6,000 Catalyst vendors (third-party add-ons to Sun systems).
- In-depth product information

REDUCING INFORMATION LOAD

Some of the key features that make Sun's web site special are the use of concept indexes to find things in the sea of data, special links to the most important items, and the use of Java to enhance understanding of the icons.

The home page is busy, but it is organized in such a way that many people with many different goals can each get something out of the page. The magazine style was chosen with a monthly update cycle to encourage return readers.

Another key item to notice here is that there are a limited number of options. It is true that there are 13 clickable places on this page, but they are clustered into three distinct groups, standard company info (products, services, corporate info), What's New highlights, and a set of specialty areas. This keeps the choices manageable.

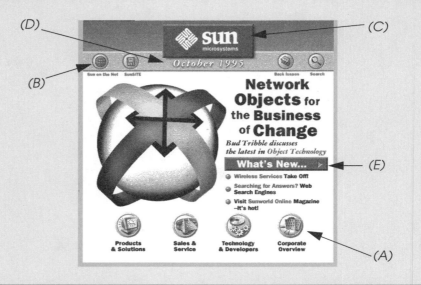

(A) At the bottom are the main unchanging categories. These elements stay the same from month to month. Their beveled edges give them a button-like appearance that cues the user into their function.

In addition, when Java is used with this page, the elements come to life, and an audio track announces their function.

(B) The top bar has another set of buttons that are unchanging from issue to issue. These are key areas. They also have a button-like quality that encourages users to click on them.

> •Back Issues and Search are functional additions to the site.
>
> •Sun on the Net is Sun's showcase of network expertise.
>
> •SunSITE is an FTP repository that offers value to the Internet community. The SunSITE button is complete with the disk icon that is often interpreted as downloadable files on the Internet.

(C) The logo is prominently displayed without being large and overbearing.

(D) The web page is dated. This tells users when they can expect to come back for new material. This practice encourages return visits and clues the user in to how timely the material is.

(E) The **What's New** bar has an arrow on it like a menu does when a secondary menu can be displayed. This cues the user into the fact that the items below the **What's New** bar are not the only new items, just the most important ones. This practice encourages the user to click on the arrow to see more items.

(F) This page is a single image. Text is not rendered in HTML here. The links do not have to be blue, but they are. The user associates blue text next to black text as a link to somewhere.

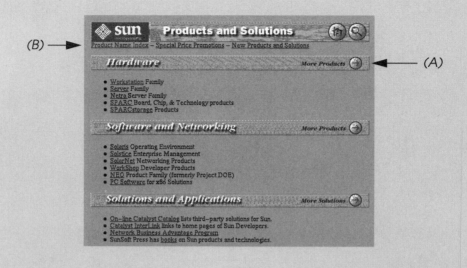

(B) →
(A) ←

ORGANIZATION

The Products and Solutions page also organizes a lot of options into a manageable set of clusters.

(A) Some of the more obscure items are still one more click away under the prominently displayed **More Products**, **More Services**, and **More Solutions** buttons. Considering that the site has more than 10,000 web pages, offering a limited number of choices to cover the bulk of the material is important.

(B) Three specialty areas that don't follow the logical breakdown appear just below the site and page identification to offer alternative organization of the material for those that have a specific goal in mind.

For example, the bargain hunters can be drawn immediately to the Special Price Promotion area without having to click through each selection to see where the best buys occur.

New items can also be showcased in the **New Products and Solutions** area. This again saves a lot of clicking on the user's part.

The Product Name Index offers a distinct advantage over sites that only offer a free-text search engine. By offering a list of concepts to the person who doesn't know quite what something is called, the page can meet their needs, too.

274

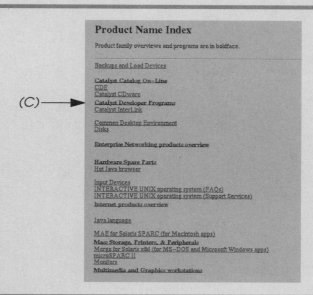

(C) — By subtle changes, such as making some items bold, additional information is conveyed. In this case, bold items offer product family overviews.

CONCLUSION

Sun has used several subtle things to improve the communications of their site. Considering the size of their site, the fact that most things can be found in three or four clicks is a credit to the designers.

Point Communications

URL: http://www.pointcom.com/
Purpose: (1) Value-Add directory listings
--------->**(2)** Timely Internet new source
Audience: All Internet Users

BACKGROUND

Point Communications established itself as a web site review service, listing only the top 5 percent of the web sites. They evaluate web sites for three criteria:

- Content
- Experience
- Presentation

It is fitting that a web site of the crème de la crème be equally outstanding. Point Communications exceeds this goal admirably. Their design is low impact, structured, cognitively appealing, timely, laden with content; it proves that you *can* create a site that doesn't slight the less endowed browser.

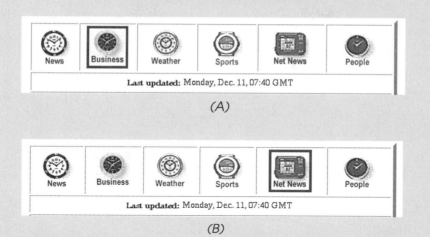

(A)

(B)

NAVIGATION AND LOCATION

(A) Point Now, the timely news information service of Point Communications, uses every image at its disposal to emphasize time. Each navigation icon represents a different style of timepiece, from the old-fashioned wall clock (often seen in newsrooms) to represent News, to the rugged, functional athletic watch to represent sports, to something out of Dick Tracy to represent the news of the Internet itself.

(B) This navigation bar serves two functions. It not only offers navigation capabilities, but it also offers visible location information. Without much examination, it is easy to discern Figure A, above, that the user is viewing Business information, and in Figure B, the user is viewing Net News.

This is an effective method for combining functions.

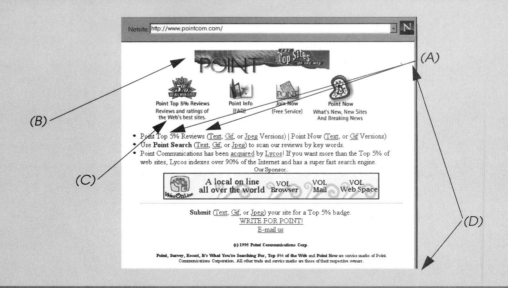

HOME

(A) One of the first things that a user will notice here is that Point Communications endeavors to meet the diverse graphical needs of their Internet audience. They offer the choice of

- Text for the graphics-shy
- Gif for the average user (Web standard default)
- Jpg for the graphics-hungry, visually oriented user

Their interest in meeting the needs of the entire Internet audience is evident here.

(B) In the interest of being low impact, the banner at the top doubles as the site identification (**Point**) and the title or topic indicator (**Top Sites of the Web**).

As a logo, this little image takes up a modest 12 percent of the page.

Behind the Scenes

(B)

Pixel Size: 293 pixels wide by

------------> 58 pixels high

Byte Size: 8 Kbytes

Color Size: 64 color palate

Pixel Size: 480 pixels wide by

------------> 109 pixels high

Byte Size: 14 Kbytes

Color Size: 225 color palate

(B)   This little image weighs in modestly in all categories: byte size impact, color size impact, and screen size impact.

(C)   Like the site identifier image, the main navigation imagemap is equally compact and fits comfortably in all categories.

(D)   This page is longer than most of the other Point Communications navigation pages, in that there is a little bit that doesn't fit onto a laptop screen. Nonetheless, this tight page still finds plenty of space to include an advertisement in the laptop visible area, giving their paying customers top billing without slighting the users.

(B)

45 Pixels

(A)

162 Pixels

(C)

60 Pixels

TOP OF REVIEW TREE

This is an ideal navigation page.

(A) It is small enough to fit completely on any screen. The three images involved only account for 267 pixels in height. Adding in the text still keeps the page below 300 pixels.

(B) The site identifier again doubles as the page title. We also see a pattern here. The site identifier/page title has a distinctive landscape theme. A few more repetitions of this will imprint the shape/scene and the user will no longer need to read the text to associate the landscape header with the site.

(C) Five items to choose from is a manageable number. Each item is clearly labeled with a meaningful title.

The acronym FAQ is not the primary definition for the label. This gives a meaningful name for both the Internet novice and the seasoned user.

```
<!DOCTYPE HTML PUBLIC "-//Netscape Comm. Corp.//DTD
HTML//EN" "html-net.dtd">

<HTML><HEAD><TITLE>Point Communications </TITLE></HEAD>

<BODY bgcolor="FFFFFF" link="0000FF" vlink="871F8"
text="000000">

<CENTER>
<IMG SRC="hometop.gif" WIDTH=288 HEIGHT=45><BR>
<A HREF="home.map">
<IMG SRC="homebuts.gif" WIDTH=402 HEIGHT=162 BORDER="0"
ISMAP="ISMAP"></A>
.
.
.
```

Behind the Scenes

(D)   The background is customized to a simple white. This adds contrast
and makes a page easier to read. The plain-colored background is
chosen over a noisy image that can compete with the content of the
page.

Another technical point is scored by defining the text color to be black
even though that is the default on virtually every browser. This ensures
that the page will display properly on the rare browser where the user
has configured the default to be something else that may be unreadable.

(E)   Because HEIGHT and WIDTH values are defined, the page will be
drawn even if the images haven't been downloaded yet.

CONCLUSION

Point Communications offers users a site where they can control the
level of graphics that they receive. Users are offered a consistent content interface at all levels. The site is recognizable by the landscape
site identifier and the thematic icons.

GolfWeb

URL: http://www.golfweb.com

Purpose: Provide golfing information to golfing enthusiasts

Audience: Golfers

Design Focus: Content design

BACKGROUND

GolfWeb is the Internet's premier golf web site. GolfWeb is committed to providing "Everything Golf on the World Wide Web!" GolfWeb offers something for everyone with an interest in golf, from the latest professional tournament scores, to extensive course information, to an on-line pro shop.

GolfWeb was recognized as the **Best Of The Net** in the Sports category at the Global Network Navigator (GNN) second annual Best Of The Net Awards. GolfWeb's was recognized as a comprehensive and well-crafted site, featuring up-to-the-minute coverage of the major tours and a database of 14,000 golf courses in the U.S.

DESIGN FEATURES

The content of Golfweb is a superior example of creating a site with rich content. It excels in the following areas:

- Content, content, content
- Internationalization
- Emphasizing important information first
- Layout supporting content
- Interactivity
- Common look and feel
- Appropriate use of language for the audience

COMMON LOOK AND FEEL

GolfWeb has put together an elegant common look and feel to make their site distinguishable. The graphics are subtle and the pages load fairly quickly. The textual appearance is aesthetic, using <h2> headings, <h3> bold subheadings.

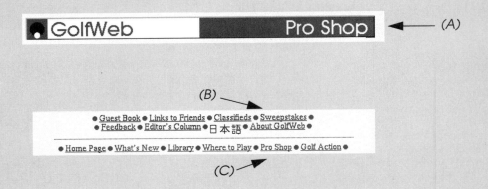

(A) **Common Banner.** To make it easier to orient the user, the banner repeats itself on all of the pages. On the left side of the banner, the designers used green letters with a white background that sports the simple GolfWeb logo and name. On the right side of the banner, they used a reverse color scheme, white letters with a green background. On this side, you'll find the subordinate link name to remind you what link you took to get here.

(B) **Common Footer.** At the bottom of each page is a recurring text-based footer, that keeps all the major subsections together in two lines, separated by green bullets—or are they green golf balls? The Japanese equivalent characters are available for an international flavor.

(C) **Common Home Page Contents.** Below the footer menu are the original six items from the home page, Home Page, What's New, Library, Places to Play, Pro Shop, and Tour Action. Having these three navigation bars makes for good navigation throughout the site.

(A)

(B)

MAKE THE SITE INTERACTIVE

(A) **Interactive Search for Courses.** GolfWeb provides OnCourse, an interactive extensible information resource for over 14,000 courses in the United States and a growing number of courses worldwide. You can search for specific courses that match your search criteria, such as courses that have 'WOOD' in the name, in the 713 area code, courses in a ZIP code that starts with 7, courses that start with C in Florida, and all courses in my area with a slope > 140.

Once a course is located, you can pull up a wealth of information pertaining to that course, number of holes, championship yardage, fees, guest policy, slope, and golf season.

(B) **Friends of GolfWeb.** Another, more in-depth feature of the GolfWeb that inspires interactivity is the Friends of the GolfWeb program. In this program, you can share your home pages with the GolfWeb and mutually increase the traffic to your pages. You can look at home pages of other golfers, places to play, golf sites, and golf equipment sites, and a host of golfing advertisers.

(A)

APPROPRIATE USE OF LANGUAGE

The designers of this web site obviously spent some time profiling their audience. The golfer can certainly feel at home here, with `Library`, `Places to Play`, `Pro Shop` and `Tour Action`. It is clear what kind of information lies behind door number one.

(A) **Conversational Tone.** The language is easy to read and is conversational in tone. You feel as though you were socializing on the green. The sentences are well written, so you don't feel like you're reading all the time. Instead, you feel engaged in the material. The subject-verb-object format with the obvious absence of prepositional phrases or long, sweeping clauses makes the content on this site well worth the visit.

Rule 21. Cleaning Ball Rules Decisions	**Rule 22. Ball Intefering with or Assisting Play** Rules Decisions
Rule 23. Loose Impediments Rules Decisions	**Rule 24. Obstructions** Rules Decisions
Rule 25. Abnormal Ground Conditions and Wrong Putting Green Rules Decisions	**Rule 26. Water Hazards (Including Lateral Water Hazards)** Rules Decisions
Rule 27. Ball Lost or Out of Bounds; Provisional Ball Rules Decisions	**Rule 28. Ball Unplayable** Rules Decisions
Rule 29. Threesomes and Foursomes Rules Decisions	**Rule 30. Three–Ball, Best–Ball and Four–Ball Match Play** Rules Decisions
Rule 31. Four–Ball Stroke Play Rules Decisions	**Rule 32. Bogey, Par and Stableford Competitions** Rules Decisions
Rule 33. The Committee Rules Decisions	**Rule 34. Disputes and Decisions** Rules Decisions
Miscellaneous Decisions	Decisions Applicable Only in The United States of America
Appendicies	
Appendix I – Local Rules; Conditions of the Competition	Appendix II – Design Of Clubs
Appendix III – The Ball	Appendix IV – Rules of Amateur Status

(B)

(B) **Text is short and concise**. The designers also realize that the users are educated, leaving no explanations under items like USGA Golf Rules. Once you get to the rules, a simple table takes over and provides straight-from-the-hip information, with golfer questions and answers to help understand the decisions that made the rule.

North American	Amateur & College	International
PGA Tour	United States Golf Association	Australasian PGA Tour
LPGA Tour	NCAA Men's / Women's	European Tours
Senior PGA Tour	American Junior Golf Association	Japan Tours
Nike Tour	Royal Canadian Golf Association	Asian PGA Asian Tour / Omega Tour
Hooters/Jordan Tour	**Computer Tours**	South African PGA Tour
Canadian PGA Tour	NEW Links Tour	

(A)

EMPHASIZE THE IMPORTANT FIRST

(A) **Tables and Font Size.** Golf is the name of the game at this site. The site is content-rich with tour schedules, information, schedules, statistics, equipment, frequently asked questions, a rule book, and information about the different courses. Wading through all this would seem impossible. Yet GolfWeb has designed their site to emphasize their important information first. Notice the use of tables and font size to encourage easy scanning of the page. Your eye goes quickly from Last Week, This Week, and Next Week, emphasizing that chronology is important on this page. Then, location is emphasized with the larger fonts highlighting North American, Amateur & College, and International.

(B)

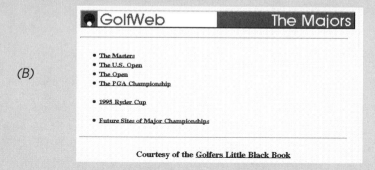

Courtesy of the <u>Golfers Little Black Book</u>

(B) **Cognitive Bullets.** Whenever you get to any major links, you are immediately greeted with just a bullet item or two, or some quick graphics. This indicates to the user that these are the important areas to access first, eliminating the feeling of being lost in cyberspace. Instead the user's mind is focused, keeping content linked to context.

Books and Videos

- The Golfers Little Black Book, a guide to all the golf games you can play during your round.
- Heroes of the Game – A new four volume collector video series from the USGA and Time Warner Entertainment.

Clothes and Other Golf Apparel

- Astro–Back – Lumbar support by AirWorx.
- Golf Gremlins – Tee Shirts.

Golf Collectibles, Antiques, & Memorabilia

- Cambridge Golf Antiquities – Select from 25,000 books, clubs, trophies, prints, and more.

Schools

- Atlanta Golf School – 1,2 3 or 5 day golf schools.
- John Jacobs – Golf schools.

Score Keepers

- GreensFinder – Electronic golf course guide and scorekeeper.

Training Aids

- PC Driving Range – By Bengston Company.

Travel Packages

- Best of Scotland Holidays – Play golf on some of the world's oldest and most famous courses.

(A)

CONTENT, CONTENT, CONTENT

(A) **Everything Golf.** You cannot leave this site not knowing practically everything you wanted to know about golf. The What's New page maintains a week-by-week history of what has been added to the web site, so you get a running commentary on the site. But, the Pro Shop offers it all: Books and Videos, Tour Packages to Scotland's 16th-Century Golf Course, Clothes and Apparel, Golf Collectibles, Golf Equipment, Golf Schools, Golf Training Aids, Accolades and Recognition, Golf Sponsor Sites, Classified Ads, Professional Golf Statistics, Staff Profiles at GolfWeb, Corporate Overview with Staff Photo, Golf Associations…

(B)

Stop, stop, stop, enough golf

(B) **Javatized GolfWeb**. If all this isn't enough, you'll have to visit the site to see the Java-enhanced GolfWeb. GolfTicker, GolfWeb's first JavaGolf application, scrolls the contents of the What's New page at the top of the GolfWeb home page.

1996 Japan Tour Schedules

Men's	Ladies
JPGA Regular TOUR	JLPGA Regular TOUR
Senior PGA TOUR	Step Up TOUR
Grand.Gold Seniors TOUR	Other Relevant Tournaments
Support TOUR	
Growing TOUR	
Cooperation Tournaments	

日本語によるトーナメント情報

● Golf Action '96 ●

(A)

International

Australasian PGA Tour

European Tours

Japan Tours

Asian PGA
Asian Tour / Omega Tour

South African PGA Tour

Argentine Tour

(B)

INTERNATIONALIZATION

(A) **Do you speak Japanese?** GolfWeb does, and with one of the most innovative tools, Shodouka mediator. The Shodouka mediator was developed by Ka-Ping Yee of the University of Waterloo, Canada. Shodouka is a World Wide Web mediator that renders the kana and kanji on Japanese WWW documents in real time for any graphical browser.

Using Shodouka, you can view Japanese documents without needing a Japanese browser or any particular Japanese capabilities in your operating system. The mediator replaces each two-byte Japanese kana or kanji character code with a graphical bitmap of the character, then returns the page.

Take a look at the Shodouka mediator to translate a site into Japanese characters. See `http://csclub.uwaterloo.ca/u/kryee/shodouka/`

Try This!

(A)

This is the launchpad for **Shodouka**, a World–Wide Web mediator that renders the kana and kanji on Japanese WWW documents in real–time for any graphical browser. Using Shodouka, you can view Japanese documents without needing a Japanese browser or any particular Japanese capabilities in your operating system. Each document you request has its links changed so that further requests will be passed to Shodouka as well.

To use the **Shodouka** Japanese text renderer, give a URL in the following entry field and select the version button. If you're going to use a URL that is just a hostname (like http://www.ntt.jp/), please be sure to *include the trailing slash.*

[I   ] [0.6e] [0.6f]

Version 0.6f had improved image–breaks for wrapping, but turned out slower than 0.6e by too wide a margin because of the increased number of requests, so the default version is back to 0.6e. Select this link to check server status.

But what does it *do*?

To save you some typing, here are a couple of places you might want to try visiting with **Shodouka**. Select the ⑤ icon next to a hyperlink to mediate the linked document.

- ⑤ Asahi Shimbun (Japanese newspaper)
- ⑤ Mainichi Shimbun (Japanese newspaper)
- ⑤ Yomiuri Shimbun (Japanese newspaper)
- ⑤ Hitoshi Doi's anime database
- ⑤ NTT home page in Japan
- ⑤ Kyushu Institute of Technology home page

(B) **Golf Everywhere.** GolfWeb understands the need to incorporate the international environment. There are sites that refer to places all around the world.

- Australian Open
- Zimbabwe Open
- Meiji Nyugyo Cup
- Hong Kong Open
- PGA European Tour

This kind of recognition appeals to international audiences.

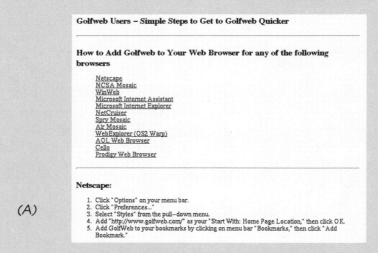

Golfweb Users – Simple Steps to Get to Golfweb Quicker

How to Add Golfweb to Your Web Browser for any of the following browsers

Netscape
NCSA Mosaic
WinWeb
Microsoft Internet Assistant
Microsoft Internet Explorer
NetCruiser
Spry Mosaic
Air Mosaic
WebExplorer (OS2 Warp)
AOL Web Browser
Cello
Prodigy Web Browser

Netscape:

1. Click "Options" on your menu bar.
2. Click "Preferences..."
3. Select "Styles" from the pull–down menu.
4. Add "http://www.golfweb.com/" as your "Start With: Home Page Location," then click OK.
5. Add GolfWeb to your bookmarks by clicking on menu bar "Bookmarks," then click "Add Bookmark."

(A)

FIVE CONTENT TYPES

Facts, concepts, procedures, processes, and principles.

Facts. Facts and statistics are a way of life with golfers. This web site is complete with a great set of course statistics in almost every corner of the site. Concepts are always well defined. For example, before accessing the search tool called OnCourse, the two bullet items say:

- What is OnCourse
- Access OnCourse

What more could you want? An explanation of the interactive database and the link to using it.

(A) **Procedures.** One of the most useful additions to web pages are procedures for doing something that the user wants to do. GolfWeb has included a great set for making GolfWeb your home page in almost every browser out there.

(A)

(B)

LAYOUT SUPPORTS CONTENT

(A) **Whitespace.** Another aspect of using layout to emphasize how to navigate content is seen in the site directly after clicking on Pro Shop from the home page. When you go to the Pro Shop, you immediately see `Equipment`, `Contact Information` and `Everything Golf`. What else could a golfer want? To help emphasize the important first, make the layout clean, with plenty of whitespace, pushing important content to the top.

(B) **Advertising.** At the same time, the site leaves ample room for advertising to its clients, referring to Shivas Iron Society surrounded by whitespace and encased in the common look-and-feel design that GolfWeb is famous for.

CONCLUSION

The GolfWeb site, winner of GNNs Best Sports Site, exhibits a clear understanding of the need to include content on the topic. Not only does the site provide Golf Everything, but they do so in a way that makes the golf enthusiast come back for more. It would be no surprise to find many a client site with `http://www.golfweb.com` as their primary home page when they boot up their web viewer.

Index

A

`<A HREF="#{jumppoint}">` 152
abstract, adding as meta-information 212
access, automatic generation 143
acronym
  adding to glossary 259
  overuse 121
activity log 266
alignment, using standard tags 175
analysis phase 6
animation
  in foreground 81
  marques 82
  pausing 82
  Shockwave 81
audience
  age, designing for 115
  analyzing expectations 118
  bandwidth considerations 131
  browser needs 129
  categorizing 115
  clickable graphics 128
  cognitive expectations 116
  content preferences 118
  cues for novices 128
  international 131, 132
  jargon 121
  layout for diversity 169–171
  lowest common denominator 132
  needs analysis 6
  neophyte 120
  novice 110
  search preferences 114
  skill level 110
  sophistication 129
  surfing experience 113
  systems 112
  technical expectations 117
  technology skills 112
  web page, providing two sets 170
  Web skills 124

authoring team
  multimedia members 8
  user participation 9

B

`Back` in linear document 137
background
  color 68, 92
  contrast with text 174
  elements 92
  experiential site 251
  image size 186
  modifications for Netscape 1.1 174
  use 80
balancing message and design 93
balancing needs and wants 74
balancing text and images 23
bandwidth
  criticality 131
  error messages 265
  full media 49
  outside U.S. 264
  saving, with URC 218
  speed guarantees 189
  VRML solutions 247
`<BANNER>` tag, for navigation bar 168
banner
  contents 66
  size strategies 187
  use 66
Being Digital 106
beta pages 232
blinking text, use 81
blocking methods 87
`<BLOCKQUOTE>` tag, layout control 171
bookmark 217
brainstorming
  chunking information 96
  content importance 48
  design development 7
  identifying logical patterns 76